Soul Revolution

The Trinity of Humanity

Shmuel Asher

SOUL REVOLUTION

THE TRINITY OF HUMANITY

COPYRIGHT © 2013

PUBLISHED BY CREATESPACE 2016

EDITED BY MJS GROUP LTD

CONTACT – AHLC@MIDRIVERS.COM

PRINTED IN THE UNITED STATES OF AMERICA

ISBN-13: 978-1522903505

ISBN-10: 152290350X

Printed in USA by Amazon Books

Dedication

To my grandparents, and mother who taught me a deep respect for those wiser than me, to find the good in everyone, and to treat others as I would expect to be treated.

To my loving wife, who has been at my side since her early teens; for her great love and strength, for always standing with me regardless who may come against her, and for her consistent and tireless support of my endeavors. Because of her support, many more people's advancement into The Eternal Creators original truth, and the growth of their spiritual walk was made possible. Moreover, for her greatest gift to me, our son, the next Hebrew Scholar to the Asher lineage.

I would also like to thank the following people for their aid and undying enthusiasm and support for this project:

Michele, Yvette, Sonja, and Jenna; for their aid as beta readers, and in the source proofing, and *pre* and final editing several versions of this book. Without their help through many stages, this work may have never seen the light of day.

CONTENTS

"Every so often, to prove the existence of Free Will, a person must force themselves to change and believe something they wish to believe, remembering that the future is determined by the character of those who shaped it"

The problem with false paradigms is such that, as long as you remain in yours, you will never see or identify anything you hear or read differently than you did previously.

The bodies of all men are, indeed, mortal, and *are created out of corruptible matter;* but the soul is ever immortal, and is a portion of the divinity that inhabits our bodies. . . . Do not you know, that those who depart out of this life according to the laws of nature . . . enjoy eternal fame; that their houses and posterity are sure; that their souls are pure and obedient, and obtain a most holy place in heaven, from whence, in the revolution of ages, they are again sent . . . into bodies; while the souls of those whose hands have acted madly against themselves are received by the darkest place in Hades?

The Works of Flavius Josephus translated by William Wiston

Foreword

By Bill Mack

For me, it is a great honor to write the foreword to a book by a talented scholar and teacher that has inspired and enlightened me.

Learning and living the Everlasting Agreement is a choice that positively changed my physical and spiritual life, and inadvertently those close to me. The collection of books by Dr. Asher is quite timely and I believe his previous books (Land of Meat and Honey, Greater Exodus) and now Soul Revolution to be very important works today.

I have spent my entire life as a trained Scientist seeking the truth and understanding about the interactions, influences, and consequences of living organisms and the environment. This is also true in my spiritual life where I struggled with what science and organized religions had to offer in regards to creation, the soul, and the minute interactions of life. All of which to me has been quite perplexing and mysterious. All of what I believed, in both science and religion, was based on direct observation, memorization of facts from established authoritative sources, blind faith, assumptions, and "fudging of data" in the gray areas. Many conflicting, duplicitous sources of information exist, in science and religion, which can lead to incorrect conclusions and even disastrous outcomes attributed to not having all the facts and evidence presented in a logical way, coupled with blindly held beliefs.

Raised in an Eastern Orthodox religion, I was blindly immersed and lead to believe what "they" believed because it was *written* and *professed* to be so; and thus, anybody to challenge, question or scratch their heads at all the duplicity in their written truths would be considered a heretic.

When my dear friend Michele introduced me to the works of Dr. Asher, it felt like my world was shaken and turned upside down until I realized that I believed what I believed because that is what I was *supposed* to believe, no questions asked. My journey in seeking the truth required me to deposit my beliefs, expectations, religious baggage, biases and socially driven narratives at the "Door Step" and approach the topic with an open mind. What Dr. Asher offers in his collection of extremely important publications is an approach that is logical, based on distilled fact, with the symbiosis of *theology* and *scientific* proof. This approach, without keeping an open mind may be painful, and as it is said, "Sometimes the truth can bite".

Once I continued with an open mind and the approach of a trained scientist, I was able to see through the veil of lies and half-truths. I then felt enlightened, almost overzealous with this new found knowledge and truth. However, I put the *brakes* on to prevent confrontation from those who don't want the truth shared, and kept an open mind and positive frequency for communication with others as it presents itself.

As a trained Watershed Ecologist I analyze situations using multiple layers of data analysis, trying to link large quantities of *past, current* and *grey* data in order to present a big picture and holistic understanding of systems/communities, all of which are linked and influenced by the interactions of other organisms, entities and environmental stressors. These stressors may be natural or manmade. However, linking much of the *gray data* requires a degree of open-minded thinking in order to interpret complex interactions within this physical world. Just because you are taught and trained to believe something and discouraged to question why doesn't make it right or the truth. Education and training like that impede progress and enlightenment. Without the ability to identify another path, and open minded enough to accept all data while on that path, those fringe *gray* data portions attributed to those stressors remain unabated and continue to impair the community.

With advances in modern science, especially physics, answers to some of the most mystical ideas are now being revealed. Additionally, the translation of ancient scriptures using more modern terms brings into the picture some great wisdom and truth which has been lost, *hidden* and or manipulated for those who seek power over the masses. Dr. Asher masterfully compiles scientific fact, hypothesis, ancient historical text, and logically links the dots back to the ancient truth with a strong supportive argument for the facts, providing the reader the information to decide to explore further.

I look forward to the release of *Soul Revolution!* While knowing well his previous publications, I assure the reader, you will need to leave your religious and academic baggage at the door, strap in and get ready for another exhilarating journey for the truth. Seeing the world as it is now, I believe the publication of this book is quite timely in that, the world/society in which we find ourselves is becoming more fanatical in their beliefs and actions, resulting in great death and suffering of all souls, which continues to devolve us as collective souls. Do living souls created out of love and given the free will to choose, really want to choose *evil, death, suffering, poverty* and all of the other negative realities projected by our conscience thought? The information presented in Dr. Asher's books and teachings provides the information to the reader to decide. Hopefully, the choice is to live the way of The Everlasting Agreement and teach others so that the wave of enlightenment can become a tsunami eliminating all that is not *in perfect order.*

The *original instructions,* which have been long hidden are so simple to follow that our living souls do not need a long list of *Levitical* laws created by those who prosper from their adherence! Many of which lead to the violation of the Creators original agreement; as you will come to know. All truth revolves only around *Love, mercy, equality* and *compassion* for the souls that we encounter daily. *Life* and *Good* should be the free will choice.

These instructions for reaching our correct/original destination, *who, what* and *where* we are, has been presented in this talented scholars publications.

Take the facts, and find the courage to decide before it is too late to separate you from all the false truths and find yourself trapped in darkness, suffering, death and evil. As living souls, the Prime Eternal Creator gave us the choice of Free Will. Are you ready to break the chains of *organized soul slavery;* to deprive the disconnected souls of their power and energy, and regain *who, what* and *where* we are supposed to be?

What Will You Choose?

Authors Elucidation

Of

Soul Revolution

T his book is about reality and truths, both long forgotten, and hidden, and certainly not to suggest or institute yet another religious narrative. It is my hope however that the reader be opened up to our modern reality of incredible emerging science finally reuniting with, and proving out the wisdom of our ancestors'; metaphysical beliefs that have long been taught as fables and myth, reemerging again to verify our literal reality. One major step forward in recently verified areas has centered on the **"living soul"** within all people!

However, even amongst all the great science which is now beginning to illuminate the metaphysical, I believe there still exists yet one major gap in all of man's understanding concerning our living-soul; _a consciousness gap to our true identity;_ a **"Metaphysical Missing Link"**, so to speak.

Many people – **souls**, live their entire lives confused about their existence, and tend towards religions to fill that hole. While many plagued by _personality traits, phobias, and fetishes_ on a scale ranging from mildly affected to that which Western society's limited medical disciplines tend to label as acute psychosis, remain mostly unanswered and unfulfilled, regardless of religion.

However, I believe it is time to explore a new enlightening and liberating understanding of who we truly are, compared to that which our Western physicians and dogmatic religionists misunderstand and label as mere medical or spiritual dysfunction. Issues which they haphazardly treat with chemicals or worse, or by their religious superstitions, they demonize certain groups or individuals as evil, sinful or deranged.

The limited information which has been largely controlled and propagated through **controlled narratives** by those few in control throughout history, and specifically concerning the Living-Soul of man, is not the truth that existed originally. In our so-called *modern times,* most perceived issues in a man, woman, or child which our mainstream physical or psychological medical establishment and ultra-conservative religionists misdiagnose as biological or mental dysfunction are not physical at all, *but in fact the undiagnosed condition of the soul!*

Remnants leaking through, and that soul's inability to navigate past its previously stored, most dominant memories without the conscious awareness that they even exist, much less why they exist! Almost all Western physicians and Theologians, as well as the individual people who are adversely affected by this still unrealized fifth dimension phenomenon, will continue to be affected until we collectively; laymen, scholars and scientists, culturally worldwide decide to care less about our Doctoral degrees, position in society, and dogmatic superstitious beliefs, and begin to allow ourselves to perceive each *living- soul-person* differently, and from a more, corrected ancient perspective.

The true nature and original condition of our souls through the ages has been thwarted by cultures of narrative controlled religions. By these, people remain unaware, in most cases enslaved and crippled spiritually by seemingly innocent beliefs, and not so innocent prejudices'.

Predominantly no longer spiritually attune, we lost the

understanding that all souls are in need of immediate *identification* and ongoing *guidance*. This great cultural loss of basic *"soul identification"* has in fact been engineered out of our collective awareness from more ancient times, and further amplified by our spiritually shallow Western culture. It is not by chance that most of the people reading this book may have themselves pondered the reasons for our Western cultures ever expanding spiritual devolution, while at the same time feeling small in their ability to effect positive, meaningful, or lasting change within it. So far all of this can be traced to the **Metaphysical Missing Link,** which at its core is the lack of knowledge of certain original, key spiritual truths — **Who we are as** *soul-entities!*

Whether it be in this physical reality or the spiritual in this life or the next, you will never affect positive, lasting change within yourself or upon this world reality until you first become aware, believe, assimilate and ACT on the understanding that a major *Soul* identity crisis exists within us. Coupled with the corrected knowledge that certain forces perpetuate that condition within us for their own gain by teaching and re-teaching all souls to blame our condition on other entities.

I warn the reader that the correlations made in this book between the modern scientific data and the ancient wisdom reconvened from the multitude of long scattered paths as I have reassembled here, will be fearful to most, and confirmation to some.

But, as you will learn later on herein; our skin must be removed in order to free our light once again!

Many of the world's most renowned Scientists continue ascending through greater heights of undeniable verification on this ancient mountain of previously lost knowledge for all to see.

At an equal pace, but unfortunately in the opposite direction we have most theologians' ever receding tide of understanding, resisting the proven scholarship of the few truthful academics in that field, along with emerging science, for continued superstitious slavery. Herein I will try to show the reader how both certain emerging scientific proofs, along with our most ancient spiritual knowledge, can, in fact, cohabitate holistically. I am not attempting to prove to you that I have found a complete skeleton in the sands of time, and use it as proof that XY&Z always existed in such a specific way, but only forgotten or hidden by some hand. To the contrary, my work is to point out how the animals have scattered most of our skeletal remains, leaving few remaining original bones at their point of origin. My expertise will be used to find the rest of those chewed and scattered bones, clean off the years of residue, bring them back, and fit them together in the hopes of rebuilding the original remains so we can see what that original body looked like.

To that end, as much as possible I humbly ask the reader to restrain any dogmatic, material scientific prejudice and long-standing religious superstition for a short time, to allow this reemerging ancient truth the attention it deserves. We stand at a crossroad of expanding enlightenment in our time once again.

However, our prosperous, peaceful future depends on breaking some bonds by re-learning and accepting what our eternal *living-souls* true identity is, along with the realization of our past choices, and their consequences. Providing us collectively the clarity to *choose* more correctly going forward.

Mankind's current worldview is a world of objectivity and naïve materialism, once believed to be as solid granite, is now seen to be as seeping lava through its fatal cracks. For an ancient comparative religion scholar like myself, this is a long-awaited opportunity to intercept coalescing knowledge streams.

With his "two-slit experiment" Nobel laureate Max Born demonstrated in 1926 that all matter particles exist as only mere **statistical predictions**. All matter in which all things are made exists as nothing but a likely outcome – **(potential),** until they are literally observed by the human *soul-consciousness*, they have no real existence. That in fact only when the *mind-soul-consciousness* sets the framework in place by its **projection** of our **intention**, can any particles be understood as existing for any duration, or in any position in space.

Continuing experiments have proven further, that even foreknowledge in the experimenter's own soul-consciousness is sufficient to convert *matter-particle-possibility* to reality. Way before his time, the intuitive Immanuel Kant showed us that everything we experience, *all the colors; sensations; and objects* we perceive to be "real" as we have determined this word to mean, are nothing but *representations* in our mind <u>constructed through the souls ability to interact with all matter to create</u>, along with space and time being the means by which the mind places it all together. Only in recent years have many scientists been dragged kicking and screaming away from their mechanical bindings to recognize that these are in fact the rules making all existence possible. In fact, as you will see presented later herein, experiments ongoing prove that objects only exist with "real properties" *if they are observed by a consciousness*.

Kant knowing this intuitively approx. 200 years ago, only to be proven correct more recently, must be uncomfortable to many scientists. However still defying our common intuition, it thankfully, and finally suggests that our soul is immortal and exists outside of space and time. The science also suggests that our souls can *receive* and *collect* previously unknown data from an outside source organically. If this were not so, how *Kant* or anyone else could intuit such profound and detailed knowledge so long before any scientific construct of measurability or context, should be the question.

I believe your indulgence will be well worth your energy as this expansive and enlightening picture unfolds. It is my understanding that the widespread knowledge and reemergence of certain important spiritual missing links can and will save lives, souls, as it were. I also know that it will take a fairly sizeable number of people who **learn, exercise,** and **teach** this awesome understanding to cause a long awaited and greatly needed metaphysical Big-Bang to occur.

Although much of the supporting information herein,

whether scientific, ancient religious texts, cultural superstitions, or metaphysical ideas are not new concepts; know that the primary hypothesis of this book, which is a lofty endeavor to free the spiritually and physically oppressed by a societal paradigm shift, *is a new holistic application of ancient knowledge and modern sciences.* One which I hope will become culturally reiterated across all borders and languages used to break out of our induced slumber and to identify each person's soul in order to redirect his or her embedded proclivities, or accentuate their innate talents early on.

To identify who our souls are and where they need to be in the future is our way home!

A word on the ancient texts used herein

I would like to mitigate any religious or academic concerns up front by pointing out; that the ancient Gnostic, Babylonian, Egyptian, Hebrew and or Christian texts to which I refer and use as examples throughout this book, have not been used to prove or force some God-given authority of said texts or religion. These texts, like all of the superstition, folklore and Mythos in which I also refer to herein, can in most cases be understood by the reader as ancient, scattered remains being found and returned to the puzzle for further scrutiny.

The main point that I wish to show concerning all these texts and their *corrected translations* is, to bring the reader's attention to the existence and clear similarities of highly advanced knowledge spanning cultures, great geographical distances, and thousands of years of time. Most of which have been completely misunderstood out of their true context for at least 2000 years.

Additionally, to show ideas that seem impossible for them to have had on their own and so long ago, only to be expressed in their writings as best as they could be provided through their thoroughly limited vocabulary and conceptual ability to express such advanced concepts. These points especially cannot be forgotten by the reader as I present these texts herein.

As well, the texts I do present herein are by far not all that exist on the subject. I implore the reader to continue their education and familiarity with the world's ancient writings and within this re-emerging narrative stream.

Everlasting Agreement Synopsis

Although it is highly recommended that for those who have not already done so to read *"The Land of Meat and Honey"* (D. S. Asher), for the best and most complete understanding of the Everlasting Agreement. However, because the concept and understanding of it are also important to and woven throughout this book, I will provide a short explanation for clarity.

The Everlasting Agreement is an all-encompassing set of original instructions; an immutable legal framework initially designed and implemented into all creations by the Prime Eternal Creator, a fence around all created beings-souls. These minimal, original instructions have always been known and remain identifiable for the few who seek them. Cleverly obscured by the Babylonian-Judaic cult whose scribes edited and redacted them from the earliest Hebrew writings. Thus, leading the world further astray by mere commentary versions known as Western language bibles.

Most people's tendency is to marginalize the Everlasting Agreement as a mere dietary restriction. However, at its essence, it is a deep, unrestricted devotion and love for our Eternal Creator and His creation, acted out through obedience to it. More importantly, in direct connection with His first law of *Freewill,* as you will also soon come to see more clearly.

The foundation of which is; *we are to treat all His creation with the soul of life, whether human or animal, as we want to be treated ourselves.*

Thus, we do not partake in anything associated with the killing or intentional destruction of His creation, *which ultimately is our usurpation of another's freewill.* It must be comprehended that this is not a simple action of "doing" but intrinsic to how we live from our soul, and *<u>directly related to our Souls return trip and reunification with its original Creator</u>.*

This life-consciousness change as described above is easily identifiable to us as being an initially inherent consciousness in all children – (Life abundant!) Its contrary behavior, of which is NOT a naturally inherent behavior for any *living-soul* - within a child, to seek to inflict death on any other living thing. If you do not believe that, you should seek help. In order for this anti-life behavior to seem like a natural behavior in any human soul, those *narratives* must be nurtured by the parents and society early on and continually. In making this life change, which by definition is our return to our source both in the physical and the spiritual, turns out to be a path which cleanses and thereby clarifies our soul's sight.

This change/return enables us in this physical dimension, to break away from the enslavement of this usurped creations false narrative controls.

Before I continue there is the need to solidify specific entity identifiers that will be used to depict precise esoteric beings and their intentions throughout this book.

- Rebellion leaders *and* Rebellion Souls, Elite Souls, etc.
- Archons

These first three terms and any derivations of them will be used interchangeably to identify those *ancient entities* that most Judeo-Christians, Jews, and Muslims have determined to be *"fallen angels, Devs or Jinn"* etc.

Additionally, these entities can be correlated directly with those 200 entities that the patriarch Enoch specifically confirmed as being the original soul-entities also known as the *Watchers. It is imperative for the reader to recognize that these Rebel-leaders-Archons, fallen soul entities, etc., to be those who manipulated and corrupted the multitude of souls <u>already living within this creation level</u>. Which is to say that none of the parties will be presented in the usual manner as our three major religions have depicted them.*

- Adam-Eden matrix
- False heaven matrix
- Creation level

The first two terms above will be used to describe *"humanity & earth"* as well as what I will present to be the *"false heaven"* construct. The *Adam-Eden* matrix makes up, *but not limited to,* the *reformatted* Archon earth system control-narratives, as well as man's physical construct; all working in conjunction. All of this will be expanded on in more detail as you go! Both *above* & *below* systems are being used to *enslave* and *manage* all souls; the reasons why will become clear herein. At this point, humanity has believed this to be The True Eternal Creator's *original heaven* and *original earth systems*. This idea as well will be discussed in great depth throughout. So without further ado, I shall continue with our topic.

Chapter 1

I remember it was cold, December I believe, just before the holidays. I was there to speak to the parishioners of a Christian Church about our collective ancient superstitions, everyone still bundled up, although I was set to heat things up very quickly.

Right off I expressed that they were about to learn a new spiritual ritual, asking everyone to stand up with their feet together, both hands on their hearts, eyes closed, and repeating this phrase three times – " I am an Evolving soul".

Of course, I do not do this to embarrass anyone, but to prove in a very obvious way just how open most people are to following the direction of a perceived authoritative figure, especially if it involves any type of ritual. The proof is in the fact that no one asked me to either explain or show them this new ritual before agreeing to learn, and do it.

Humanity has been driven by diverse religious superstitions for far too long, and most of it all continues to be rooted in monumental intolerance, veiled in false humility, wrapped up in a thin layer of faux unconditional love. Throughout this book, I will refer to *control narratives*, *false narratives* and sometimes just *narratives*. All derivations understood to be deliberately fabricated story narratives most generally known to us as *myth, folklore,* and *superstitions.* All most generally found throughout the world's religious writings and revered as the literal words, and or instructions from some god, but not limited to religion. Paralleling the religious, we have scientific, geopolitical and socioeconomic control narratives as well, and their sub-narratives.

There exists an original instructional understanding for all mankind, simple and equitable for both man and animal alike. Sadly, the majority of people who have access to this information lack interest, instead they prefer to close their eyes to its simple justness and true spiritual freedom. However, the refusal to accept these soul-freeing directions alternatively places them under the control of the super-religious, and various other narrative controls which ritualistically enslave the masses still, and drive us to the brink of annihilation as we are seeing now in 2016.

Regardless if it is our own Levitical heritage, modern Christianity, Muslim or other cults, the common thread that runs through all the earth religions are embedded with long-standing superstitious roots. This is accomplished with *controlling narratives* used to grip their followers, most generally by fear. In addition, and especially so in our more modern times, the few Archon sycophants, and their overlords have been *allowed* to exert a good dose of control over the other non-religiously related segments of our populations by ever expanding means.

Latent, but ever expanding control narratives that on one side socially control and persecute *scapegoated* segments of our populations, but then also adversely affects the souls of those who lovingly persecute them.

Both of these have been made slaves by the orthodoxies. *Soul-Slaves*, induced by the implementation of cleverly controlled narratives! But who gave us the first narratives? Who is really in control?

What if while exploring one of the many caves in *Canaan* a long lost scroll was discovered? What if this scroll had been secretly hidden back during ancient times attempting to protect and preserve its contents? What if that scroll depicted all of The Creator's original work and systems in far greater detail than presently known? *Original laws which are the polar opposite of all other spiritual or religious laws as we have come to know them.*

Such detail would afford the possessor leverage, and at the very least great power if used malevolently. For we all should know by now that great power to create, can also be used to destroy.

However, the most conniving use of such knowledge would be to completely hide it with intent to promote and propagate various *opposite* narratives. Having access to the knowledge of the inner workings of the *Prime Creator* that created this place and its systems, would surely afford them great insight and the ability to manipulate those systems by *creating new* and *amending old narratives,* therefore *reformatting* the Prime Creator's original wisdom for all generations to come.

By doing so, these entities and anyone they have brought into their inner circle could eventually effect and control larger segments of the growing world's societies, but don't forget to ponder...*where did the original narratives come from, and by whose hand, mind, or creative-intention?*

Why would anyone stop short at controlling only your physical body for the duration of one typical human life cycle, when they could exercise control over many lifetimes? This would mean having domination over your very soul! *It is impossible you say?* Because you believe a person's soul exists for only one lifetime?

Well yes, of course, you believe this way. This is because the entities, who believe they wield the power of the *control narratives,* were those who presented that religious dogma in the first place and that which remains in effect now. All as you will come to see, perpetuated by our own consent! These are the hidden half-truths perpetuated through man's unconscious consent! The masses give their ever-expanding permission by participating in the cultural and faith-based superstitions purported by the control narratives of these nefarious entities. This is further amplified by the prophetic events conjured up by these controlling entities themselves. As I will show herein, the unaware populous of this world will literally "believe & speak" the plans and prophecies for these Archon controllers into existence by their own creative souls *"intention!"* The manipulators need only stand by, watch, wait and tweak control narratives as needed.

Even more amazing is that through this ancient knowledge they are able to thwart original benevolent systems, as well as design new schemes, conning good people into participation by their own consent. These people have no direct knowledge of their being utilized in this manner and hence remain continually ignorant of the desired end goal. *Sound like science fiction to you?* Soon you will understand it is not at all science fiction, as I connect newly verified quantum and biological physics with ancient knowledge that was until recently, thought to be myth.

As documented throughout history, in the natural events of civilizations there exists a very limited number of elite sycophants associated with on-going and identifiable evil tendencies. This is regardless of culture, language, or generation. Of these propensities, the most prominent is the drive by the few to control the many. This is initially accomplished through religious superstition and rituals migrating into government brute force. An observant historical scholar will be amazed at just how similar in *thought, belief,* and *action* the *evil minority's* procedures and endgame proves to be, compared to what most perceive to be true religious faith.

Unfortunately, mankind's lack of retention and awareness to these evil elite's strategies remains unrecognized in the day-to-day struggles of life. A life that is always *driven* hard by their narratives!

Many philosophers and religious scholars tend to coin this protracted behavior as the *"evil stream of consciousness"; a* continued conscious behavior, which at face value only appears able to inflict control over *willing people* <u>by their consent</u>. However, there is another more probable scenario. This would be that people remain unaware that a control system of false narratives actually exists at all, *and consent tacitly!*

The three major religious cults of this planet, along with their many offshoot sects have their varied superstitions and folklore concerning who these entities are that drive the consciousness of humanity to the brink, and as we find ourselves today.

As we progress, these available chosen programs which drive the *evil stream of consciousness* have become more easily recognizable. Additionally, this becomes more evident as science uncovers, correlates and demonstrates what has long been misunderstood and clandestinely passed down through the generations of elite priests, and passed off by them as, *hidden knowledge!* And although it is my area of expertise to expand on these religious misunderstandings at great length and historical detail, I will not be doing so in this book to the extent possible. Rather this topic far exceeds the dank confines of man's misguided religion alone.

Despite whether or not we believe that some unseen entities exist, or identify their malevolent and detrimental effect on a chosen elite key people, or mankind in general; most in one way or another will concede to the existence of some influencing supernatural or super-technical entities. Thankfully, once again in human history, with each passing day our collective souls are awakening to the fact that something very grave, and even yet unseen is wrong!

Your Freewill always has a choice. First one must become aware that the consciousness, the *Living-Soul*, has the literal ability to create. As will be shown later in this book, the direction of conscious thought (focused intention) has the ability to change an individual's and collective society's immediate and long-term physical & spiritual realities! And no! I am not presenting to you any New Age fiction!

It all started with a single bone!

The Saturn Narrative and Kubrick's god-monolith!

The first body, first narrative!

The *evil stream of consciousness* had to come from somewhere.

The author and filmmaker Jay Weidner has proposed that legendary film director Stanley Kubrick created his masterpiece *2001: A Space Odyssey* as a visual depiction into the ongoing transformation and ascension of man to our so-called Star-child destiny.

Kubrick's film is set against the backdrop of a space mission sent to the planet Jupiter, *originally Saturn,* to investigate a massive monolith. If one pays very close attention, this movie incorporates elements of *extraterrestrial life, early human existence and their manipulation of us through a violence narrative provided by the god-*

monolith, technology, artificial intelligence; the bonus is that it even shadows the *Kayin & Habel* biblical accounts we have today.

It is evident that in mythological and esoteric occult traditions that *Saturn* is recognized as the original prime creator or god entity. This is ever present even within our current world and its many corporate logos depicting and giving homage to the planet and its rings. Many are just unaware of its presence. As you will see further into this book, there was an ancient shift by the early Hebrews away from the True Eternal Creator, with the Saturn deity being substituted. This is made evident within the Hebrew texts as well as other Canaanite writings. Then again later, there is yet another diversion depicting the cult of Judaism continuously promoting Jupiter as the supreme creator but never again Saturn openly.

It is believed that Stanly Kubrick was somehow forced to change his movie theme from depicting the planet Saturn, as being the origination point of the *god-monolith,* to the planet Jupiter.

Allegedly pressure imposed by high-ranking occultists concerned that his depiction would obviously point to their human metamorphosis scheme. However, there remained a Saturn "connection" within the movie and that was the black monolith.

This standing stone, although differing in shape, can easily be equated with the black monolith cube of Ancient Saturn worship throughout many of the world's religions.

The first Controlled-narrative!

Excerpt: "Alchemical Kubrick", by Jay Weidner – filmmaker.
"The next episode, after the monolith appears, is the famous scene where the ape-man leader is sitting in a pile of animal bones and realizes - again clearly defined by Kubrick as an intervention into the mind of the ape-man by the monolith - that the bone can be used as a weapon. To the music of the World Riddle theme, again from Strauss' 'Thus Spoke Zarathustra', the ape-man suddenly understands that he can kill animals by using the bone as a club. The next scene shows that the ape-men are no longer scrounging for seeds and leaves, instead, they are

eating raw meat, presumably from an animal that they have just killed with their bone club.

Kubrick clearly shows this action in a way that makes the meat appear extremely repulsive, and specific to a change in their overall intention.

Finally, he ends the first sequence with the confrontation by the water hole, again, with the other tribal ape men. This time, though, the leader of the ape-men has a bone club in his hand.

The other tribe goes into their ritualized shouting and gesturing in order to show that they can dominate the water hole. The leader of the other tribe runs up. He yells at the ape-man with the bone in his hand. The leader of the tribe of bone-wielders places both hands on the 'handle' of his weapon and strikes the other ape in the head, killing him instantly. (The first murderer) *The leader of the rival ape-men falls down to the ground motionless. This stuns and frightens the ape-men in the other tribe and they run away. Kubrick then brilliantly shows the other ape-men in the tribe come forth and pound their bone weapons on the body of the dead ape-man. Kubrick pulls no punches here. He wants you to know that this first murder is an act of cowardice.*

He shows the meek ape-men pounding their bones on the dead body and acting as if they had done something incredible in this act of murder. The leader of the ape-men howls victoriously and throws his bone into the air. This is where Kubrick magically transforms the bone into a spaceship and rejects all of human history in one-twenty-fourth of a second. In his audacity, Kubrick is telling us that all of history is meaningless. He dispenses all of civilization as if it were insignificant. And, in a way, that is the complete point. He is telling us that the ape-man's encounter with the monolith and whatever is about to happen in this film is vastly more important than all of the wars, famines, births, marriages, deaths, disasters, discoveries and art of the last 4 million years." (Emphasis added) Weidner, Jay. "Alchemical Kubrick." Web. 2015.

Whether Kubrick intuited this sequence of events or had a view of the greater picture, his depiction was more astute than most people have had the depth of wisdom to see. Although Kubrick does not go to the length of showing our original previous *light-soul-bodies* prior to enslavement in whichever type of humanoid body we may have been forced into during our earliest times, his depiction of the *god-monolith-entity* presenting the first narrative of death by way of *intention,* clearly exposes the first murder. *The portrayal of the god-monolith presenting that first control narrative by way of creational intention to the inquisitive man is quite profound,* considering that the god-entity could just as easily provided a more useful and positive intention to that man. This is proof of the low character of that god-entity.

That account could just have easily provided an intuition showing the man how to use the bone to dig for roots and other food sources, but the proof of character is easily identified as the ever present *evil stream of consciousness,* and the redirection of our programming begins! This "start" point *proved the character of that false god monolith. Conversely, that man-soul did NOT have to <u>consent</u> to the evil one's intention!*

If we look close enough, this directly correlates to all negative behavior being influenced by the world's *control narratives* and propagated by the same counterfeit gods' *anti-creation* character. Moreover, it should not be lost on anyone that in the exact sequence as Kubrick portrays, once the first man or *Adam* understands the power of his single swinging bone, it is used for murdering the first animal; *it isn't long after the taste of flesh and blood that they murder one of their own.* For those aware of my teaching on *The Everlasting Agreement,* this same violence precedes the ongoing contamination of our DNA and spills over to our souls. This is the force of the narrative!

This homicide by the sand pond against his rival with his new found weapon is not unlike that of the biblical Kayin and Habel story. Clearly, these creatures were few enough to comprehend that they were very possibly of the same lineage. As seen in the days preceding the murderous event, anger was expressed but never unto death. Once a new "intention" was introduced, killing became justified as a means to settle a dispute. The bone weapon is then almost incidental. All expected and in perfect sequence when set in play by some *negative narrative* wielding demigod! The black god-monolith.

"However vast the darkness, we must supply our own light."
Stanley Kubrick

Why is it that people continue to use their awesome gift of Free-Will to make choices for Evil, more times than for Good?

Evil inclination is REAL, and the task of man was originally such that our living souls would to navigate the creational maze without being defiled by the Evil therein. **This is the core of Free Will.**

As you can see thus far, I believe it is easily proven that the main answer to this all important question can best be expressed as follows: *Many original truths, which were set in place to promote LIFE abundantly have been hidden. Then only to be replaced by less than "life" promoting dogma, ritual, and governmental systems - "control narratives."*

The key to breaking their chains of control is to finally learn whom humans truly are − (living-Souls), and who we can be collectively. A knowledge which they still mostly control!

WHO YOU ARE

This book is not going to be some new age metaphysical self-help diatribe that ultimately leaves you searching for the literal nuts and bolts of how to get there from here. When all is said and done, the objective is to unveil an uncomplicated, complete understanding of the following:

- The true identity of the soul
- Why our collective souls are here
- Our soul's true origin and condition
- To where our soul was intended to return
- How to recognize the control narratives and those who impose them both in life and death.

The simplicity of these realities has nearly been lost since ancient times because certain self-appointed entities have kept it hidden under their authority. Unfortunately, for some time our Western culture has been used as the main vehicle to perpetuate this control of very basic knowledge. For the most part, two opposing strategies are utilized as *divide & conquer control narratives*. The first employs religion to segregate people through what I call, *Levitical Intolerance*, while the second counter punches with faux political correctness directed at only certain politically driven chosen groups or races.

Nonetheless, without the knowledge of this deception, it would be easy to fall prey and become hypnotized by their doublespeak as they play both sides intending to keep the masses off balance and unaware. Regrettably, thus far they have succeeded in capturing most souls by passively manipulating us by our individual free-will choice to remain unsuspecting and ignorant. *Think of what they do as magic.* Illusions work because YOU, the observer, actually do most of the magician's work by paying attention and looking in the wrong place. Our perception is easily manipulated because of our individual lack of knowledge and our naiveté to the subject matter.

Although this is an oversimplification; nevertheless, this is how they accomplish their work. They have used the very same ideas and tactics for thousands of years. Within all cultures, many wise men and messiahs have come and gone attempting to enlighten those who might listen to the same truths I will be presenting here, but so few are ever open to hearing. It is my hope that this book will speak to those whose religious doctrines teach and encourage *righteous intolerance and prejudices* against select individuals and/or factions of the world's populace under the ruse of being righteousness. I and a growing number of souls know, that despite what many have been lead to believe, our religious institutions embody neither "love nor mercy", much less as endorsed and sanctioned by the character of our loving Eternal Creator. To those victimized by the aforementioned religious zealots, the goal is to impart information and healing. Additionally, there is also a desire to provide insight to the many scientists and researchers who seek deeper truths for the understanding and meaning of mankind's existence within the fabric of this creation space.

As I progress further into the depths of the distinctiveness of our souls, both present, and past, you will garner a sudden realization. Much of it will be based on the scientific theories that are currently becoming proven reality, and how they can make such sense when formerly esoteric knowledge is brought back in and recoupled to the science in a holistic way.

> "A fundamental conclusion of the new physics also acknowledges that the <u>observer creates</u> the <u>reality</u>. As observers, <u>we are personally involved with the creation of our own reality</u>. Physicists are being forced to admit that the universe is a "mental", <u>spiritual construction</u>. Pioneering physicist Sir James Jeans wrote: "The stream of knowledge is heading toward a non-mechanical reality; the universe begins to look more like a great **thought** than like a great machine. Mind no longer appears to be an accidental intruder into the realm of matter, we ought rather hail it as <u>the creator</u> and governor of the realm of matter.
> (R. C. Henry, "The Mental Universe"; Nature 436:29, 2005) **Emphasis added**

Thus far as a species whose souls were created to be the *microcosm-souls* of the true Primary Eternal Creator's *Macro-soul*, we have yet to embrace such a lofty proven concept as spoken by *R.C. Henry*. However, once enough of us awaken and recognize the truth of our reality, a renewed peaceful heaven and earth of equity should emerge before our very eyes. In that day, there will no longer exist any form of enslavement. Neither by our own deafening recklessness nor the evil intent of those yet unseen entities currently yoking our *living-souls*.

I end with a quote that expresses a very true concept, often spoken by a very good friend to remind me that it is not our inability to persuade people despite the presentation of provable verifiable facts. That the burden of keeping an open soul and a willingness to look beyond their own learned paradigm lies with them. It's all a matter of perception. I repeat this to encourage you, the reader, not to become discouraged when faced with those unwilling to look at their soul with different insight. Remember, I am merely a messenger. What another does with the information given is entirely their responsibility.

"A man convinced against his will; is of the same opinion still."
                                                                                -Anonymous

My greatest hope is that the Eternal Creator reestablished His connection to all the souls of this creation!

S. Asher

Chapter **2**

Souls Above, Souls Below

The Cosmic Separation!

Although I am only able to speak for this lifetime coming from a heavy scholastically Hebrew influenced background, looking back over my life I can identify always being strongly driven to know and do what I now tend to believe I have done through many lifetimes. This has been to seek absolute truth for the sake of it alone regardless of where it leads or forces me to cast off. To relinquish that which is provably not of the True Eternal Creator. It often separates not just spiritually, but socially as well.

They say the truth hurts, but the realization of these truths is devastating, as it should be. However, without its realization the continued lack of knowledge only works to serve our slave masters; those who make us forget in order to keep their claim on us, and hold tight their own imaginations, the eventual total reformation of this creation to their kingdom of lies.

It grieves me as I even try to write the words to describe what I know most will not yet accept, and to a depth not yet realized by most of you who read it, because I, both fortunately and unfortunately at the same time have been privy to the greater picture of it all; so much more than mere words in a book can convey. Moreover, in the end, it is simply this; all of the Prime Eternal Creator's truths are always simple and available to those who truly seek them past their personal, limited narratives and comfort zones. *Meaning,* whether you are a Doctored scientist or scholar, talented researcher or layman, the equality among us all is, that we just have to decide to *see* the truth of it! Then *un-consent* from their many narratives, and "<u>Return from them</u>!"

Before we embark on this in depth and lofty subject which spans ancient cultures, languages, and ideas, to finally couple them together in a holistic fashion with our modern scientific discoveries in physics and other disciplines, and in the hopes of weaving them together to gain a new and possibly divergent view from the sum of their parts; I feel I must begin by clarifying one particular set of ancient texts which have been the basis of so much misunderstanding.

In this chapter, I will clarify the Hebrew texts that most of the Western culture believes it knows and understands.
Misunderstandings which have created new narratives, largely due to poor scriptural translations and grammar issues. *The purpose of all this and especially that of this book is NOT to fabricate a new religion or to uphold any New Age cult, God forbid.* My ultimate aim is to renew an important understanding, possibly one that many once possessed but by force has since been lost. <u>The identity of our Living-souls</u>!

The immediately following grammatical correction and later dissection of biblical Genesis chapter 1 texts is to provide a better, more comprehensive understanding of the ancient law of freewill as given in its original context before I move on to correlating any other extra-biblical ancient texts or cultural understandings, with our modern science. The hope is that it will provide greater clarity concerning the capture and continued manipulation of our living-souls generationally, and why.

Later on, after exploring the first chapter of the Genesis account, I will posit the argument that the *second chapter* of Genesis exists as a literal depiction of a *second* literal *re-formation* story. More accurately, a *reformatting* of this original creation through newly devised and injected control narrative streams of consciousness.

Genesis 1 – The Grammatical Error!

As you will see after this section, when I render the Genesis 1 texts grammatically, contextually and literally corrected, the story is quite a bit different, and it isn't painting the historically accepted picture. It should also be noted that the higher practitioners' within the Orthodoxy know the context as I corrected it, although their practice is to deny it.

It should also be known that certain ancient Jewish sages who were forced to deal with these flaws publicly, pretty much gave nothing more than apologise for the alleged grammatical errors, and highly biased personal opinions on the contexts. I use the word *alleged* here because of course, I believe it to be subterfuge. To prove it as such, I need only point to the well-known and highly touted rabbinical constant; the belief and teaching *that not one letter or vowel point is out of place in the Hebrew bible;* which is based on the strict scribal criteria of creating these texts via the *(Masora – Traditional discipline of rules for writing or copying – 7th CE).*

We are then left to believe that such a blatant and obvious mistake such as this, and that which I am about to show you, has gone unnoticed all this time. Of course, anyone who has read any of my other books already knows that I have pointed out hundreds of textual and cultural falsities, text story doublets and triplets that don't match, and a plethora of contradictions throughout the English and Hebrew bibles.

Now, using basic facts and logic a second time here, we can refute the additional apologies, opinions and excuses about what vowels were used where, and or which vowel marking (or Nikud) were added under which letter, etc. Because again, the (Nikud) – *vowel markings* did not exist when the earliest Genesis stories were penned out of our long oral tradition. Which points to the obvious, that the prefix in question was added much later, along with the vowelization markings, and along with its subsequent and alleged meanings, both grammatically, and spiritually.

The Aleppo Codex dated 900CE is the oldest Hebrew Torah/bible in existence that we know of. And it was my lineage namesake Aaron *ben'*Asher in the 10th century who designed and added the vowelization and cantillation notes to those texts based on their traditional Tiberian system. So in any case, for now, this is as far back as we can go with any complete Hebrew Torah text. *Strangely enough in the English/Hebrew concordance's, I have seen how they tend to leave the Hebrew prefix in question out of the Genesis 1 text.* That is interesting.

I would like to preface this before I start by reminding everyone that the later scribes for many generations had their own pens and opinions all over our texts.

In the be'ginning?

Everyone knows, that within all Western language translations and the Hebrew alike, all render the first line of Genesis as – *In the Beginning*

Reshiyth = (Raysheeth)

"בראשית ברא אלהים" - **"B' reshiyth bara Elohim"**, always translated as, **"In the beginning, God created..."** However, from the first Hebrew letter/word (bet-ב) this is a blatant grammatical error! Having that understanding now, if you pay close attention as we progress through this teaching, later you will see how its letter/word addition and subsequent translation, changes what could very well be one of the most important points of our entire existence here. Even hiding the truth of what was being created, and by whom.

Many of you may also have heard people say that, yes, it should really be translated as – **"In the beginning of...."** This is based on the reality that the two-word construct, or **(Smichute)** of *Be'reshiyth*, should have had a different vowel mark – *(be' – has been depicted with the* **Sh-va** *vowelization mark),* but should have been depicted with the **(Kamatz)** vowelization mark under it.

However, the real issue is the word (Reshiyth)-*it's true literal meaning we will get into shortly.* Had someone added the correct (Kamatz) vowelization point under the letter (Bet), making it (Ba-Reshiyth); then this might start looking like – *"In the beginning God created..."* – However, now we run into another major issue.

Problem two – Created What?

Simply stated, for the *construct* word "Be-Reshiyth" to exist grammatically correct here, the next word after it would need to be a "noun" describing **"what" was being created**! However, the next word is **"bara"** which is a verb! *(Bara means create or created).*

So now your mechanical translation of *"B'-reshiyth bara Elohim"* would be closer to - **"In the first beginning of God, created."** Obviously that can't be, but there it is in black and white worldwide, mistranslated to something it is not. Was it done on purpose? Was it just a mistake added so long ago no one wanted to fix it?

Reshiyth – (Raysheeth)

The elder and more literal meaning of this word can be expressed several ways in English -
Chief part of a year or reign; first phase, step, or element in a course of events; first of a thing or of a kingdom; first king; first god, segment or cycle of crops; first or earliest segment of a nation or place; first of a harvest, etc. (First!)

To narrow it down as meaning "In the Beginning" is both limiting and not in the correct context with what comes next from the literal translation of the rest of the words in this Genesis text. This will be more evident within the actual translation to come.

However for most religionists, it will remain a grammatical mess which they believe to have very purposeful spiritual intent and significance. While waving their hands using *Jedi* mind tricks they will say – *"you don't see any grammatical or temporal errors here, you seem confused, tired, go now and return to your slumber..."* But in the end there remain 49 lines of Bible text where this word is used 51 times, all predominantly used to express its true literal meaning of **"first"**, as it is correctly translated even in the English as FIRST among those 51 depictions, and not, *"beginning"*.

Now that you understand that a massive grammatical error has always existed in such a key section of scripture, which has been used to influence two of the world's largest organized religions; we can now move on and see the corrected rendering of those ancient texts which have remained so misunderstood.

More importantly, how they pertain specifically to *who our souls truly are, who the rebel souls are,* and *what they are still doing with us.* Then we will move on to the modern emerging sciences that are correlating all of this presently.

Creation of the Freewill System and Separation of Souls
Part 1:

In part one, contrary to all Western language bible transliterations and understandings taught within its many religious factions, you can expect to see <u>no</u> words used that express the physical properties of <u>light</u> or <u>water</u> within the first section of the Genesis account.

Rather, it should be understood as the **Prime/First** Eternal Creator forming His "<u>Freewill</u>" system by <u>dividing</u> the <u>extant darkness/chaos</u> = (lack of light/good), from His "Good"= (lack of darkness/chaos). This will also show the elements He used <u>to separate certain souls</u>. *Make no mistake, the adherence to His Freewill system is tantamount above all else for the existence of any and all creations or created beings to exist.*

The following is a literal text translation. The specific relevant phonetic English has the corresponding Hebrew in (parentheses before the English). Some Hebrew words have extended definitions after them. These delineations reveal what the Western language context understanding should be. In addition, any words in <these brackets> depict the need for a further clarifying explanation to come.

Creation of Souls; Creation of the physical, and the Creation of 1st Law of Free Will

Gen 1:1 "(**Reshiyth**) the **First/Prime** (Elohim)-**Eternal Creator** (bara)-**created** (et) <Shamayim>-**Obedient Souls**, and the (Eretz) **earth**." – Eretz = *DRY-hard-Ground, no presumption of water with these words* - (If anything it is particle-matter in general)

> **NOTE:** The Chaldean word "Sheema", Hebrew - "Shama", the root of "Shamayim" is usually used to mean "HEAR" - *i.e. Hear me oh lord* - But more literally it means ***"to obey with great intellect and discernment"***. So, if "Mayim" as I will show below in Gen 1:6 is depicting "the Souls", then "Shamayim" in this context is meant to depict the creation of all "Obedient-souls". As all souls were created and knew the law before being negatively influenced.

Gen 1:2 "and the (eretz)-**earth** was (To'Hu)-**without form**=*Desert-Waste*, and (Bo'Hu)-**void**=*Empty;* and (Choshek)-**darkness**=*Chaos/Wickedness* was upon the face of the (T'hom)-**abyss/***depth*" - *Not water!*- And the Spirit of The Eternal moved upon the face of the (Mayim)-**waters/souls** – *Mayim is also used as* waste *in certain contexts, also water/springs, and souls/people prophetically.*

Gen 1:3 "And (Elohim)-**The Eternal** (amar)-**spoke** saying, (haya)-**exist** (Ore)-**light** =*Goodness, or a light generating star:* and light existed."

Gen 1:4 "And (Elohim)-**The Eternal** (ra'ah)-**saw** the (Ore)-**light/good** was (tob)<**good**>,and (Elohim)-**The Eternal** (Badal)-**separated,** (Beyn)-**distinguishing** the (Ore)-**light/good**, (Beyn) **distinguishing** from the (Choshek)-**darkness** = *Wickedness*

Gen 1:5 "And (Elohim)-**The Eternal** (Qarah)-**published** the (Ore)-**Light/Goodness** as (yom)-**Day** = *(period of time - perpetually),* and (Qarah)-**publishing** the (Choshek)-**darkness**=Chaos/*wickedness* He called it (Lilah)-**Night**=*adversarial in some contexts;* and the evening existed. And morning existed, day one."

Tobe as seen above in Gen1:4 for the word - <good> = In Prefect Order: This more exact literal Ancient Hebrew understanding is very unlike the English or any Western language. This word is vitally important within all creation understanding, "good" is a far too inferior interpretation. This leaves the need to clarify and identify a very important and specific point. It must be understood that all that the Prime Eternal Creator, created, is viewed and understood by Him in *finalized, absolute terms* of **"Perfect Order!"** This now concludes all human arguments that somehow "imperfection" was initially created and/or found to be imperfect based on religious dogma. *(Any change in this perfect order is due to later Archon manipulation, or re-formatting of certain aspects in the original creation by those entities – In their image!) And our consent to them!*

Consequently, this lies to rest some severe condemnation

concerning His created souls. There can be no saying that in our original *soul-light-body* state, or within this physicality of man after that, or any higher soul entity, possesses any authority or is capable of UN-creating what was originally created by The Eternal Creator in the perfection of - *perfect order.*

In perfect order means precisely just that and cannot insinuate the opposite in any way, shape, or form. All souls, as they were created, are created *in perfect order,* which means <u>naturally obedient to the Eternal Creators systems</u>, but still having the free will to disobey them.

All of these Archon narratives and man driven falsities must be burned out of the collective misunderstandings like the dross from metal before we will be able to move out of this false reality and enslavement. It is imperative to understand that each soul has been equipped and is suitable for what He created it to do otherwise it is *"ra"* - unstable/evil. The living-Soul remains in perfect order. The post creation of these *Trinity-6* bodies in which our living souls have been encapsulated is the imperfection in which we need to be released from. *Scientific proof of the origin of the 666 is to come.*

Deciphering Part One

Part 1 sets the foundation. First is the creation of all *obedient* souls for this creation level, along with the creation of all dry ground, *matter.* All formed from The Eternal Creator's literal speech. Understanding that His speaking is in actuality a *frequency,* which science shows to be exactly what forms and holds together all plasma core based particle matter realities.

Additionally, that this 3rd dimension earth was reformatted in their *Archon* image using the dust or elements from the ground. Versus the Prime Creators original intent for this place, to be occupied by us in our original *soul-light-bodies* to live and cohabitate as equal souls.

Continuing in part one, we also see that the *abyss* was only *chaos or wickedness* and NOT specifically physical water or open space as most have considered this section to depict. Take further notice of His description in verse 5 of the *darkness as "adversarial"*.

We then see the Prime Creator-force create *light* but not the physical light of the sun or stars as we see depicted as being created on the 4th day. More accurately, His creation of *light* was the direct opposite of *chaos*, therefore denoting *Good-Correctness-Order!*

(This "light" was and remains the creation of His Free Will System!)

PART 2:

This section can be understood as the separation of souls above and below the expanse. As it would appear there to be an expanse zone set between all creation levels. In addition, a distinction is made between differing "souls/waters". So far we have seen the extant darkness/Chaos *and His* created light/Good; *more accurately, the potential for both with the ability to occur via our choices within His Freewill system.*

As you continue down through these next few verses, take special note of the word *Shamayim*. Remember this word is understood to depict that all *souls* were originally created obedient. Watch now for the Non-obedient souls to be separated below *under* His created *expanse zone* and referred to as "mayim", (having no "Shama") - *i.e.* obedience. Also, note that since Shama is missing in conjunction with these souls it also signifies the inability to *hear* The True Creator's voice. *I.e. a level of separation!*

Gen 1:6 "The (Elohim)-**Eternal** (amar)-**said**, '(haya)-let **exist** the (raqiya)-**expanse** (Tavek)-**bisecting** the (mayim)-**souls**, existing as (badal)-**separation,** (Beyn)-**distinguishing** the (mayim)-**souls** from the (mayim)-**souls**." **(Water=SOULS!)** *As seen in other prophetic texts.*

Gen 1:7 "And The (Elohim)-**Eternal** (asah)-**accomplished** the (raqiya)-**expanse**, (badal)-**separating**, (beyn)-**distinguishing** the (mayim)-**souls** (ashar)-**which** *were* (mineh)-**from** (tachat)-**under** the (raqiya)-**expanse** (beyn)-**distinguishing** the (mayim)-**souls** (ashar)-**which** *were* (mineh)-**from** (al)-**above** the (raqiya)-**expanse** (hayah)-**existing (ken)-rightly**."

Gen 1:8 "The (Elohim)-**Eternal** (qara)-**published** the (raqiya)-**expanse** as (Shameh)-**elevated**; and evening existed. Then morning (haya)-**existed**, day two."

Deciphering Part two

Part two is where we see the actual *living soul* portions being specifically separated out to *above* and *below* the greater expanse that separates our creation with another. It's important to recognize that these obedient living souls *already existed* as the microcosm-soul portions from His Macro-soul.

Important note: Most people view all biblical texts as events that occur close together in time and in a linear order, however, that is just not at all true in many cases. In this case of the *separation of disobedient souls* and their creation or birth before that separation can appear to be out of order. *Our issue here then is elapsed time.*

For now, we should understand that souls are being created all the time by the Eternal Creator. And for this overall picture of the *obedient souls* being created, and then appearing to be immediately separated for some incursion, is obviously not the case.

Going forward you should understand that all the souls created for *this creation level,* were living on this perfectly ordered creation level without incident *prior to those few disobedient souls arriving here.* That is the order of these events.

As expressed previously, there are other ancient texts which speak directly to this exact idea of separation, however, they tend to lend more specific details for the division. Justifications that later, for one reason or another expanded into larger myth or superstitions concerning fallen angels and wars in heaven against the Prime Eternal Creator and other such explanations. As I have always taught, *all myths and tales do tend to have an original root of truth,* so no doubt these may contain some degree of accuracy.

Therefore, since it is prudent not to throw the baby out with the bathwater, then sometimes the best method is to take a step back from these myths, folklore, and other superstitious expansions in order to identify the original roots of truth. The *Babylonian Emunah Elish* is one such text that has proven to be valuable. Consider the following:

> The first Genesis Hebrew text of "mayim" depicting the "waters-souls" of above and below has an equivalent in the older Babylonian *Emunah Elish*. This "water-souls" is described as *"Tiamat's substance/body" being overcome and split in two by Marduk and placed above and below the expanse as a separated pair.*

The Nag Hammadi codices of the Common Era's early 1st century reveal even more detail on this subject. Also, take note that there is little doubt that the English translation of these texts has an obvious early orthodox Christian influence. We in the modern era like to believe ourselves to be more advanced and better educated than those civilizations that came before us, however, the knowledge and specifics possessed by these ancient people defies even our most current understanding.

Following is the Nag Hammadi Library, Codex II, *The Hypostasis of the Archons,* paragraphs 1-3, (underlined emphasis and parenthesized clarifications by the author of this book):

> *"On account of the reality of the authorities, inspired by the spirit of the father of truth, the great apostle – referring to the "authorities of the darkness" – told us that "our contest is not against flesh and blood; rather, the authorities of the universe and the spirits of chaos." I have sent this to you because you inquire about the reality of the authorities.*
> *Their chief is blind because of his power and his ignorance, and in his arrogance, he said, with his power - (technology), "It is I who am god; there is none apart from me." When he said this, he sinned against the entirety - (Prime Creator).*

And this speech got up to incorruptibility - (above the expanse); then there was a voice that came forth from incorruptibility, saying,
"You are mistaken, Sama'el" *– which in the Hebrew tongue means - "ruler of the blind."*
"His thoughts became blind, having expelled his power by the blasphemy he had spoken he pursued it (his will) down to chaos and the abyss, (with) his mother, at the instigation of Pistis Sophia. And she established each of his offspring in conformity with its power-(Soul) - after the pattern of the realms that are above, by starting from the invisible world the visible world was invented.... (Robinson)

The Nag Hammadi texts reveal a story that seems far advanced from its contemporaries. How could they articulate such awareness if they had not received it from someone with direct extensive knowledge of both, our *original* and *re-formatted* heavenly realms?

You don't have to be a scholar to discern that the above text clearly speaks of another entity other than the original Primary Eternal Creator. This *realm* we find ourselves in was formed by the Primary Creator and should not be confused with the fact that it has been partially *reformatted* by the other entity spoken of here.

Another amazing imagery detail is how they depict the original created living-souls being used to animate the physical bodies they created - *And she established each of his offspring in conformity with its power-(Soul).*

- *(she established each of [his] offspring)* – [his] is referring back to **Sama'el.**
- *(in conformity with [its] power)* - [its power] must be referring to the living-soul light body, and them producing physical bodies that "conform" and accommodate the soul for use as a power source = [offspring]. Thus, the *imagery* of [its power] is of the power provided by the living soul which they enslaved to animate these bodies.

Additionally, the upper levels of heavenly creations are being revealed and contrasted between where this *below* realm is, to those other levels of *incorruptibility above.*

Also depicted is this now *reformatted* creation reality continuing in the fashion, and *after the likeness* of the one *above;* but as you will see most amazing of all is that this, and most likely all creation levels, in reality, are *holographic* by nature, which is a highly important feature to fully comprehend on this subject.

Specifically, how that is used to advance their *reformation process* by using us to do it! I will get into this in detail later! Thus, it is a manipulated hologram *"...by starting from the invisible world, the visible world was invented."* "Or more accurately **"Re-invented".**

As we can see, this Nag Hammadi text provides some additional verification to what was revealed previously in the corrected understanding of the Hebrew texts of Genesis one, as well as the view from our modern scientists.

Arthur Schopenhauer, Philosopher and author of *The World as Will and Representation*:

"Consequently, a way from within stands open to us to that real inner nature of things to which we cannot penetrate from without. It is, so to speak, a subterranean passage, a secret alliance, which, as if by treachery, places us all at once in the fortress that cannot be taken by attack from without."

Schopenhauer believed that all was a manifestation of WILL (meaning consciousness). **This WILL or consciousness was intrinsically evil** and blindly strives towards its own nourishment and propagation. He viewed human desire as futile, illogical, and directionless. Therefore, by extension, all humanity in this world is comprised of these same attributes.

Schopenhauer also deemed the Will/consciousness as a *malignant, metaphysical existence,* which controls not only the actions of individuals, intelligent agents, but ultimately *all observable phenomena;* it is an evil to be terminated via mankind's duties – *i.e. self-restraint and chastity.*

Since the Nag Hammadi Codex was not discovered until 1945 and Schopenhauer lived in the 1800's, clearly the influence this document could have provided would have demonstrated how the will/consciousness was misdirected by the *control narratives*.

The Archons created and supplied these narratives to rule after the *consent* of all souls already within this creation level.

Despite the lack of Schopenhauer's information and his stance as an atheist, oddly he still believed and made reference to an *evil entity force* that resided among us. He proposed that these *evil* powers were the driving force of knowledge and *conscious will* in this realm. (Control Narratives!)

The presence of this *evil* clearly abounds here in *this* world as Schopenhauer further intuits that all life on earth feeds off one another to live.

"The Will must live on itself, for there exists nothing beside it, and it is a hungry will"

Although both *Immanuel Kant* and *Arthur Schopenhauer* were very close to exactly what is being discerned in this book, they came from opposing religious biases. Kant's perspective was colored by Papacy dogma, whereas, Schopenhauer attempted to apply no religious narrative points whatsoever. Yet, look at just how close Kant comes to showing exactly what is being stated here about control narratives:

"...new prejudices will serve as well as old ones to harness the great unthinking masses.
For this enlightenment, however, nothing is required but freedom, and indeed the most harmless among all the things to which this term can properly be applied. It is the freedom to make public use of one's reason at every point. But I hear on all sides, 'Do not argue!' The Officer says: 'Do not argue but drill!' The tax collector: 'Do not argue but pay!' The cleric: 'Do not argue but believe!' Only one prince in the world says, 'Argue as much as you will, and about what you will, but obey!' Everywhere there is restriction on freedom."

Are new prejudices any different than new control narratives? **Does Kant not make an excellent point about how well a new prejudice will serve in replacement of the old?**

Now I would ask - *Does not one religious control narrative serve to enslave as well as another?* **This is very evident when ancient religious** *scripture* **is taken into consideration alongside today's current dogmas and doctrines.**

Let us not forget the time periods in which these men lived. Kant came first in the late 18th century and Schopenhauer in the early 19th! As stated earlier, it is evident that they weren't deducing and recognizing the use of the *false narratives* specifically, or their details as the major tool for the evil ruling entities of this creation level, *but intuiting that all evil is derived from our Will!* Not quite connecting those dots, that our *will* to do good or evil is most generally driven by what we *learn, know and believe.* Even further lacking the understanding from the *soul* level, that, *even what they and we perceive in many people, even all people in various percentages, are the layers of past life cycle scarring which emanate from a person consciously, but remain unperceived by those people because it does emanate from their souls-subconscious.* However, due to the changes in language, vocabulary, and context that occur from one time period to another, it is easy to miss the details of what these two men were intuiting.

Perhaps neither Schopenhauer nor Kant is given their due credit. For each possessed pieces to this secondary matrix puzzle.

One clearly intuits the existence of *control narratives,* while the other speaks of another *original* place of existence. Their words and attempts at explanation may appear somewhat veiled to us but they did use their generation's vocabulary, context and palette of verbal colors to paint the best picture. We do not know whether those of that day were capable of discerning the details which these souls intuited.

The following is another very telling bit of insight by Schopenhauer with a detailed explanation to follow.

"Consequently, a way from within stands open to us to that real inner nature of things to which we cannot penetrate from without. It is, so to speak, <u>a subterranean passage</u>, a <u>secret alliance</u>, which, as if <u>by treachery</u>, <u>places us all at once in the fortress</u> that cannot be taken by attack from without."

He begins his entire quote by intuiting that the ability to discern all resolutions comes from within *our souls* and that it will NOT be found by other means. Moving on and keeping in mind that his work revolved around our existence here and our consciousness, let's dissect the latter portion of this quote:

"… <u>a subterranean passage</u>, a <u>secret alliance</u>, which, as if <u>by treachery</u>, <u>places us all at once in the fortress</u>…"

- *"a subterranean passage"*- This Re-formatted creation (below) as the literally translated Genesis One texts depict.
- *"secret alliance"*- The alliance of belligerent souls who led our souls to rebel as they did.
- *"as if by treachery"* - The essence of all ancient soul-rebellion narratives culminating to depict this *below* creation level as a prison or "fortress" in which all (will/consciousness/souls) are entrapped!

In all this, it would appear that we stand on Kant's and Schopenhauer's shoulders. Only now do we have modern day vocabulary and more access to ancient texts to clarify the contexts in far greater detail, and to show how it correlates with other ancient texts.

Now we begin to have a far greater picture as to why the human forces who work with the *chaos entities* of this realm hold close their corporate pronouncement - **"As above, So below". It is a mocking mantra!**

Their team motto **"As above, so below"** refers to their reformatting of this matter based holographic creation level in the *reflective image* of this creations originally perfected condition, and that of the original Heavens, **"above the expanse"**. It should remain understood throughout this book that the creation these entities reformatted here, is now a cheap rendition of the original, and of those creation levels *above* us. *Understanding that these imposed reformation narratives are "opposite!"*

PART 3:

This is where <u>it could</u> appear that the Prime Creator changes from creating the non-physical *Freewill system* as seen in Genesis 1:1-1:8, to the physical properties of this creation level.

Please Note: *The Hebrew masculine plural ending of "im" pronounced (eem) in both* mayim *and* Shamayim *does NOT apply in these cases to make them plural, as in other cases.*

Rather, "im" is specifically employed <u>to indicate elevated-abundance</u>. The words in this context can also be understood as *reflective pairs* in the Genesis account, as in "<u>waters above</u>" and "<u>waters below</u>" with a separation between them. *Note* that verses 9 and 10 are now showing the creation of actual physical land and water mass. As promised, we will also explore the second perspective of this next creation text directly afterward.

It all comes full circle

Gen 1:9 And (Elohim)-**The Eternal** (amar)-**spoke**, let the (mayim)-**waters** (mineh)-**from** (tachat)-**under** (Shamayim)-**heaven** (qavah)-**collect** (el)-**towards** (echad)-**unification**, to be (mukam)-**situated** on the (yabasah)-**desiccated land**; Perceiving it existed rightly."

Gen 1:10 (Elohim)-**Eternal** (qara)-**published** the (yabasah)-**desiccated land** (eretz)-**Earth=hard-ground**; *and the* (mayim)-**waters** HE (qara)-**published** Seas: And The Eternal saw perfect order."

Gen 1:11-19 *"And The Eternal said, Let the earth sprout grass and herbs, the plant seeding seed, the fruit tree producing fruit according to its kind, whichever seed is in it on the earth. And it existed rightly.* [12] *And the earth bore tender sprouts, the plant seeding seed according to its kind, and the fruit tree producing fruit according to its kind, whichever seed is in it. And The Eternal saw that it was in perfect order;* [13] *and the evening existed. Then the morning existed, day three.* ¹⁴ *The Eternal said, Let light exist in the expanse of heaven, to separate and distinguish the day, distinguishing the night; existing for signs, seasons, days and years.* ¹⁵ *Existing as luminous bodies in the expanse of heavens, light upon the earth, existing rightly.* ¹⁶ *The Eternal made two great luminous bodies: the greater luminous body to rule the day and the small luminaries to rule the **night-(Lilah)**, the stars.* ¹⁷ *The Eternal gave the expanse of heaven light on the earth* ¹⁸ *to rule over day and night; separating, distinguishing* **light-(ore/good),** *distinguishing* **darkness-(choshek/evil)***; And The Eternal saw that it was in perfect order;* ¹⁹ *and evening existed. Then morning existed, day four.* "(Emphasis added)

There is a very interesting conflict of terms used here in verses 16 and 17. Genesis 1:17 returns to using The Hebrew word *Choshek*, meaning *chaos* and *evil*, whereas verse 16 the word *Lilah*, commonly used in this context, meaning *night* is used. Why the change? It appears this is making a direct reference back to the beginning where HE made a clear distinction of *separation* between good & evil, *i.e. light and dark within His Freewill system.*

This presents further proof that His Freewill system is exactly what was described as being created in the texts of Genesis 1:1-8.

Specific (concrete) Hebrew words used, allow us to understand the meaning to depict it all coming full circle. Now all light, *both physical* and *spiritual goodness* within His Freewill system, are fully created and operational systems. Also, His later parting of the souls, where some remain in His higher creation levels *above* our expanse, while all the souls in this creation level are locked here *below* for a time - ***Choices were made!***

The idea of souls being kept below the *expanse* division begs to question *why* and *who*. I have found most ancient texts and cultural beliefs to depict, that the Primary Creator did not create the ideas for all the control narrative systems we find ourselves enslaved by, but *allow them to exist* after the fact because they were *chosen* by the free will *consent* of the souls here. At the same time, Christianity clearly poses that another evil entity is the ruler of this creation, as do many other religious cults depict their various demigod rulers from the stars. However, generally, none of the religious orders give us any clear cut and believable reason for such a hostile takeover. Judaism and its subsequent Christian cults do come close, but as you will see they have also left much of the needed context out. Taking that into consideration here, and pushing past the many known religious narratives on this subject:

- Why did the higher souls rebel against our Creator?
- What was their great offense?
- Were our souls coaxed to agree with them later by trickery and then enslaved within these bodies after we chose incorrectly?

It seems prudent to pause here and explain the accepted *academic formula* for allowing what some might depreciate as being minor proof of an event or belief from an academic standpoint. *The formula for circumstantial information to be considered by scholars <u>as literal proof</u> is based upon the amount of recurring comparable information from varied sources that are gathered to substantiate the validity of the subject in question.* This formula, along with other factors surrounding the event, such as *sociological, religious-political*, and *geopolitical pressures* of the era are collected to build a tangible rationale. In such cases of antiquity, modern scholars tend to fall on the number **four** as being the tipping point for circumstantial evidence of an event or belief required to categorize it as *true or extant.* You will find in this book that the material provided or referred to will exceed that number by a considerable margin.

Duplication or Reformation?

Most learned scholars of the ancient Aramaic-Hebrew texts consider Genesis two to be a *duplicate version of the previous creation account.* Most mainstream scholars have long believed the alternative second version to have been scribed at a much later date by a different Hebrew tribe, while the two tribal units were separated for a time.

However, there have been and remain many professional

teachers and scholars who truly believe that our Genesis texts, beginning in chapter two, *to be literal separate accounts of two different creations having occurred in two literal separate locations and times - i.e. Completely different worlds!* However, I do not concur fully on that. I believe the preponderance of evidence as outlined in this book, although certainly not all the evidence available, proves the picture of an Archon *usurpation* and ongoing *reformation* of the originally created earth, and with the addition of our physical bodies, created in their character image.

Both of those theories being understood, when we break from the classical paradigm and consider other paralleling ancient information on this topic, we discover detail gap filling information.

The Secondary Creation "Reformatting" in Their Image!

*Now ponder the possibility that this Genesis 2, "second creation" story, may be a completely separate, totally independent, and different account specifically illustrating the **Re-formatting** of this creation, and even the known universe, in another entities "image".*

I fully understand why most learned scholars believe, or would rather believe these two stories to be two accounts of the same story from an oral tradition separated by time, which provides an easy answer for the story's existence *and various differences.* However, most of their determinations on this have been derived from textual understandings and translations that were provided to them from very early Judaic scribes who did not provide anyone with a word for word direct translation. This was done because they deemed everyone outside of their cult to be pagan, and not worthy to possess the data as they had it.

For many years now, not wanting to overburden my own students with the great weight of this book's topic, I strove with the accepted understanding by using the verified and recently proven *Documentary Hypothesis* concerning this second creation story.

Scholars of the DH identified the second creation story by what they determined to be the (Y-Source) or (Yahweh) source. This (Y) source identification is equally important to the *second creation* hypothesis because it isn't until Genesis chapter 2, vs. 4 that the differentiation of *some* gods depicted by a *change in name* is identified. This new title-name designation is known as the *Tetragrammaton* – (YHVH) or Yahweh. This new *3rd* person title-name designation is important because it can be understood as being the false god-entity who *reformatted this* original creation-space *below* the expanse which separates that from *above*. *He is also the second voice identified by his destructive demeanor depicted throughout the Hebrew & English text bibles.*

It should also be stated and remembered throughout the reading of this book, that regardless whether the standard Genesis creation narrative is true, near true, or believed to be true, or this second creation hypothesis is true in connection with the way I depicted our original creation within the Hebrew texts at the beginning of this chapter, the end result and larger picture I am attempting to depict here will not change. Souls in which The Prime Eternal created, rebelled, and were in fact separated from those who did not. This is a fact that many of the ancient texts, just as the most literal understanding of the Hebrew texts depict, and as many religious cult narratives also certainly depict.

Clearly, these *creation* accounts differ greatly. The writing style, content, and change in events highlight these variations. Can it, therefore, be said that the Genesis one and Genesis two renditions of creation are the same occurrence just merely separated by time? Let us not forget that the original Hebraic text hasn't any chapters or verses assigned to it. In fact, there originally was no modern punctuation, and the vowelization was added much later as I depicted earlier.

Realizing this, I want to refrain from becoming too concrete or set on the idea of chapters, verses, and so on.

Consequently, many may identify Genesis 2:4 as the beginning of that reiterated creation story from "another source" or "perceptive state" deeming it an expanded version clarifying the chapter one account, but being in the same book doesn't make that assumption true.

As identified previously, the verses from Genesis 1:1 to 1:8 clearly establish the overall understanding of:

- The existence of an Original Prime Creator
- That His higher creation levels do exist
- The creation of (light = free will)
- The creation of the *expanse* that separates the levels
- The separation or *quarantine* of souls occurring
- Lastly, that this lower level still exists in chaos, ruled by wickedness

As you may surmise by now, I tend to believe that the Genesis 1 account, possibly from verses 1:9 all the way through to chapter 2 verse 25 are entirely depicting the *usurpation* and *reformation* process by those Archon rebel souls. In fact, I have proposed along the way that Genesis 1:1 to 1:8 - *day two* - to be the only original account given of the Prime Eternal Creators overall greater heavenly creation of this level; His creation of the Free Will system, and subsequent Everlasting Agreement, and this earth.

Another major point that may go unnoticed is the fact that the Prime Eternal Creator set His immutable and overriding legal precedent <u>by establishing His Freewill system **first**</u>, even before creating the expanse and this creation level. This simple legal construct being established as *first above all others* forces all who may come after it to be thoroughly constrained by it in all manner of ways. It forces all entities, *and the laws or constraints they imagine to hold over others* to be hemmed in tightly by its existence regardless of time, space or lust.

I reiterate by the text of the Nag Hammadi –

> *"His thoughts became blind, having expelled his power by the blasphemy he had spoken – he pursued it-(his will) down to <u>chaos</u> and the <u>abyss</u>, (with) his mother, at the instigation of*

Pistis Sophia. And she <u>established each of his offspring in conformity</u> with its power-(technology) - <u>after the pattern of the realms that are above</u>, by starting from the <u>invisible world</u>, the <u>visible world was invented</u>.

Although arguing the providence of the secondary Genesis creation event stories from the purely scholarly position myself, while attempting to remain transcendental-neutral when guiding Jews and Christians to the more pure path, I always made certain not to encumber them to early with such profound ideas that might set them back.

Whether it is the Qur'an, the Hebrew writings, Egyptian, Babylonian, any number of Canaanite tribal beliefs, or the later Christian, the core story remains intact; someone else is ruling this usurped creation level, and although we do not recall this data consciously, the fact remains, we are here quarantined *below* the expanse with them. Most importantly, as you will see going forward, *memory* plays a major role in all this!

When the various ancient cultural and modern day creation tales are taken into account, we see veins of truth that support the validity of these Hebrew texts depicting one original creation event, followed by a subsequent and continual *reformatting event reflecting the low character of other entities.* All levels of creation came into being by the true Primary Eternal Creator before the establishment of our particular quarantine. However, for the time being, this level was and remains mostly controlled by those who originally defied and removed themselves by their own free will from The Prime Creator's upper realms. This, in fact, does tend to fit all of the later super-spiritualized religious accounts, which are strewn among many civilizations and geographical locations.

Moreover, it also fits within the confines of our new emerging scientific models of this universe, and of man's soul-consciousness.

Schopenhauer – 1788 to 1860 said:

> *"Consequently, <u>a way from within</u> stands open to us to that real inner nature of things to which we cannot penetrate from without. It is, so to speak, <u>a subterranean passage</u>, <u>a secret alliance</u>, which, <u>as if by treachery</u>, <u>places us all at once in the fortress</u> that cannot be taken by attack from without."*

Consulting Schopenhauer again, it would appear he very intuitively began to understand that it might NOT be science alone or possibly at all that finally allows us to SEE the very make-up of our perceived reality here. A reality that is more and more referred to as a *holographic matrix.* Even more compelling is his early 1800's ability to actually describe the matrix of a holographic universe as our modern science has come to see it, and not only identify, if only by sheer intuition that one exists, but that we exist inside of it ' *by alliance'* and *'by treachery!'* – *"It is, so to speak, <u>a subterranean passage</u>,* - (below) - <u>*a secret alliance*</u> *– (consenting to another will), which, <u>as if by treachery</u> –* (Manipulation of consent) - *places <u>us all at once in the fortress</u>"* – (Place of captivity below) - **Thoroughly compelling!** Emphasis added.

So, now it appears all of the ancient knowledge and new scientific discoveries on several major fronts within the sciences are finally coalescing to prove some incredible and even disheartening facts that our ancient ancestors believed as absolute; *that we live in a momentarily separated, reformatted universe that we may have in the beginning <u>consented to join</u> in with, but have since had the institutional, false narrative wool pulled over our collective souls-eye's and made to forget.*

By manipulating our souls to forget our not so distinguished past, the original masters of this universe have trodden the True Eternal Creator's immutable and eternal Freewill system like so much grass; and just as most ancient religious texts and superstitions attest, the hubris of those celestial leaders of chaos who have breached the boundaries of His Freewill system so deeply and so often, forcing our souls to forget in order to keep their reign in the hopes of fending off their own judgment like so many human kings throughout history, have actually done us the greatest of favors in a way. A favor based on another law, that, *"for every action, there must be an equal and opposite reaction"*. In our case, the action laid against immutability, *freewill*, has allowed the opposite action that guaranteed and hastens their demise, and our eventual freedom to remember. One that will afford all souls the ability to *choose* to return home again.

I believe the Christian prophecy of Revelation 21 also speaks directly to this - *"And I saw a new heaven and a new earth, for the first heaven and the first earth, did pass away, and the sea [abyss] is no more ..."*

Not only proving further the existence of the created *expanse* made to cleave this holographic universe from the creation levels above, but also that when the predetermined allotted time has run out for this event, a portion of this alleged prophetic Revelation depicts the collapse of the expanse which holds us apart, and the complete restoration and unification of this creation level to the Prime Creator's upper creation levels.

Like Genesis one, further proving the two exist, proving the separation of souls one from the other, proving by default that all other creation levels continue to exist *in perfect order*, while this refashioned creation level, although retaining some of its original form and character, is, in fact, a *reformatted* and opposite facing facsimile of our original estate.

The moral, leave this world's dogmas of fear behind you, shed the false and confusing religious and geopolitical narratives, and allow greater understanding to seep in. Our souls are far more than most understand them to be. Created as a gift from our creator source, they are micro-soul portions from His Macro-soul! Which, as you will see more and more in chapters to follow, how our captors use the power of our living-souls to their own ends.

Gen 1:1 , *In the beginning, God created the heavens and the earth; 2 and the earth being without form and empty, and darkness on the face of the deep, and the Spirit of God moved gently on the face of the waters, 3 then God said, Let light exist! And light existed. 4 And God saw the light that it was good, and God separated between the light and*

darkness. ₅ *And God called the light, Day. And He called the darkness, Night.*
And there existed evening. Then existed morning, day one.

₆ *And God said, Let an expanse be in the midst of the waters, and let it be*
dividing between the waters and the waters. ₇ *And God made the expanse,*
and He separated between the waters which were under the expanse and the
waters which were above the expanse. And it was so. ₈ *And God called the*
expanse, Heavens. And there was evening, and there existed morning. Day
two.

Chapter 3

Access by Consent

Often times we believe the best course of action is to remain silent when faced with situations that require us to speak. We may fear the repercussions, however, in the end, it really is a form of disobedience. In fact, truly the first form.

Disobedience is Consent, allowing other disobedient entities' to have their way with this creation, and all within it!

Let me begin with perhaps the origins of why we so readily comply with the authorities we imagine our soul is to submit itself under. Most of the religious texts of the world are very patriarchal in nature. They consist of some form of male dominance over the female, especially within the marital union and family life. We see the evidence of this within the different cultures spawning from the ancient societies. Although the ancient polytheistic cults had their goddesses along with their gods, there was male dominion represented within those realms as well. Clearly, patriarchal thought did not spawn solely from western religion but was present in the ancient religions of man. This has trickled down into many governmental systems, employment structures, and all the way down to our children.

This is humorously evident in the following true account of a squabble between two children playing on an elementary school playground. Upon the little girl telling the little boy too, *Shut up!* His forceful response was, *No! I am the man! You don't tell me to shut up! You shut up!* It just so happened that this little boy was being raised in an orthodox Christian environment. However, the concept of males being given dominion over females is not restricted to this specific religion. It is often believed that females are an inferior gender and thereby the weaker, even less intelligent, of the sexes.

As stated previously, this is not restricted to Christianity. We see this repeatedly in the texts of Judaism and Islam. As the story goes in Christianity... the *man is the head of the house because Christ is the head of the church.* Therefore, man is head of the woman with her being required to submit to his authority.

Obviously, this youth was learning this doctrine all too well, and one day he would grow up to be the king of his castle.

Despite our perception that we are an advanced culture and civilization, this did not truly disappear with equality for women anywhere. It is as I have seen it many times, expected that a Christian woman consents to *obey* her husband. Is this the truthful model and depiction of The Creator's Freewill system, or is it the model of another false deity's structure?

Moving forward from here, we will take a look at the militaristic manner displayed within societies. Again, the military originated with very patriarchal roots. It would seem that this would please and play into the Archon system of order because it sets into motion an expectation for people's need to be commanded with a hierarchy in place. A soldier is required to obey the commands of his superior officers. This is not accomplished in this or any country without an individual's free-will consent. We know that Kings/Presidents/Prime Ministers are leaders over earthly governments.

As we know male domination is no stranger to the religions of the world either; Priests, or other religious leaders, are heads of religious governments, whether they reside globally or locally. Now we come to spiritual *laws*, specific *control-narratives* that aid the Archon agenda. As can be seen, this is very specifically outlined within the Christian New Testament along with similar ideas in the Jewish Tanak. Leading to the general idea of, *"Whatever you do, do not displease god or speak against his anointed ones, or you will suffer great rejection and be cast away from him forever."*

Romans 13:1 *"Let everyone be subject to the governing authorities, for there is no authority except that which God has established. The authorities that exist have been established by God."* (NIV) Emphasis added

Psalms 105:15 *"Touch not my anointed..."* (ASE Tanak), **or as others misquote,** *"Do not speak against god's anointed!"*

The all-important question no one ever asks is – Which god?

This gives way to perhaps the utmost misconception of man. Many believe that having *husbandry* over all the other living creations to be or mean *dominion or authority* that gives way to their destructive use, however, this is a gross mistranslation from previously manipulated Hebrew texts. Because of this error, the idea of authority becomes completely transferred into a hierarchy whereby there is a need for all to be controlled and governed. Thus, the delusion of man's superiority now transcends that initial instruction towards *husbandry* by establishing supremacy over all of mankind and the earth itself. **"Reformatted"**.

This use of religion to institute ascendency is further evident when within Western Religion you are your brother's keeper, rather than your brother being responsible for himself in all things, and thus must be controlled! When we consider this humanitarian patriarchal narrative it all depicts a caste system of hierarchy, which effectively bi-passes the True Eternal Creator's free will system even unto their soul recycling system. Although in all honesty, it originally began and continues by our own consent!

The concept of controlling the masses to a given agenda by way of religious means is nothing new. Many methods have been utilized to trick humans into using their freewill choice to consent to what is in reality nothing short of a smoke and mirrors facade.

The documentary, *Century of Self* (Curtis) reveals the American Nephew of Sigmund Freud, Edward Bernays, promotion of his uncle's theories about human beings to manipulate the public. During the 20th century Bernays taught Corporate America how to appeal to people's desires instead of rational thought to persuade them into purchasing their products for the sake of profit alone.

While many people have difficulties parting with their Western religious traditions and concepts, I will defer to an Eastern concept that is prudent to keep in mind as you advance through this thesis. Be sure to remember the structure of the patriarchal system depicted above as you progress through this chapter and book as well. It is key to all domination structures on this planet.

The Sanskrit word, "loka" best translates to *world, locality, or plane of existence and consciousness.* In Hindu cosmology, this term is applied along with "tala" to designate seven higher worlds and seven lower worlds. In 1947 there was a worldwide UFO convergence. By this, I mean that there were *alleged* alien flying discs seen and described similarly all over the globe and by people from all walks of life, including Military pilots. This was the year of the ever-famous Roswell crash and the world was abuzz with UFO sightings.

Is it any wonder that a Google search of the terms *Lokas* and *Talas* produces many hits of this era including a July 7, 1947, internal FBI memorandum (Federal Bureau of Investigation) and an article in *The Round Robin Publication* (Layne), which gives an enhanced version of the FBI document. The FBI memo states that an individual, who gained his information via a spiritual medium sent this to them along with several other professionals. Now to some the validity of this evidence is instantly discounted just as it was at that time.

However, some of that which he depicted, as you will see, is just now being proven by science almost 70 years later. Not to mention that by July 7, 1947, these same flying discs were sighted in over 34 different states.

These documents also mention the presence of a specific *vibration rate* in this world with visiting beings from other etheric planes. I know that this too is something that science is beginning to prove out. Although I neither ascribe nor promote the adherence to any religion narrative, this bears mentioning so that you, the reader, may see that there are some root truths in the many *control narratives* of the various faith systems. Furthermore, this in part would explain those Archon entities that interrupt and confuse the Freewill system of The True Eternal Creator.

It has been proven throughout my earlier teachings and books that our Hebrew texts do depict the existence of other entities having direct interaction with men. Where they come from, how they get here or what their technology is compared to ours is something we can only speculate about. What we do know is that there is much-documented evidence confirming the existence of other beings occupying the universe.

This idea of other alien life forms has been strewn throughout many ancient cultures, religions, and despite many that don't want to believe, even Christianity is beginning to accept this reality. As you will find in my other books, the existence of *"two voices"* are shown to be present throughout the Hebrew texts, nevertheless, the majority of these entities have been mistakenly depicted as the true Eternal Creator and/or His messengers. Unfortunately, these false assumptions have been promoted generationally.

In or out of control of the greater plan!

The fact is that most Tanak (O.T.) stories of godly encounters have never referred to the true Prime Eternal One or His Malakim (messengers), i.e. *angelic beings/higher souls*. Rather, most stories refer to and are depictions of the false god entity "Yahovah" / "Yahweh", by Jews and Christians, additionally, by other ancient cultures this entity is known as Moloch or Marduk, among other names.

This entities name is most generally depicted in all Hebrew texts by their ancient Babylonian Judaic "Tetragrammaton" - **"YHVH" or "יהוה"**. This 3rd person title and all other derivations of the YHVH title were manufactured by the later false *Shelanite-Judah* cult and salted throughout their revised texts, while culturally hiding the true identity of the false deity they actually followed - **"Molech"**, the god associated with the planet Saturn.

Either way, no biblical god or angel entities, as they have been taught and propagated throughout time by these false *control-narratives*, have ever acted alone; nor have they been allowed to act directly against the free will of all other souls – humanity.

Another misconception or deliberate *false narrative* concerns our collective misunderstanding of the nature and status of these long lost *rebellion leader-souls* who continue to act out their evil intentions against all other living-souls - humanity. Those souls who mankind has long misunderstood to be literal *special* angelic creations standing for either good or evil were and remain only equal *living-souls* like you, and everyone else! All living souls, of both man and animals, are of equal power and value to the Prime Eternal Creator; as all living-souls were originally created from within His own Macro-Soul.

More specifically, this means that those anti-life Archon rebellion leaders who evidently reside in one of the higher realms of the heavens above ours have only *appeared* to ancient men as gods because they still exist within our original *light-body* soul form. Many throughout time have referred to this form as *light-bodies*. This was our soul's original form. To give one biblical evidence of how our living souls came to reside in these corruptible biological bodies, a quick portion and more literal translation of the Garden of Eden story is very appropriate here:

- **Gen 3:21** *"To Adamah and the woman, Jahovah-Elohim brought forth, <u>covering their light</u>, wrapping them.*

- **Gen 3:22** *"And Jahovah-Elohim said, Behold; man existed once from perceiving good and evil: henceforth, lest he cast off his hand from taking again <u>the power of flesh eating</u>, and be revived forever…"*

Thus, our souls currently live in a *state of demotion* caused by this original coaxing and manipulation to go against the first law of Free Will, which continues unabated. More details on this temporary demotion for the majority of all souls, and the eternal demotion of the few orchestrating it, will become clear as you progress. The rest of the stories are merely progressions of our ancient and modern superstitions guiding many to deceptively believe the *false control-narratives,* and thus continuing this dark cycle.

This manipulation of The Eternal Creators free will system by their passive redirection to gain our own consent has been the greatest deception. By people's ongoing *consent*, this hoax results in allowing most people to remain deluded and enslaved through our collective lack of knowledge. A lack of knowledge which continues to be driven by the negligence to investigate, which is further compounded by our individual unwillingness to know or accept something different than the comfortable superstitious dogma we already cling to. These *control narratives* are engrained from an early age just as we witnessed in the opening account of the playground squabble. They can be political, religious, economic, etc., although, for many they are one in the same. Humans simply do not always recognize them as such.

> *"One way or another, we spend our whole lives being conditioned into accepting some line or order, some position of domination or subjection. It's hard to unlearn such hierarchy, to undo such control. It's implicit."*
> — Cliff James, *Of Bodies Changed* (James)

Obedience to The Prime Eternal Creators original and most minimal instructions for all creations is required, but obedience to whom, and what law is the question never asked?

Let's consider this not where religion is concerned but rather the structure between The Creator and the creation, versus that of the Archon rule and the reverse impetus of this usurped creation space. This is the essence of the soul's existence.

Obedience to the True Eternal Creator's original and most minimal instruction is required for all past, present, and future created beings – 'Behold; <u>man existed once</u>' *from perceiving good and evil*:

It is often assumed that this obedience is one and the same as that foundationally taught within all religions and cultures. The vast majority within these paradigms never think to question if the *whom* or *laws* instilled are from the Prime Eternal Creator or <u>*another entity*</u>! This is evident within the story of the first Adam's & Eve's, who, *while still existing in our original soul-light-bodies* equally decided to turn from The Eternal's original mandate. *What is lost and or hidden is* *the reality that <u>it was we/souls that chose to turn away</u>. Just stay with me, you will grasp the how and why later.*

As expressed earlier, it would appear that the biblical narrative is showing us that misery required our company *by consent* in order to gain control of this creation. A control that will eventually prove to be quite elusive in the end; *a burdensome stone!* The original rebellious souls in question, *now Archon's*, needed to get all souls within this creation level to knowingly or unknowingly usurp the free will of others, *thus breaking the Everlasting Agreement exactly as the rebel Archon souls originally did within the higher levels of the heavens before coming here!* **We consented to** hear **another voice, and the Everlasting Agreement was broken for the second time!** Yes, as it is written, the first *living-souls*, prior to becoming physical men and women, and all who came after them, have consented to *hear* and *agree* with the alternative policy and procedures, of another entities voice!

Our living-souls, as all are created by the Prime Eternal equally, already possessing the knowledge of "Good & Evil", our collective and continued consent to another entities will, rather than that of the Prime Creator, resulted in the immediate self-induced exclusion from His presence and direct communication. This Edenic period most certainly depicts the second time any living-souls consented to rebel against the instruction of our Creator.

Additionally, our many prophets appear to depict a future time where, many, many more of us will, **by way of deception,** agree to hear and follow that other voice again for the **third** and final time. Strike three... YOU'RE OUT!

My aspiration is, that from the realization of this knowledge that people will learn to withhold their *consent* from those same dark chaotic entities who currently believe they rule this *lower* creation. It is because of our ongoing consent to their narratives that they still hold adverse jurisdiction and control of our original soul-sources. This hypothesis of the *soul-sources* will also become more apparent later.

The Mercy of Prophesy!

Identified throughout man's history long prior to any Hebrew, Christian, or Islamic experience, in His merciful compassion and yearning to teach and elevate all souls by the instruction and function of His *first law* of Free-Will, The Prime Eternal Creator sends His benevolent *messenger-souls* periodically to <u>reiterate</u> His original instructions so that they will never be totally unavailable to our souls. Should the ruling rebellion leaders have had the power and ability to circumvent the absolute first law and process of His Free-Will system, it would most likely have brought about permanent soul-enslavement within this usurped lower creation long ago.

As I previously touched on, since the first men and women, all *souls*, consented to the Archon manipulation, this left the Archon entities free reign to take adverse control of all souls within this lower creation. Hopefully, this is contained for a finite period of time as spoken through our many prophets. From the beginning unto this present day, they have created many *narrative* systems, using the freewill of consenting people to change all original thought and understanding through those false *control narratives.*

This has thereby provided only very small remnants of the Prime Eternal's original truth woven amid highly misconfigured written works present throughout all of mankind's various cultures.

Most refer to them as *scriptures.* These tainted texts with all manner of false rituals and superstitions concerning man's true origin were designed to further entrap and enslave us through <u>memory loss</u>, as I will discuss in greater detail in a later chapter.

As stated at the beginning of this chapter within the patriarchal narrative, they accomplish this through our ongoing consent to their lies and trickery, via contrived narratives.

These Archon oligarchs have placed over this world a cooperating labor force of both man and other entities which they created in their image and character. All of whom are most generally misidentified as aliens from other worlds or dimensions. These helper entities appear to be used to further ensnare us by continuously working their deceptions and divisive tactics. Thereby giving way to their destructive nature, they possess and continue to hold this lower creation and all in it with the aid of our <u>individual and collective consent</u>. Our consenting approval made by way of the Prime Eternal Creator's original and ongoing Freewill system.

These degenerate forces have found a myriad of ways to reteach mankind using false narratives on a continual basis; with most seemingly small choices being the direct cause of our individual and collective nations unfolding future.

Manipulating us in such a way that we *(choose, consent, agree, permit)* them to do their will every waking moment while deceptively believing we are submitting to the Prime Eternal's original Will, and as directed by ancient religious narratives! Again, it should be understood that within every deceit that these rebellion rulers present through their labor force minions, there is always a thread of truth. This is then assimilated by an individual soul-person, thereby being lead to presume the entire duplicity to be authentic. Ultimately, this is their baited soul-trap and re-trap, originally perpetrated through all religions. These are again expanded and paralleled through many narrative tributaries.

I have explained for many years that Free Will cannot be Free Will if another entity of any kind has the ability to force you knowingly to do their will. To manipulate us unknowingly after so much time has passed without a conscious memory of what transpired is surely skirting the edge. In order for those chaotic entities to keep what they themselves re-created in this lower creation, they needed to re-write the Prime Eternal Creators original doctrine for all souls; in this way it is used as a *redirection* of His Freewill system producing an intolerable, and barely legal, gray area.

Their lies are found in - the *reformatted image* of this creation through their ancient paradigm of - *As above, so below.*

For example: *If no blood sacrifice for "sin" atonement is performed within the "original heavenly levels", as our many prophets have clearly stated, and as well clearly stated in the Christian book of Revelation, then there should be no kind of animal or human sacrifices whatsoever here in this lower creation level either.*

However, in this *reformatted image* we have the *opposite*

image and character written within their false control narratives.

Consequently, instead of the Prime Eternal's true original instructions, their *replacement* endorses the animal and human sacrifices of the blood cults worldwide, spanning all continents and cultures. Thus proving to me that their catch phrase *"As above, so below"*, is referring to their totally fabricated, false heaven station above, to be working in connection with our now reformatted creation level we know as earth. I call this secondary system, *the heaven way-station!* The great relevance of this *way-station* complex will become evident later.

Pretending by their own authority to be *as god,* they give the inhabitants of this lower creation their mock *narratives* and *laws* as if it were the true Prime Creator's **atonement system** for alleged sins. This is a false system promoted in various ways through diverse cultures over time alleged to bring the soul back into unity with its creator, *"at ONEment"*. *All the while being the reverse image, 180 degrees out from the original.*

All designed primarily to induce fear and inflict harm upon all souls, both man, and animal, all of whom share the same exact micro-portion *living-soul* from their Eternal Creator.

The *atonement* scheme actively urges the shedding and consumption of blood in this lower creation through sacrificial memorials, wars, and as a food source, to name the most common. By participating in these deceptions and in conjunction with the genetic code of their Adam-Eden matrix - "Hu-man body-hardware", their blood in our blood becomes a nearly impenetrable firewall against the soul's capacity to resist recognizing their lies!

- **Gen 3:22** "And Jehovah-Elohim said, Behold; <u>man existed once</u> from perceiving good and evil: ***henceforth, lest he cast off his hand from taking again <u>the power of flesh eating</u>,*** and be revived forever…" (Asher Literal Translation)

By their false control narratives, they cast all their destructive ways upon the feet of a Creator who hates the shedding of blood and the destruction of all that lives. As pretenders to the throne, they use magic and trickery to, again and again, retain the consent of the majority of souls who generally believe all that they know and see has always been and remains to be coming directly from the True Eternal Creator entity. This is part and parcel to the greater lie and entrapment! *"The Word of God!"* – BUT, Which god?

We often view our own ancient texts as being the first augmented instructions used to gain access to enslave men through fear and trickery. However, this is not entirely true, is it?

When these Archon entities distorted the Eternal One's original mandate by dark reformation, with the intent to keep all souls forgetful, submissive and acting in opposition, that act was the first rendition of *revised* oral-instructions in contrary to the original laws our souls previously knew – Gen 3:22 *"And Jahovah-Elohim said, Behold;* **man existed once from perceiving good and evil***: henceforth, lest he cast off his hand from taking again the power of flesh eating, and be revived forever..."* (Asher Literal Translation)

Therefore, ever since we have had what has only been the continuation and expansion of that original false program.

Their *program* must be maintained in its entirety through ancient, revised, and newly instituted *control narratives* if these entities are to remain in power over the souls of mankind. To accomplish this, mankind's *soul-impetus* must be shaped to continually *consent* by our freewill choice to behaviors that are in clear and continuous rebellion to The Creator.

Understandably, the only reason most of this is lost or outright denied by the earthly multitudes is because of their deep belief in the *control narratives* as being truly "God-given", all based on the *control-narrative* of underlined text infallibility! As I have long distilled and proven out of the Hebrew and English bible texts, there has always existed - *Two voices, by entities giving two laws, from two mountains!* The sad commentary as pointed out earlier is that few ever see the need to ask, "Which god?"

Nothing changes over time other than mankind's perceptions and the continuation of deliberate false religious and social narratives. If man is willing to look outside of these various chronicles, they will find them to be tailored for specific purposes, all containing similarly added misconceptions. Regardless how we slice the narratives, they all incorporate the same entanglement; that is the individual and collective soul obedience or disobedience to the True Eternal Creator's original system of life, *in lieu of the death and chaos* that we now reside in. We remain enslaved by our own consent, including our tacit approval to their false system of death and destruction.

Provide for the Freewill of all those around you, especially those weaker than you!

The ancient Hebrew understandings of *"Live by the sword, die by the sword"* and/or *"Treat all others as you would have them treat you and yours"* are actually the same underlying concept. It has been in the re-teaching of these ancient understandings that the purposely-orchestrated definitions have been altered to dictate how we apply them today. Too often humans lack the comprehension of the world around them as anything else besides belonging to them to dominate as they please, and *regardless of the free will of others.* This is not limited to our treatment of other humans only but also includes the other created souls, which occupy this temporary home with us.

The Animal Narrative

At first glance and by the manipulated text narratives many people may get the idea that the animals may have been the Prime Eternal Creators original *narrative* provided to test the impetus of all *young* souls within this creation level! However, I ask how that can be true?

If we can plainly ascertain that our souls original form was and remains as plasma-based *light-bodies,* and meant to exist as such requiring no physicality in any form to sustain us, then why are we to believe that any animals were created in their current physical form at all, also to be infused with the same living-souls; much less to sustain us or work for us, etc., as incorrect bible translation, exegesis, and myth would have it. Obviously, a disconnect derived from later false narratives exists here, and anyone who has read my first book already knows most of this is due to blatant text manipulation. The obvious logical argument based on the texts we have dictates that no *animals* were created by the Prime Creator for this place or any other, but only living-souls!

Then who created them, when and why?

As I continue to posit by our deeper understanding of those ancient texts, and as you will see much later proven via our modern sciences, it can be ascertained with substantial accuracy that these physical human bodies were specifically fabricated by the Archon leadership in order to *house* and *firewall* the great power and capacity of our living-souls; in conjunction with their great need for as many souls as possible living negatively influenced lives for them to be sustained by our energy output. This also provides the generational karmic disaster brought on by their narratives of death which keep us *consenting* against the rule. Especially so through our now institutionalized and culturally entrenched reign of terror on most animals and unborn children alike.

In the *reformatted, reversed image* and *character* of this current creation, man is not cognizant that where the Archon's are concerned, <u>mankind assumes the role of the lower animal</u> to be manipulated as they see fit. Remaining ever vigilant to their original rebellious momentum, these *higher* evil souls acted on impulse instead of their direct knowledge of our shared Creators all-encompassing love and mercy. From the first hearing of that horrific news of being cut off from His sustaining force as presented to them by the man Enoch, and rather than falling down further into a deeper contrite heart condition, even unto their near critical state of complete demise, they turned more fearsome and malevolent! Had they just remained aware that their own *soul-impetus* was <u>still</u> being tested further on that spot! Had they just fell down and accepted that *perceived* fate of death for their actions against Him, to die forever. The Eternal One would have reached down in His awesome mercy and plucked them all out. And the perfect order would have never been disturbed.

Even now they continue to be judged by how they treat those

less developed below them. Thus, even though the evil Archon souls believe all they have done and continue to do to the souls below them to be within their own omnipotence, this is also not accurate. The greater truth is, the Prime Eternal One who creates all things has been *allowing* them, as He allows all souls at all levels to exert the true impetus of their individual living-souls!

His Freewill system demands nothing short of this action-reaction process. The main difference between them and us is, that they knew better and _took advantage of our perception of their superior ranking_. No souls above them manipulated them or dumbed down their understanding generationally to manipulate their non-compliance to that immutable rule of free will. *Their rebellion and willingness to usurp ours were premeditated and sustained!*

As most are aware there are many ancient texts outside of what was canonized as the accepted *authoritative, holy,* or *word of god* scriptures. These are classified as "Apocryphal" or other writings and many refuse to view them as valid, or trustworthy.

More often the issue is that these contain conflicting information from what they were taught to believe as truth within their religious doctrines, most of which _demand us to believe the infallibility of these texts_. Text infallibility is yet another false idea that I have proven as such in my previous works. This is especially true in regards to their ritual, dietary, and sacrificial narratives.

Where western religions are concerned this perception of their alleged *God-given* domination which allows them to kill anything under any condition perceived to be socially acceptable or biblically legitimate, is met with great opposition! *An opposition which should seem to be derived from a sociopathic nature to any critical thinker.* Many do not know that this is also true within what western religion would deem the *pagan* or *eastern* religions as well.

As I author this book there is a much-heated debate being waged within the Wiccan community concerning the practice of animal sacrifice by some of their members. It would truly shock many in the Jewish and Christian circles to discover that the justifications for the *humane* slaughtering practices of the intended sacrifice are very much the same, if not identical, to those they present or believe to be acceptable to *god* via our ancient Levitical laws. Wicca is an earth-based religious practice that believes their mandate is to *harm none*. Many people within their practices have not only dedicated themselves to the vegetarian/vegan dietary lifestyle but practice holistic natural medicine as well. There are also sects of the Hindu, Buddhist, and other Eastern religions that deal with this same internal conflict of not harming the non-human sentient beings, while others still participate in the sociopathic behavior of ritualistic animal sacrifice, or waiting to be able to do it once again to their god.

In several places within the Jewish Tanak/Old Testament, there is an instruction to *not consume the blood*. Unfortunately, it is mistranslated, edited and mingled with the lie that the blood can somehow be fully drained from the victims flesh, and thus rendered – *Clean?* Moreover, teaching that those texts are speaking about only the blood, which they are not.

This is absolutely impossible to accomplish and yet they allow themselves to be fooled by this false narrative, even though it has been proven that this is not what those Hebrew texts are saying. As we saw at the beginning of the chapter, once man believes the deception that he is over the animal kingdom, *domination over other men ensues*.

Try to remember Stanley Kubrick's depiction of the rise by intuition within the first man's soul-impetus as suggested by that false god monolith, to use his new tool to first murder the animal, then consume its flesh; with his ascension to murdering his own kind and subsequent domination of the tribes through force ensued directly **"Live by the sword, die by the sword"**

The eldest available Hebrew texts of Genesis, when translated literally and correctly, prove that ALL the souls of men and animals are from the same source and equal. There are no new texts or instructions as many are lead to believe. Also, as it is plainly written in the Hebrew, both are equally responsible for their actions. Therefore, if The Prime Eternal Creator **never changes or modifies**, then this ancient understanding of *The Golden Rule* cannot, and does not, pertain to only men or the souls thereof, but to all His creation endowed with eternal 'souls of life'. (D. S. Asher)

I believe these points have and continue to be lost on most people to our collective detriment *because most people continue to identify their physicality as being all they are.* The religious people give lip service to the *soul,* with even fewer of them truly giving the soul its due consideration above their assimilated superstitious beliefs, much less understanding it in the correct context with their ego bound physicality. Going forward we must start understanding the great reality and power of who we truly are as – *living-souls* – and acquiescing to the fact that our limited and fleeting physicality is far less important because it plays such a minimal role within this current reality.

Our soul memories have been *reformatted* by the generational intake of false control narratives. By feeding our physicality the pabulum of controlling *narrative* superstitions they have been able to slowly accentuate the negativity output from our physical existence individually, which is then exacerbated by our *collective projection* of it all into our world reality. On the part of the Archon's, this is a direct disobedience to the Prime Eternal Creator's original instructions; while the negatively programmed physicality of men remain deaf to the simple, unified instruction found in most all world religions, *"Treat (all) others, as you would have them treat YOU"*

As I explained prior, the original souls now being housed within these Adam-Eden, *Trinity-6* bodies find themselves in this physical dimension state because they consented to follow a different narrative which was presented by a voice other than the True Eternal Creator. The direct result was that their/our *soul* communication line with the Prime Eternal Creator has been temporarily dialed back.

This condition persists because of man's lack of knowledge and overwritten paradigm. The good news is, that it appears their grasp is growing weaker. I have been curiously watching as the souls of this creation awaken more each day to the truth of the Prime Eternal Creator's original thoughts, ways, and true character.

The rebellion forces of chaos are aware of this trend, just as they were aware of it during other epochs within their control, which I believe they nearly destroyed to perform an utter *reboot* against the souls of mankind. *Thus, forcing us into yet another beginning, a reset.* Their use of such a mechanism would seem plausible if the re-awakening soul percentage of those alive during a high population density era such as we have now, was the impetus that utterly forces the release of their grip on this creation. Try to bear in mind as you forge through this work that where it pertains to these evil soul entities, virtually all of this has always been for one main reason, **"to be as God"**.

Ask yourself, *what better way to "be as God" than to control billions of His "living-soul" portions?* As mankind has advanced, the opportunity to peek behind the Archon veil of deception becomes more of a threat for them with our expanding ability to explore such things as *"Past life regression"* & *"Near-death experiences"*, in more scientifically proven ways. These have the potential to prove to millions that there is far more occurring than most were ever willing to accept, leaving behind considerably more questions than answers for most. *However, never forget that these procedures, and the data coming from them can also be in part contrived, control-narrative tributaries.*

No doubt this is why we now see those like *Mr. Ray Kurzweil* informing the world that they are very close to being able to "capture" the human soul from the human body with potentials of soon possessing the ability to install the soul into, and I quote, a *"better body"*. Better for whom? It has been my experience that when they tell you they are close to any evil technology, this is code for, *we already have it perfected.* Do not be confused about this!

The only logical reason for those rebellious souls to explore this prospect of a *better body* is their need to secure a superior *enslavement vessel* for our eternal living-souls. This then enables them to maintain full and complete control with zero possibility of opposing organic human attributes like *memories* or *natural law morals!* Stick with me and you will see just how this plays out.

This is the only plausible motive for the current depopulation agenda as publically announced by several prominent governmental leaders and declassified documents. As insane as it sounds to most, it is understood that it has been determined that certain elite factions fully intend to exterminate approximately 90% of this world's population. In contrast, certain, specific, and limited few *beautiful elite* and their loved ones are to be spared this tragedy – *As in the days of Noah.* These are the very humans who have always been aware and directly work with the rebellious Archon souls. *Just like in the days of Noah,* these Archon sycophants have all been given *Arks* to take refuge in from this mass genocide.

As time and newly revised world narratives evolve, or devolve as it were, humanity will be required to begin anew. Therefore, it isn't too difficult to see how depopulation and the introduction of new, high technology *cyborg* bodies for mankind's souls could go hand in hand. Now as silly as that may sound to most, truth is if you don't have the power to kill or create new souls that you require to live on, then you must prevent as many as you can from *evolving, waking up* and *ascending* back to the True Eternal Creator as requested, and as it is available to them.

Clearly, as some can holistically see through man's history or at least the history we are aware of, the rebel Archons have worked to capture ever-increasing control over the souls of man. However, this is not because they wish to control the *human form,* but their intent is to control the *souls within the form.* This time, it appears their goal is to house our souls inside these new *better bodies,* which they have secured by teaching their technology to our earthly rulers. Their elite will produce a far more efficient, more **governable body** than our current physicality allows. This then affords them a higher level of prevention for *leak through* of our soul consciousness unto any level of enlightenment. The Eternal's Freewill system disconnected from our perception, securing us to be all the more controlled captives in this usurped creation.

Allegedly in Noah's day the world's population was such that only eight carbon-based bodies were required to restart mankind at a very slow and controlled pace, or more likely (eight types).

Additionally, as scholars know, the Hebrew texts very clearly depict a far larger population existing almost immediately after the flood event. Evidently just as we see in those texts, this time many thousands of people will be required to ramp the human population up again upon emerging from their deep underground *Ark safe zones;* Unless you believe the U.S government and several other major powers have spent the last fifty years building extensive deep underground bases equipped with massive food and supplies stockpiles, as mere exercises. Either they are insanely paranoid, or they *believe* they have data that we do not.

As I continue to point out, it has always been about the false narratives used to keep as many souls as possible throughout all generations from finding their way out of the maze.

The Devil Steals the Soul!

As I will continue to point out; *all superstitions, myths, and folklore have a root core of original truth within them.* As much as we want to believe this is different from our religious text, it is not.

Consequently, this means all religions such as Judaism, Christianity, Islam, Hindus, Wiccan, and etcetera possess not only a verifiable element of misconception but of truth as well. For this discussion, I want to consider the lore concerning the universal *devil* entity and what is seen as the attempts by this alleged demonic kingpin to *capture* the souls of all men, which is one of the oldest universal beliefs among men going back as far as our history provides. In conjunction with this entities soul stealing operations, we have the ancient belief that the *Moon* is his tool used for attracting and capturing all souls – *The trick of light!* This overall understanding from ancient times is where the reformatted souls of mankind came up with another universal belief wrapped in various cultural rituals - *Moon worship!* Deriving their core understanding for said beliefs and rituals, as well as nearly all world calendar systems prior to and after the written word to this day, *from some original core of truth!*

It should not be dismissed as mere ancient superstition that so many major and minor civilizations spanning all of our histories share the same specific tendencies concerning the moon and the god that owns it. This belief being so widespread among civilizations to this very day, should at the very least give everyone cause to inquire as to why so many people over such a span of time have had these beliefs. The next question then should be; *who gave them or directed them all towards such specific information?*

Remembering, that vast oceans have kept many of these great civilizations separated! Therefore, we know they did not come upon these ideas organically. Thus, even without filtering all of the above through our various religious narratives as most people do in different ways, man's general historical data alone proves this concept of evil entities being real, and even forcing these ideas for worship upon us. Concurrently, our world history proves that evil among us and through us, regardless of the outside influence, has always continued to grow worse, and never better, not yet! Ergo the reason for this books lofty endeavor; to wade through all the added layers upon the roots of these superstitions to arrive at a more holistic and original understanding for the, *who and why.*

We can only determine this answer by considering the sheer number of cultural myths, religious, and historical writings which are present in the many cultures and have spanned history.

All myth and superstition generally have a root point of original truth. It has been man's inability to distil these core truths because they knowingly or subconsciously <u>consent</u> *to* <u>perpetuate</u> *and even create additional false control narratives by their continual adherence.*

They pass these counterfeit chronicles down from generation to generation and it often becomes a thing of pride to have a long family heritage in a particular religious affiliation.

One major overriding point of truth traversing most religious cultures is the concept that "God is in us". More accurately understood, but generally misunderstood, this equates to our souls being the *microcosm-soul portions* from the Eternal Creators *Macro-soul*. Quite literally, we are not made in His *"reflective, reversed"* image; our soul is His <u>direct image</u>!

It is then our *impetus* which is chosen by our own *consent* and *driven outward* through the availability of the Prime Eternal's freewill law and system, which more than not shows our *characters* to be *projecting* an *opposing* image, outward. It is our individual choice to *learn, love* and *live* the Prime Creator's character of total love and mercy towards all, *or we consent to the polar opposite, both knowingly or unknowingly!*

The Who

In these contemporary times, many thousands of alleged victims of alien abduction tell researchers that their abductors depict humans as being *unique among all other races in 'this' universe system*. However, the why never seems to be answered.

Moreover, and of far greater importance to all souls is the discovery of who these *entities'* actually are. *Are these alleged aliens our rebellion leaders in disguise or a lower creation provided with technological advancements who are also created from the dust of this or another earth by those rebellion leaders themselves?* My thinking is that they are both, the rebellion leader themselves, and other soulless beings that they created to aid their endeavors. As it is their ultimate and unchanging goal, they perpetuate yet another false narrative of an advanced alien culture visiting earth. However, as always these false narratives are used to divert mankind from seeking its true Creator. *Later used to prove these alleged aliens as being our original creators no doubt!*

It must then be, that we are considered unique because we, *unlike* them, are a direct creation of our original source Creator entity. We are eternal *living-souls;* they are not! My educated guess is that no other *demigod* created entity within this creation level has been afforded a living-soul to go with their *Trinity-6* bodies, making us unique even within our temporary physicality.

Truth is, no created being can create as the Prime Eternal Creator, but rather they are only able to emulate and manipulate what has already been created. Essentially faking it, a mere reflection. You are wondering what a *Trinity-6* body is aren't you?

If we take into account other ancient texts, such as the *Nag Hammadi previously used in example*, then it may be seen that the rebel Archon souls who present themselves as demigod rulers of this lower level creation, have never possessed the ability to bring our *dust of the earth, devolved* bodies to life by the mere capture of our souls, in their own power.

This understanding is very important to the understanding of our soul's free will choices, and to the overall topic of this book.

"The [Archons] rulers laid plans and said, "Come, let us create a man that will be elements from the earth." They modeled their creature as one wholly of the earth." (Emphasis added)

"Not understanding the force of The Creator, because of their powerlessness, they breathed into his face; and the man came to have a soul [installed] but remained upon the ground many days [unanimated]. They could not make him arise because of their powerlessness. Like storm winds, they persisted [in blowing], that they might capture that image [soul], which had appeared to them in the expanse, but they did not know the source of its power." (Emphasis added)

"Now all these things came to pass by the will of the father of the entirety. Afterward, the Creator spirit saw the soul-endowed man upon the ground. And His spirit came forth from the upper heaven; it descended and came to dwell within us, and man's [Physicality] became a living soul." (Emphasis added)

For most hearing this idea it will be a bitter pill to swallow because it sounds like our loving Creator knowingly allowed His created living-souls to be subject to and enslaved by an entity, which rejected Him.

However, it behooves the reader to remember that our *light-body-souls* were convinced to make the wrong choice which resulted in the *self-imposed occupancy* of these physical bodies. That our consent was given and has continued to be given even tacitly, ever since.

What we are seeing here in these ancient texts, as well by other ancient texts and cultural lore is, that by the true Eternal Creator breathing His *Breath of Life* into these lower *Trinity-6* body constructs, enabling our souls to animate these bodies for a time, is actually Him performing by example the highest form of Free Will!

Reanimating our souls to work within such a physical construct as they were never meant to be constricted within, *He allowed our free will choice to remain our choice,* and He allowed the Archon forces choice unto eventual judgment to remain their choice. Most importantly for our captured souls is the wisdom that The Eternal Creators, creative *intention* is always in control; and that the Archon systems of captivity and rule are the mirage and the measure by which they will be judged.

The most realistic scenario in my opinion, being based on the ancient texts and cultural beliefs of many cultures spanning generations and geographic locations, is that all of our souls here in this lower creation, *not being the lowest creation level*, were provided this creation as a place for our young souls to learn and progress into the higher levels. Creation levels which are *mechanically governed* far less than this level. *Learning the boundaries of and willful adherence to The Creators first law of freewill is our soul's primary function.* This first law is the primary duty of all souls. It transcends and regulates all levels of His creation. All ascension and all judgment of souls are determined by this single, and most simple law. *I will get into the scientific proofs of the governing mechanisms that greatly regulate this lower creation level in later chapters.*

To gain a greater understanding of all this from within a religious paradigm that most are aware of, we have to look at the corrected Hebrew texts of Genesis:

> **Gen 3:6** *"And the woman saw that the tree was good for food and that it was pleasant to the eyes, and the tree was desirable to make one wise. And she took of its fruit and ate, and she also gave to her husband with her, and he ate."*

It must be understood that large sections of this story are given by men as allegory and that the English versions are more commentary than they are literal translations from the Hebrew.

The tree was not a tree, and the fruit was not fruit, *but a living, sentient, physical creature with a living-soul* as all the context prior to this point clearly provides.

The transgression was the <u>usurpation of another soul's free will</u>! And as this can most likely only be achieved while that living and most powerful soul-entity is restrained within a physical body, so the animals were created first! *In this case, our living souls being led to murder them.*

In all such cases of Torah exegesis, besides knowing the most literal definition of the ancient Hebrew words within their specific contexts, we must also look further into other details in order to extrapolate the actual event.

Gen 3:7 *"And the eyes of both of them were opened, and they knew that they were naked. And they sewed leaves of the fig tree, and made girdles for themselves."*

At this point the nakedness that these living souls experienced was the immediate understanding that they just separated themselves from their Creator, *i.e. no longer covered! This is not a representation of a physical naked body, as they/we were not physical beings at that time.*

Gen 3:21 *"And Jehovah god-[Archon] made covers of skin for the man and his woman and covered them."*

The corrected and most telling literal translation from the Hebrew of the Gen 3:21 verse above proves what I am saying here –

*"To Adam and his woman, Jehovah god covered their **light**, wrapping them."*
Asher translation)

The Hebrew word for light is (ore). It is absolutely specific to mean and depict *(any source or entity which generates and emits light),* like a star, a candle, or in this case the *living-soul* still in its original *plasma light-body* form.

Remembering that the later manipulated texts with their added allegories' of only two physical body humans falling away by eating apples, is not nearly an accurate depiction. It is more accurately understood from the greater Genesis context that the *Adams'* and *Eves'* referred to, to have been the multitude of souls already present here at that time, *not only two!* All living-souls existing here in our original *light-bodies.* Moreover and quite, unfortunately, by their/our consenting to a deceiver's voice and direction, our *Light was covered, in skin*!

Meaning - the physical body which was made *"in their image"* was the vessel produced to house our living-soul by adverse possession due to our consent!

Our action, or *sin* as it were, like this deceiver's action previous to ours, *was the usurpation of the free will of another sentient entity,* namely the animals that they also created here in order to facilitate this destruction. We failed that test miserably, with most of us continuing to fail that same test daily ever since.

In all my years of re-teaching religious people, and conversing with many scholars, priests, and rabbis, I have heard the occasional musing among them pondering with no clear proof or good answer concerning their question of why *god* made all the animals first. Why, if Man is the alleged *"apple of His eye"*, did He not make Man first among all? To be sure the conjecture runs wild! *The answer;* because the True Prime Creator did NOT make any physical entities for this place! Only living-souls resided here in tranquility, abundantly. The Rebel Archon souls produced the animal physicality's' first in order to provoke all living-souls into breaking that first, immutable law of free will! *Then your light was covered in skin!*

Christians and Jews should not remain fooled by these texts any longer. The entity who came looking for them in that garden place after the transgression *was not the Prime Eternal Creator at all.* We should all recognize this because by that point they/we had already forced our separation from Him by our transgression of His free will system so willingly, as described on the previous page.

Thus, the entity who we see depicted in that garden forcing our *light* into *skin-physicality* was the same evil transgressor that tricked all souls into consenting with his extended program of death in the first place. A program that all those living souls had no detailed knowledge of. Souls which still remain unaware because of that entities array of false religious and social *control-narratives* ever since. We consented to the program before reading the fine print, and that program is all about *soul-control!*

For those who are missing the sequence, these physical bodies were produced *after* our transgression of the first law. Breaking that law allowed them to capture us in those bodies.

Meaning, the Genesis texts are out of order, depicting men and women's physical bodies *being animated by a living-soul* prior to our original *light-body* form-souls transgressing. The law was broken and after that, the covering of our *light-body-soul* with the skins of physicality occurred. You will be surprised and amazed by modern science later when I delve into how the number 666 proves these physical bodies to be the so called, Beast Mark, as created *in their image & reflection – Trinity-6*

Note: Before the *experts* comment negatively on my suggestion of the Genesis texts being out of order, understand that I and other scholars have proven many such accounts to be out of place. Not the least of them being the existence of the alleged *Ark of Testimony- Covenant* as clearly depicted in Exodus 16, long before said Ark was alleged to have been *fabricated* by the specific instructions of god much later! Additionally, for those who rather believe that the *Testimony* spoken of in that chapter to be depicting the actual *Commandment Instructions*, then be advised, this as well would be a major key feature now found out of order. As most Hebrew scholars understand that textually, no Commands other than the specific usage of the Manna as collected on the 6th day, as well as the command to remain in their dwelling for the entirety of the 7th day, were provided yet.

Gratefully, The Eternal Creator being who and what He is, mercifully created a simple workaround to free all souls from our previous poor choice. This, however, requires us to do our part in the physical here and now, and it has absolutely nothing to do with any religion! Since The Creator is genderless, having no need for us to be encased within a physical body or to reproduce, then clearly it makes little sense to believe He cooperated by breathing our souls of life into a disobedient Archons physical creation without a plan. *As I stated just previously, it is an exceedingly important point to remember as you progress through this book, and especially when I start correlating the ancient texts with our modern scientific discoveries; those rebellious Archon souls are also being tested in real time.* Just as we are tested and judged based on the mercy or lack thereof towards those created beings *we deem to be lower than us.* So are those soul entities above us within the higher creation levels so tested and judged. They are the ones retaining and perpetuating our existence in this lower creation space, not the Prime Creator. *His part then was to provide all souls a way back.* As most understand this to occur, the Prime Creator sends His messengers as needed to *replant, reiterate* original knowledge for guidance along our way. Our living-souls and not our physical bodies are the prime targets. And somewhat like our ancient stories have brought it forward, although mostly super-spiritualized and overwritten, the root of truth remains that we are unique and sought after – *Living-Souls!*

Because of His first law of free will, no *devil* figure has the ability or authority to manipulate our soul outright without our consent. If an evil entity is to keep our souls enslaved, it is by our consent as stated previously and throughout this book. Therefore there is no *stealing* but rather it boils down to our *giving* ourselves over and away, even if by the *tacit consent* of ignorance. Let's face facts, just as with the Edenic garden event, it is all too easy to point the finger at the other guy and state that it was their fault. However difficult it may be, this requires each of us to take responsibility for our own actions then and now. The *devil* may have asked you to do it, but the reality is, we are the perpetrators.

The Gnostic Archons

It is curious how the majority of world-renowned scholars tend to generally disassociate the various entities within most cultural religious texts, this is not logical. Simply look at the obvious similarities between Greek and Roman Mythology. The *gods* of the ancient world were shared across the differing nations by varying nomenclature. It appears the question of whether *these alleged gods* vs. *those alleged gods* to have literally existed or not existed, etc., is not restricted to the experts, but also trickled down to many people throughout the various faiths and cultures today. It appears to me that most religious people do not believe any of them existed literally, and at the same time never connect their personalities to be in league with their own superstitious *fallen angle* personalities.

Such is the case when both of these groups consider the gnostic texts. I must again state that I am not claiming these texts to be authoritative down orthodox religious lines, but rather when viewed side-by-side there appear to be very specific similarities, and they correlate. This seems to be the case with the Gnostic *Archons;* otherworldly dimensional beings – *aliens;* the mythical *fallen angels, Watchers, Jinn, Devs* and the like? I tend to believe the misunderstanding is derived from a lack of holistic perspective and a deeper understanding of all the available ancient texts and superstitions across cultures.

By direct translation from the Greek, the word or title Archon means *ruler*. In the ancient Hebrew language, *Nazi* also means ruler, where have we seen them before? Better yet, why did those who allegedly hated Hebrews', name their movement with a Hebrew word? The majority of contemporary researchers regard these Archon entities today, to be *Energy-Vampires*. Those who feed on the *soul output energy* of all humans, but few if any can tell you why. Again, as I stated earlier, all myth and superstitions have some original core of truth and this misconception of these so-called Archon entities is no exception.

Make it easy on yourself and collate all of the evil entities you have ever known of or read about into one troop of beings working within the same system. *Tall grays, short grays, tall whites, winged or wingless reptilians or shapeshifters, angels of light, or dark Jinn,* it matters not. As I postulated earlier, I suspect that these alleged alien entities may be those who are mere creations of the original Archon rebels. Just as the devious leaders here on this planet work, not to leave themselves exposed they send in their minions – *expendable cut-outs!* Therefore, it stands to reason that these other entities, generally thought to be *aliens,* are not those higher Archon entities who the majority on this planet understand to be interacting, and even manipulating our affairs.

As I quickly mentioned above, it is the understanding of many researchers that these Archon entities actually live off the vast energy output of our souls! It is thought that they require us to generate *negative energy* more so than positive. This negative energy output that we provide is evidently a literal life and death issue to them. *Why negative instead of positive?* Negative emotions (Plasma frequencies) rooted in fear expend or release more energy from your body; just think about how much it takes out of you after you have had a negative experience. Negative frequencies are destructive, depleting, and known to actually significantly shorten life span. Whereas positive energy, which emanates from love, energizes you internally with minimal output.

From where I stand, looking at the scientific evidence of how human body plasma energy is displaced and revitalized, I concur on all points. However, my understanding of this issue relates quite differently. Instead of taking this information and applying it to one given narrative, I take a more holistic approach.

In addition to the scientific data, the vast array of ancient Mesopotamian writings in conjunction with later religious texts and concepts, those so-called parasitic *Archon-energy vampires* would equate to the ancient spiritual adversaries as we also see them more specifically described in the book of Enoch. Since these entities have been recast later by dogmatic religious narratives as our *demonic principalities,* we need to be very careful to identify and differentiate them correctly, or most will remain unaware.

As far as the *aliens*, these are not merely Hollywood style alien creatures from other worlds having no connection to our very ancient story. Granted, some people tend to believe these Archons as aliens, but that is just one of the more recent *false narrative streams* they impose on us. It appears many people also believe that they *rule* and manipulate mankind against their Will. Clearly, this cannot be the case based on the law of Freewill, of which all created entities good or evil MUST abide or forfeit their existence.

All Archons and their cut-outs are forced to work in the gray areas of free will by coercion. Many people also believe that these, or some entities at times literally control people's minds and bodies, and perhaps that may be true, although again there must be an element of *consent* rooted in some amount of participation or misguided belief in the entity on the part of those people for this to occur.

From our beginning to our end it has and will always come back to the consent of our souls, and hopefully our movement towards a new rebellion of our continued consent.

Chapter 4

Disconnected Lifeline, a Case for the Caste System

As previously touched on, virtually every narrative system in this creation has fabricated institutions based on a simple hierarchy, from kindergarten to the highest offices of politics, corporate systems, and religion. It must be understood that this hierarchy is nothing short of a caste system. It is that which you are born into. If you don't believe me, simply consider your own heritage. If you are not of say, Jewish decent, then by birth alone you have been made lesser than god's *"chosen"* people. This has its foundations in the manipulated Hebrew Scriptures as well and continues on into the Greek New Testament writings. This is rooted in an ancient elitist mechanism as propagated throughout the secret societies, monarchies and governments of the world to this very day. *The powers above us have promised them all the power and riches of this world.* At any point in mankind's recorded history, we see this at play. This is the reflected low character of those who implemented the control narratives.

This is fully expected, as this *Adam-Eden* matrix has been re-formatted in the reverse-*character*-reflection of The Eternal's original creation design. Thus, by default, we know that no system of hierarchy exists anywhere within the Prime Eternal's unaffected realms. In those realms, there is no need to struggle for power because all power resides with the loving Eternal Creator, Himself.

This is evident in the binding character of the first law - *"treating one another, as we want to be treated"* - Equality. That mandate alone levels the playing field and brings down the cultic house of cards, royalty and all!

As I continue to reiterate throughout this book, *there is always a root of original truth in our superstitions and myths.* The oldest account concerns a certain finite troop of 200 souls transgressing the Creators first law, later coercing a greater multitude of other souls *within this creation level* to transgress as they did – (alleged to be 1/3 of the souls in the heavens) - *Yes! The First Murderer and the captains with him coerced all the naive souls of this creation!).* There may be 7 billion souls' on this planet soon, but that number is no proof of how many captured souls remain else ware in their system awaiting rotation!

The Energy of their Immortality - "Cut-Off"

The first murderous soul and 199 additional rebellious soul entities who usurped this lower world creation have in fact been literally *disconnected* from the Prime Eternal's Omni-present *"life-force energy"* - a **sustainer.**

The rest of the souls, since quarantined within this system have been provided a reprieve from this absolute disconnect from immortality. Take into account the religious ideas of *outer darkness, hell,* the *separation from God,* and such, these all speak to the same concept. The trouble has been in discerning what that darkness or separation actually is. What I know it is *not,* is an eternal life in some *burning* or other condition. The most common perception among religions is that this is a literal place *lacking of God's presence.* Remember - Perceiving nakedness?

Those original 200 rebellious Archon souls learned the hard way exactly what being *cut-off* truly means! Their separation was and remains a literal disconnection from the Creators *sustaining force of immortality!* The very force and *tether* back to His Macro-Soul that enables our eternal living-souls to remain *eternal!* Their hate for us stems from their perception that we were not *cut-off* as they were, for what appeared to be the same offense! *However, it was not the same!* Had we all been disengaged from that sustaining tether at that time, *losing the ability to sustain our light,* no souls would remain. This is the far greater reality and truth of the Archon's great burden. To continue existing, or cease to exist; plunging into *eternal darkness* or more accurately; *eternal non-existence.*

The root of this understanding comes through the ancient patriarch *Enoch* and his story of those *higher souls* who disobeyed grievously. In short, when these rebellious souls came to know that Enoch kept the company of other higher, *but righteous soul messengers,* (angles), they requested that Enoch bring their written supplication for forgiveness back to the Eternal One on their behalf. Unfortunately for them, and upon Enoch's return, *they received their answer, not only by his discourse but through the pain of that eternal tethers severance.*

Upon their hearing of that most final proclamation, *forever denied,* as it is written, they fell to the ground screaming, inconsolable! Which to most of us would appear to be quite out of character for such highly advanced soul entities who thought they could be *as god!*

This denial response from the Prime Eternal One and its most authentic meaning has long been misunderstood by Western religious cults. The accurate ancient meaning is as I have depicted it herein; that they were not merely thrown out of the higher heavenly realms, but literally - *'cut off'!* And not merely *cut off* by proximity as the Western religious cultures teach that to mean; *as simply an eternal existence outside of God's presence.* This grievous action depicts the literal *disconnection* of their *life-sustaining tether.*

That *eternal force* derived from, and connecting them back to the Prime Eternal One. At which point even Enoch looked upon them with pity.

Are we starting to see where this is going in regards to the misconceptions of why the so-called Archons have a need to *pirate* and *feed* on the output of our soul energy? A powerful energy known from ancient times, and that which even our modern science has proven to exist to be emanating from us all.

These Archon rebellion leaders are not just some far-flung alien entities being mistaken for *angles of light* throughout history, and now little gray aliens. They are those who men have understood through the false control narratives as being the fallen angels. The very entities who have arrogantly positioned themselves higher than our souls. It is they who have required a consistent *soul-energy source* in order to sustain their very existence after the removal of that eternal coupling.

Clearly, they knowingly used their free will choice to forsake the True Eternal Creators original, minimal instructions.

They have contrived and perpetuated all manner of evil, death, and negativity narratives throughout all generations, within all epochs. Their control narratives are the tools by which they amplify the greatest percentage of negative energies out of *our still connected and sustained living souls. Pirating the eternal energy connection provided by the One who removed it from them in the first place.* Without such a system of energy vampirism, they could not continue to exist, much less create their own realm over us to "be as god". Therefore, the Archon-souls are false rulers who coerced and manipulated the great multitude of equal but evidently naïve souls, who for some yet unknown reason consented to follow and agree with their rebellious vision.

The Archon Rebellion leaders are forced to be *Energy Wraiths* to survive, and thus manipulate our circumstances inclined towards the negative in various degrees to meet their desired need.

The Extant Alien Forces?

As postulated previously, and based on the numbers alone, it makes sense that 200 highly advanced soul-beings cannot keep up or control the growing population on this planet alone without the aid of others. Question is... Who? A growing number of people worldwide, even the Papacy no longer doubt, and even expect the existence of other non-human entities. With even a little research one will generally find the stories depicting entities interacting with people and animals sporting far higher technology, as well as the expected standard hierarchical system routines. The majority, if not all of these entities, has shown themselves to be malevolent towards man, engaging the character traits of slave taskmasters.

By the decree of their Archon father-demigod *the first murderer* and his cohorts, they use slight-of-hand to sustain old and employ new control-narratives to maintain existing soul portions by their own, ongoing Freewill Consent.

Consequently, regardless of the rebellion leadership, their mInIons' technological advancements, or in-depth knowledge of the Prime Creator's great creation, they cannot bypass His Freewill system in order to enslave us openly against our *will*.

You must consent! Aware or unaware, permission is given every single day by several means, in every single lifetime since creation.

Code Revisions – Bolstering the Modern Narrative

To make a choice, or not make a choice, *you have still made a choice to be governed.* By our own consent, they have virtually enslaved many portions of the Eternal One's very own microcosm-souls. Micro-souls apportioned from His own essence! Thus, if you control a large portion of the Prime Creators Microcosm soul portions, *do you not also then to some degree control the Prime Eternal Creator Himself - To be as God?* Not true, but of this, I am certain they believe.

There is a reason why these entities work so diligently to keep us enslaved. These Rebellion leaders know that we have the innate ability of *returning* to The Eternal One who made us. They cannot allow our collective souls to be enlightened to this reality, even partially, for our soul energy is their literal life-sustaining force! The altering of original truth into their own control narrative versions recurrently enslaves the soul-masses. This produces an ever expanding emergence of differing religious orders, which then nurtures an increasing absence of the Primary Eternal Creator's original wisdom. Due to the presentation of a similar core of beliefs, the basis for falsely mandated ritualistic traditions is further developed. These are then salted by superstition updates ongoing, and the process of enslaving souls is complete... or so they think.

How is it possible still?

Answer – *"My people/souls are destroyed for their lack of knowledge."* (Prophet Hoshea)

Priest Craft – Turnkey tyranny

We have many examples of this very scenario in this creation level. Look no further than the Jewish Levitical Priesthood and their manmade sacrificial system. (D. S. Asher)

They raised the *special* (clean) animals themselves, created a market, sold them, and then accepted them back for sacrifice, of course taking the best meat portions for themselves afterward. *Why wouldn't they want to keep that system in place?* They profited on both ends of the deal. No wonder the great prophet Yehshua cleared the temple market! *Simple to see why they would pull out all the cosmic stops to keep us here.* They fabricated the system and authored the texts which now in our modern times are allegedly coming to life in new and amazing ways.

To the amazement, religious fervor and willingness to believe in and follow yet another false, control narrative stream; now in recent years they miraculously *find* this alleged "Torah Code" that so many religious people look to as being some literal miracle from God. Again I ask - *Which god?* Do you truly believe that the Creator of everything that exists; *entire expanses, galaxies, civilizations,* from *microbes* to *complex matter,* requires the silliness of some hidden, *and I want to stress this word – hidden –* basic word code puzzle to enlighten His people, really? Because last I checked He used His PEOPLE for that, we call them prophets! And even some of them are suspect.

Now, let's take a close look at the alleged *Torah Code, defined as a form of Gematria numerology that utilizes selected Equidistant Letter Sequences proclaiming to be a "hidden" prophecy of end times.*

Many religious people claim this to be a literal miracle from "God ". Again and again, "Which god? In my opinion, this ranks up there with counting the characters of the Torah to verify its authenticity, which is also done. More amazing than the Torah code phenomenon itself, is how so many totally disregard the fact that all the alleged code found is <u>AFTER the fact</u>, so it is not even prophesy. Most likely, a *god given* false narrative tool to consolidate someone's power eventually. *Beware the keepers of the god-code!*

Not Prophetic, but getting closer!

The Torah Code is not prophesy, but in many cases being made to look as if it is! It appears simple enough and very convenient for a *god* to compose a book that contains corresponding coded events woven throughout. Especially when the Archon *gods* hold the only access to the advanced technology which affords them the ability to make updates in real time by the manipulation of the Prime Creators *super-holographic, matter-based universe.* In addition, there remain within this *reflected* image creation, those human archon sycophants possessing the superior technology to carry out those alleged *prophetic* operations on the ground in real time - One supporting the other – As above, so below!

How then can anyone have any issue with a written text containing secret code predictions that turn out 100% correct after being fully orchestrated? **Not at all prophetic!** And by no means helpful, not helpful to us anyway.

To what end?

Based on all the knowledge I and many others have concerning how these Archonian usurpers work, in my opinion, these Post-prophesies of the Torah Code are merely phase 1. That in due time, their *keepers of the Code* (the chosen people) will begin to show the Torah code as 100% prophetic <u>before the fact</u>. Such a tool could easily be used to predict the names of all the people/souls not worthy to remain living due to their defiance of "god", and his alleged laws.

Even then few will ever think to ask - **"Which god"**

Parlor trick?

Consider this, upon approaching the total collapse and world destruction *year of fear* 2012, the high Torah Code experts in Jerusalem and New York were finding the use of <u>modern words</u> in the Hebrew texts relating to all things 2012. Much in the same way they found modern words like *Airplane, bombs, NYC,* etc., <u>after</u> September 11, 2001. Any person with a Hebrew linguistic background should be asking themselves, *'How can that be?'* How can there be the literal use of modern English words in phonetic Hebrew, depicting objects, locations, proper names with personal or professional attributes that did not exist within these ancient texts or language at the time of their authorship? *The fact is, it cannot be!* Not unless this creation level reality is exactly as our scientists and ancient prophets tell us it is, *a Plasma-matter based holographic construct!*

To simplify what I am saying here; what they were finding in their *codes* was nothing more than *updates,* much like your computer does on its own after receiving the real-time updates from its *computer-company-god-consciousness.*
Compelling *fear narratives,* which of course are controlled and disseminated through their media complex for *soul-assimilation and eventual projection into our world reality.*

Example: As certain specific fear narrative topics loom larger as an event date such as the 2000 *Y2K* event, *Mayan* 2012 event, or the 2015 *Tetrad blood moon* events, the collective agitation grows both internally and externally, all of which uploads and *feeds* the Energy-Wraith system, which in turn sends out its real-time updates, which are of course miraculously found in the Torah <u>after the fact</u> as proof to complete and renew the cycle.

Clearly, the Torah code becomes a control narrative all its own. Should you buy into the concept that this was actually prophetic, then we have just given our <u>approval</u> and <u>consent</u> to have yet another level of authority over us. Resulting in our sitting on pins and needles waiting for the next word that will emerge to instill fear into the world's mass soul consciousness. Additionally, as authors begin to include this in books, and as it develops into themes of movies, this becomes much like a destructive Trojan computer virus. Just as a computer's software unsuspectingly becomes captivated and controlled by an infectious virus program, our collective soul consciousness is drawn in through the power of suggestion into believing events that happen, to have been predicted by ancients long ago and driven by *god* of course. First, we hear about it, and then see it fictionally played out upon a movie screen and in books, only to have a similar incident appear as alleged truth in the news media. We begin to actually believe and more dangerously, assimilate *emotionally* that there may be some solid foundation for such clairvoyance and terror, now implanted causing imaginations, and more importantly, our *soul-intention* to run amuck. This is how their control narratives are issued into our world's collective consciousness. This installed fear gives way to an Archon feeding frenzy! Smooth and unexpectedly delivered by those you would never expect, but on the contrary have been programmed to trust!

I touched on the science of the holographic universe theory previously. This will be explained in an upcoming chapter, but please allow me for the sake of this specific discussion to clarify a bit further on how it works, and their manipulation of it. Since we live in the re-formatted reverse image reality, but retain the Eternal's originally given power of creativity within our souls, then we actually have the unified soul-power to make what is *suggested* in fear narratives, <u>to become reality</u>; you will see the modern science proving this later. This then plays into the Archon's hands.

Just as computer software permits updates, *our corporeality complies as well with being updated.* As we accept this updated *virus* version to our human software, we integrate it and now it becomes an integral part of this creation level. Thus, by giving our consent to propositions such as the Torah Codes, or horrific revelations prostituted as true and inevitable prophecy, we give access to our individual souls, which over time can by the *assimilation* and *intentions* of our collective soul's power, we manifest the input we received from them, <u>*for them*</u>. All assimilated and propagated willingly.

The takeaway here should be this; that our individual and collective soul-consciousness can be *passively* controlled, most often through *fear narratives*, which assimilate in our daily lives and minds, both consciously and sub-consciously. Then collective agitation grows both internally and externally, all of which *feeds* the *Energy Wraith* system, and brings their long contrived processes' to fruition, by our hand. This is a continuous renewing cycle. It's a matter of negative energy being drawn in and compounded instead of enforcing our Creator given power to reject the negative, which would allow positive energy to gain strength within our soul; thus reducing their negative narratives force logarithmically.

Again, I highly recommend the viewing of the documentary, Century of Self (Curtis). Research history and look for all the similarities at play.

The new mythical code

Just as the alleged Torah Code is redirecting man's soul-consciousness with the ongoing influx of updated control narratives, supported by the echoes of previously assimilated fear based religious narratives that are born on the back of their horrific reverse-exegesis and circular logic, they tout proof of both their *god,* and the authority of those who translate the codes as the high Levitical Priesthood of bygone days. Yet, we do have another witness to this amazing supernatural circus; the **"Web-Bots!"**

Developed in 1997 by Mr. Cliff High and George Ure. Interestingly enough, a "bot" is a program considered to be malware as are worms and Trojan viruses. They perform tasks on behalf of their user or another program with the intent to gather specific information from various computers far quicker that a human.

In this case, the Web-Bot system boasts the ability to collect, collate, and analyze data to predict future events. This is accomplished by tracking keywords based on *emotional queues* from humans' personal Internet communications. So in this regard, the Web-Bot program is actually more prophetic than the Torah Code. As *the Torah code appears to be instilling a stress either consciously or* subconsciously _after the event_, the Web-Bot program appears to be calculating that _collective stress_ to predict future outcomes. Make no mistake about it, this is tracking the collective, _projected_ "soul-intention" via written and verbal cues.

Simply put, the _projected_ output of each soul which has been manipulated by all the previously assimilated control narrative suggestion, is being recorded, collated and processed to formulate an expected prophesy outcome. As always predictable, and as usual, the designers of the Web-Bot program have kept all their magic a secret. Just as all good high Priests and magicians do!

Who's wagging who here?

Always remember, these details, although important, should never be allowed to overshadow the foundational point I would like to make. _It has always been about the Living-Soul!_ If our souls are a literal creative force, which is a truth that has long been suppressed, then our souls are creating _in real-time_ all that we experience; this again is supported by the modern science.

Unfortunately, the New Age movement's narrative has dominated this idea with false claims and ideas that too often connect the physical with the spiritual. This was the same error science made in the past by attributing our physical brain as that which created our life experiences. They are now discovering that it is, in fact, our souls that drive our physicality, and that without the soul, the _body-hardware_ remains unanimated. This is not news to those of us who have experienced this first hand in our own lives!

Why is this important or germane to the topic of hidden codes and Web-bots you ask? Truly none of this is prophetic or given by our Prime Eternal Creator to be prophetic. It is simply souls/people being directly influenced by controlling propaganda with the intent of gaining expected emotional responses uploaded and absorbed for later reiteration by those who want to reformat continually, and dominate. We are the only ones with the authority to end their cycles of deception by increasing our knowledge and awareness of it. Then we must refuse to consent further, rebel against their rule of fear and change to love and mercy.

A quick study concerning the energy of fear versus love will prove that love generates a calming peaceful energy/frequency. If you don't believe this just recall entering a room where people are in conflict. It is often said that *'the tension was so thick you could cut it with a knife!'* This is negative energy you are feeling! In the same way, we feel wind but cannot see it. Can you see how these negative control narratives and or special god-codes produce fear and its effects on us as collective living-souls?

As for the two code systems, I am certain they have been and will continue to be more and more helpful to those dark forces, which created them. Aiding them in keeping so many unenlightened souls wound up tight with their eye's more and more looking towards some chosen few *Priests* who yet again hold the sacred keys to the book, or in this case, the code.

Where have all the Angles gone?

The ongoing problem has been that the Prime Eternal One and all His Malakim/soul-messengers are equally bound by the same rules established within His freewill system. A close friend reminded that the words of Yehshua might be apropos here. *"Truly I tell you, whatever you bind on earth will be bound in heaven, and whatever you loose on earth will be loosed in heaven."* (Matt 18:18)

This binding and loosing within the Christian context is more than dealing with the sin in a fellow so-called believer's life. It is not simply a command but comes through the *obedience* to the Prime Creators <u>original Instructions</u>. That which the original rebels transgressed, and later got us to follow suit. Loosing means to free while binding requires *action*! By man's ongoing consent to the Rebellion leader's will and ways in participation of their control narratives, we *loose* or *free* them to have direct control of us. Only when we take action to literally bind their hands and essentially cut them off from us, do we succeed in liberating our souls from their absolute domination. Perhaps this and this alone is the only reason for the *"Elect one"* as clearly spoken about within the book of Enoch. This *Elect one's* persona was later usurped and re-casted as a *messiah figure* by the post-Babylonian Judahite cult. However, his original role as depicted by Enoch appears to be as an intermediary between the majority of yet unenlightened souls/people and the true Prime Eternal Creator whom they/we originally rejected.

Those faiths that place stock in a false messiah narration have turned the Elect one's role upside down through the unintentional mixing of ancient pagan traditions, *other control narratives*. These are then intermingled with blind trust in convoluted, erroneous scriptures. Despite these added, flawed texts much of the core information depicting his role is correct. The issue is, that by no real fault of those who are taught this dogma, that without a background in the Hebrew language and culture, it is difficult to understand or relate its origin as accurately as desired.

It is prudent to expect this type of situation within all religious doctrines and narratives. Unfortunately, these religions have been the main citadel for the dark forces continued grip on all souls.

Understandably, and as stated many times now, this is accomplished through our consent to their control narratives. Most assuredly, one cannot know an ancient text has merit until its removal from the original cannon of the Judaic-Christian authoritative texts. This requires cross-referencing those such as the books of Enoch, Jubilees, Yasher, Job, the Emunah Elish, Nag Hammadi, the Dead Sea scrolls, and many others.

Bringing things to a halt

> **Darnel** – *'A Hebrew agricultural term for the plant which has the same appearance as wheat.' Nearly identical, one cannot determine which is wheat or darnel until the ripening stage, at which point the heads of wheat bend downward. Among the Hebrew culture, this is understood as the wheat bowing their heads to the creator in reverence to Him, while the darnel standing tall in defiance remain easily spotted.*

Although historically I have rarely utilized any commentary from the Christian testament, I have found the parables of the prophet Yehshua to be quite outstanding, as I have also found his answers to the Pharisee's to be near sublime, out cunning the most cunning of their day, which I assure you is no small feat. I have written in depth on that very subject in my Asher Codex.

One of the best examples in understanding how to stop the Archons cold in their tracks is found in Matthew 13:24-30 of the Christian New Testament. This well-known passage is often entitled, *"The Parable of "The Wheat and the Darnel" or "Tares"*.
Although I believe this parable to be mostly misunderstood by them in general, in this teaching Yehshua points out that within any given time or generation, the Prime Creators Malakim/soul-messengers will know the identity of who the actual righteous *wheat* are, opposed to that of the false wheat or *darnel*.

It is depicted that an *enemy* has commingled the fake wheat within the authentic wheat in the field, but that they will be allowed to grow together until the harvest, at which time both will be gathered. First, the fake darnel will be gathered, bundled, and burned. Then the good wheat will be taken into His barn.

It should be understood at this point that the fake wheat/souls/people, were not born this way or predestined to be evil. They are those who "allow" themselves to remain asleep and manipulated by the false control narratives, by way of deception, most likely to such a depth that they are irretrievable during "that" generation. There are also those that are very few by comparison to the majority regardless of earthly religious affiliation, who will never be returned because of their knowing.

This *good* or *true* wheat is referring to those *souls* who have found The Eternal's original instructions, and thus taking the action of living them out to *enlightenment to ascension and out of this system!* As much as Yehshua taught this same instruction, few outside of Judaism understand this expressed Hebrew thought.

Due to the later New Testament text manipulations, along with the loss of original Hebrew language and culture, the true intent of this teaching became lost. Searching, finding, and doing His original instructions is the essence of *returning* to Him as He consistently requests through all His true prophets. We call this, "Teshuvah".

The common misconception of this parable is the misunderstanding that the event occurs <u>only one time</u> and at some yet unknown <u>future date</u>. However, in truth, this harvesting event has been occurring consistently, generationally. Most likely this slow harvest could be taking place since long before our current known history; and although we cannot know for sure, it does not really matter. The fact is Christianity and those who follow Jesus as Savior may recognize our souls as being part of The Creator's soul. They may even realize that we possess the same, perhaps minor, creative abilities. However, when it comes to the truth concerning all souls *recycling* through many lifetimes, they have been brainwashed to believe this to be pagan and/or a new age idea. This aversion to understanding reincarnated souls has yet become another control narrative rooted in total fear created by church doctrine.

Although long purged from the consciousness of those many sects of Christianity, a significant number of early church fathers carried the doctrine of reincarnation with them as fact. Such notables as St. Augustine, Clement of Alexandria, St. Gregory of Nyssa, Justin Martyr, and St. Jerome, believed in it fully.

The tragedy is that the world's largest religious base, *Christians*, have, ever since the close of the Fifth Ecumenical Council, been led to believe that the understanding, even the doctrine of reincarnation, to be a great pagan heresy within Christian religious experience.

From long before the Hebrew culture to the later Babylonian-Jewish cult, reincarnation as a fact has always existed within both. Since all of Christianity is rooted in the Hebrew culture and existed long before the Papacy, it only makes sense to understand that this doctrine of reincarnation originally existed within that cult of Christianity as well. It is also easy to understand why the later faux-Christian papacy hierarchy went to such great lengths to acid wash the idea from all Christian minds and hearts moving forward. Because, if they can get you to believe that *THIS* life is your <u>one and</u>

only shot at immortality with GOD in heaven, or eternal hell fire, then they can own all of you spiritually and eventually, even physically. _They are the one and only path to that immortality! They are the only special Priest, the vicar of the Creator on this earth; let no soul pass but through me and mine!_

In great contrast to that; the knowledge and understanding of your soul recycling, _even if the Archons control a secondary recycling system between here and the true higher realms beyond the expanse as I posit herein,_ will generally breed a condition in most people-souls called freedom! Freedom from the FEAR of those special priests; from the fear of some god, from the fear of death & hell; from the fear of living life outside of man's control systems, and Archon narratives, etc. And let's face it, all the special Priests, Levites, Mullahs and god-man messiahs won't have all of you outside of their daily control and conditioning without a fight. Just ask _Origen,_ the scholar they crucified for this belief!

The disinclination to soul continuance is not based on proof but rather is contrary to the amount of worldwide documented evidence available corroborating souls returning to live out another incarnation. For those who delve into this topic, the confirmations are certainly there. Instead, the "one life to live" dogma is the lie of another narrative, however not one held as truth within the early church. _Origen,_ an early scholar, and Christian theologian, is credited with teaching a _soul rebirth doctrine_ which of course he received from the ancient Hebrew culture. However his teaching was banned by the Byzantine Emperor Justinius, a non-religious entity, at the 5th Ecumenical Council in 553 C.E. Therefore this ended the concept of reincarnation in the Christian doctrine from then on. Having stripped away the rebirthing of the soul made for a very effective, strong, and controlling narrative. Basically boiled down to this, _"Just believe as we tell you and in this one incarnation you will have life everlasting!"_... In some cases, at no extra cost, we will include 70 virgins! Every religion narrative has it perks.

But are they actually telling us a lie in that last statement? No, not really! The same way no one ever thought to ask – _which god,_ they also don't think to inquire as to just _how_ they will be living forever. Or do they mean - over and over? Semantics!

Moreover, the many canonized text distortions later created about Jesus allowed the newer *special* priests to project yet another control device. Something I coined as **"Soul-Fear"**.

They designed yet another halo of superstition regarding Jesus with consideration to an alleged *salvation*. Once a Christian confesses (the magic words) *that he/she believes in Jesus as his/her personal savior, then due to the previously mentioned false messiah system, that individual is now saved from the consequence of their sin and thereby receive eternal life instead of damnation.* Why would anyone want to leave such a failsafe, secure paradigm? No matter how much I teach that this is in error, the instilled *fear* of the eternal fires of hell looms over those who even consider leaving this narrative. Soul-Fear - Perhaps one of the most effective narrative tools!

Now, as we look at this parable a little closer, let us consider the reality that crops and harvests *are not one-time events*, but cyclic. Fields are recycled anticipating a new crop to be harvested in rotations several times each season. In this same way we should understand that our souls have been subjected to this same cycle in each generation, just as with any earthly crop. It should be noted again that *some* of the "imposter wheat-***darnel***" who are ultimately burned are exactly those few in all generations whom I have been addressing all along, evil men and women who have direct knowledge and access to their Archon gods – *The knowing!* The Archon human sycophants who *consent and embrace* those evil entities' deceptive will and ways *knowingly.*

Before you can become truth, you have to embrace a terrible thought – That you have always been the responsible party!

Consequently, this parable is about the condition of the soul at the end of *an incarnation* by having chosen to live either for "good" or "evil". Searching for true goodness (light)-*the essence of free will,* finding and living it, is to embrace the Eternal One and His original instruction for all life, which is wholly rooted in the *free will system,* and <u>proven out in our lives by our merciful response towards the free</u>

will of all things living! Lack of seeking results in neither finding nor living that goodness is ultimately by definition Evil & Darkness.

It has absolutely nothing to do with any mythical warring demonic force with us in the middle. We CHOSE this! We chose to consent; we chose their will over The Eternal's original plan.

The Eternal Creator knows who is ready; His Soul-messengers are also aware as they watch. Those souls who are open to seek absolute truth for the sake of truth alone, and regardless of where it leads them; those souls who yearn and cry out for all life threatening, destructive intentions to end, giving way to mercy, in each lifetime *are the good wheat* who live among the darnel in any generation. When any soul finally becomes reawakened to The Eternal's original truth, even in various percentages, *which is an original truth solely based on His character as a creator, not destroyer,* that soul to varying degrees embraces the change and returns to His *Everlasting Agreement.* Upon the death of this flesh body, that newly *returned* soul departs, and instead of returning here for a new incarnation cycle, it is now allowed to move on to reunification with the one true Prime Eternal Creator! *Life-Energy - food removed from the mouths of those evil Archon-souls!* That good wheat being placed in the barn, its *house,* is no less than that soul returning back to *His house,* the Eternal's realm, our original estate. *Much to the rebellion leaders' disappointment and demise, this removes yet more "life-energy" vital to their existence!*

Now, when the soul that had knowingly chosen evil separates from the body, represented here by the *darnel,* it is not unlike that of the Christians idea of the refiner's fire. Just as that fire burns off impurities out of gold, the burning of the darnel at the end of any generation gives way to a recycle of that rebellious soul's continuance in this realm. That life was a result of choosing to again consent to this reformatted creations narratives. The next *new crop* of lives contains the souls that have another opportunity to choose good by seeking Him and living out His original will. However, for some time all of this has been sidetracked by our own consent to the Archon's original offer, and our ongoing consent to their false narrative

programs. *All of that has worked well to stemming the tide of souls finding the original, minimal instructions of truth, and returning home.*

There is then another harvest with yet another *darnel* soul crop cycle to follow in the hope of change. *So it is ongoing in each generation.* This is why the rebellion leaders continuously work towards a new and more efficient enslavement vessel for the remaining returning souls. In contrast to the compassion of the Eternal One by allowing the soul to use its own will to choose the journey back to Him, their objective is to preserve the energy source required to impede their extinction! They inch closer and closer to that line of totally usurping the free will of all souls, which will only hasten their ultimate and sure demise.

Here seems to be the final word on this parable. Regardless of the prophet speaking, whether Hebrew or otherwise, there will be an end to the usefulness of this usurped farmer's field. All those darnel crops/souls who *knowingly* worked for the rebellion leaders in full knowledge and understanding at that time will be cut down, bound, and burned...Cut-off! – "Soul-Lights out!" This indicates there very well may be a point in time with no further chances of return... *"Diminishing their Light unto non-existence!"*

These people knowingly exercised a true freewill choice, unlike the rest of the souls revolving captured in this lower creation whose choices were based solely on non-disclosure, lies upon lies, ever since having our memories of it all erased prior to each cycle. All very cleverly planned and continually executed to ensure the longest term of slavery. This is the same issue for all. No one, not even the rebellion leaders keeping you preoccupied by concealing truths just within your grasp, knows when the final harvest will take place.

Those who chose to be darnel by their *knowing* will be found cut off and *disconnected* until they disappear along with the first murderers they followed. No soul will be subject to some eternal, burning damnation. That was added to the narrative in order for the priests to gain power and control over you.

Those who are technologically superior mistreat us in this life and <u>yet by the same measure, we control, dominate, and mistreat all</u>

other sentient and non-sentient life forms that we deem to be inferior to us! Most of us are no different because we have been remade in their image! *Reformatted by their control-narratives.*

If all understood and lived the simplicity of the *Everlasting Agreement,* the Archonian rule would come to an end so much sooner. I believe it could occur almost instantly. Their rebellious souls would suffer a great loss of energy to pirate due to a quicker and higher percentage of souls returning back to the Prime Eternal Creator.

As the evidence will continue to prove out, our souls do recycle many times returning back to this creation. Many cultures have mistakenly assumed this *wheel-cycle* to be a benevolent mechanism created by the Primary Creator, an alleged necessity for the enlightenment of each soul. I however strenuously disagree that the Prime Eternal Creator set up such a system initially. As I speculated earlier, *I tend to believe He is using this free will inspired situation after the fact.* To allow our original free will choice to stand even though it was made without full transparency, with the majority of our subsequent choices made mostly by our tacit consent to their ongoing narrative manipulations. Beyond that, there exists the Prime Creators willingness and no doubt long-suffering to allow and afford our Archon-rebel-soul captors their lengths of rope unto the end of this production.

It does not seem logical or even reasonable to believe that the Prime Creator would infringe on His own natural law of free will _by wiping our soul's extensive memories_, which is an obvious, blatant intrusion and usurpation of our individual free will. A major intrusion which you will see as we progress, to be the main mechanism used to thwart any meaningful progress to the enlightenment of any original truth within this creation space.

Having total recall of so many past lives back to our original consent to disobedience would surely send most if not all living-souls flying back to our original state of being within mere seconds of that recall. It is my hope that you will come to realize how that is an absurd and gross misinterpretation of who we are, and who HE is. Our various prophets communicate this within their texts, just as I also illustrate within the pages of my book - *The Greater Exodus*.

Come out of her my people!

Many learned Rabbi's, in and out of their orthodoxy, along with their Christian theological counterparts, have no meaningful concept of this phrase. Likewise in over 3000 years, few to none of them inquire about or expound on why their prophets, and especially the prophet Isaiah went out of his way to *rebuke concerning the Everlasting Agreement!* The silence on the one side who know this truth remains deafening, while their Christian counterparts fill peoples' heads with fanciful thinking more suited for children.

The answer to both is actually quite simple. The soul has no need to remain on perpetual autopilot for the Archon dark side system. *Everyone houses the potential to break through the rebellion leaders' entrenched control narratives of dogma and ritual.*

The Eternal gave each of us the capability to consider and intuit the original truth that is stored within all our souls, and regardless of the negative control programming, possible memory wipes or deliberately designed DNA-based, soul firewall systems.

As some have witnessed, once a soul is ready to return to the Eternal Creator and His original way of total free will, seeking Him, desiring Him and with a willingness to live *His Everlasting Agreement which is the outward expression of His free will system,* its invariable truth flies in the face of our Adam-Eden religions. *This single ancient understanding is unlike any chosen narrative in this realm and remains alien to the most ardent religionists among us.*

That fact alone should be proof enough that such a path is decidedly something different, *even a Polar opposite!* Unstoppable to a souls return, and yet it must be experienced for there are no words to describe it.

Exactly as our own corrected Hebrew texts of Exodus prove out; as they did then, we consented to follow **another voice,** *to* **another mountain,** to receive **another law!** To comply and Consent to the will of another entities character, in clear contradiction to the True Prime Eternal's Will.

We are mistreated in life by those who are technologically superior. Just as we control, dominate, and mistreat all other life forms who we deem to be inferior to us!

Access by consent... do you now comprehend the gravity of it? Do you understand the control narrative program used to manipulate us against the True Eternal Creator's simple instructions to *treat all souls as you would have them treat you?*

It is only your own consent within His Freewill system that holds you here. The only stumbling block preventing you from even attempting to break away is your tacit submission to the dark side's fear control mechanism - "Soul-Fear".

There is an unmeasurable cavern of black space between the original path of life, freely abundant for all souls, vs. life abundant for those we deem to be equal to ourselves based on the extension of another demi-gods arbitrary system of hierarchy!

Chapter 5

The Eden Protocol

John 8:44
"You are of your father the serpent, and you want to do the desires of your father. He was a murderer from the beginning and does not stand in the truth because there is no truth in him. Whenever he speaks a lie, he speaks from his own nature; for he is a liar, and the father of lies."

This evil entity – *Serpent*– is nothing more than just another created SOUL who took his Archon position in adverse jurisdiction and possession over us all; no better or bigger than you or I, and certainly not one who was exempt from any foundational laws. As I do not believe there ever existed any hierarchy divisions within any creation levels, then this *Satan* entity could not have maintained a hierarchal position over any of the souls within the original Heaven other than within his own mind, before arriving here. If all souls were made in perfection, as all had to have been, and given to *free will*, and of course all having our own character and personalities, etc., then the serpent entity, and all others with him who appear to manipulate us from their 5th tier creation level, *rebelled in some way as many myths describe.*

The question most have never been able to answer is; **where did this** *first murder* **take place in the beginning?**

Of course, by our current ancient narratives most people will attest that the first murder occurred in some mythical garden place on *this* earth, and always attribute it to the character called Kayin.

However, I will attempt to unbind the more ancient context, understanding and more probable sequence of the *"Adam, Eve and*

Kayin" stories we received. The fact is the majority if not all souls living here now in this 3rd tier created space, originally sided with the *idea* that killing was ok.

THIS is the law that cannot be pleaded out, and it was broken long before the birth of Kayin.

Moreover, we can see how this John verse is telling us exactly as I have surmised it to be for so long. *(He was a murderer from the beginning).*

As I depicted earlier; Genesis 1:1 through 1:10 is a depiction of the original Prime Eternal Creator, creating His *free will system,* and His *separation expanse-zone* for the *separation and quarantine of disobedient souls* within this creation space. Also depicted earlier, was that starting at Gen 2:4, it is NOT as most scholars have openly taught these *other* creation verses to merely be, *'another telling of the same story in a different time and by other people, etc.'* but a lower creation level being partially *re-formatted* by another entity presenting himself as being, "THE only god".

The Setup!

To push your limits even further, wrap your head around the fact that this *other* evil entity was actually the one who *initially* commanded that (all) life here were to sustain themselves, both man and animal, by the original, righteous dietary laws as clearly defined in the Hebrew Genesis. These original instructions are nothing less than the Prime Creators original *fence* we know as His *Everlasting Agreement.* This Archon rebel allowed, and in fact, as it appears to be written, even proliferated this original, righteous *life code* within his reformatted creation; *because the best way to tell a lie is by using a preponderance of truth. It is most important to understand that this "entity" did not begin his reformation process of this creation level based on a totally separate and opposite trend of laws.* He knew that the first law of *Freewill* could never be bypassed without the consent of those now newly governed, making all accountable for their own actions, either for or against that of the Prime Creator. In doing so, this Archon created a *set-up* scenario, just as this book will show all false control narratives to have also been designed, instituted afterward and continually used as set-up scenarios. *But why, how, and who is being set-up?*

As we have seen already and will continue to see, other ancient texts bear out how this other entity *reformatted* this place in the *reverse character* image of the heavens above. Additionally, at first glance, and without the understanding that there even exists other Heavenly levels, as well as an original Eternal Creator entity; *then by the Genesis texts we all have, "this" place won't appear to be "originally" made in the reverse image.* Even students and practitioners of the enlightening law of the *Everlasting Agreement* continue to have questions in regards to the Genesis creation stories. The dichotomy appears to exist because it can be proven that the Freewill system and Everlasting Agreement laws were all original attributes of both the Heavens *above* our expanse, and also within *this* creation level as I point out in our Genesis 2 texts!

So then by that, how can it be true that *this* creation system was and continues to be reformatted in the *alleged* reversed image which other ancient texts appear to posit when at first glance it clearly appears to be created in the *same* image as the heaven above?

Well, of course, it was originally created all the same. However most of our Genesis story writings came into being long after the reformation process began, and the introduction of their subsequent false control narratives. The reformat changes of which I posit herein, revolve more centrally around the implementation of their false control narratives, and our soul's *assimilation* and *adherence* to them by consenting *thought* and *deed*. These cumulatively are the *mark* on your *forehead* and on your *right hand!*

Obedience to what you *assimilated, know* and *believe*, brought out into reality by the *intention projecting* from our souls, and to fruition by the deeds of your right hand. *All formatted within us by their false, anti-creator narratives that very few even believe to exist.*

The existence of those *original primary laws* here within this reformatted creation space <u>was the initial set-up for entrapment</u> through our consent! All based and structured on his *'first murder'* in the Heavens above. A murder for which the one called *Sama'el* and his counterparts, who clearly agreed and understood, were evicted from the heaven levels above us as most religions present to be the core of the entire matter. The Biblical Genesis story we have now of the *first souls – (prior to becoming physical men and women),* with their subsequent consent to breaking the first law, was the first *set-up* and *knock-down* in this realm which caused our temporary and lesser separation from our Eternal Creator.

Their own initial murder did not occur here. That Eden does not exist in this realm, and the souls set in place to guard its entrance are guarding it from the other side of the expanse.

The perfect, *original law had to be instituted and maintained here for a short period by the Archon souls even though they had previously broken from it.* Keeping these laws established just long enough to find a way to cause us as well to break it, and be severed completely from that eternal coupling provided by our Creator source, as they were; *or so they planned.* Their plan, which partially worked, was to cause an even greater multitude of living-soul portions to become totally separated forever from the Prime Creator. Accountable to them only - **Consent is key here.**

After which, and by our own consent as previously depicted by the corrected Hebrew Genesis texts, *our light-bodies were covered in the physicality of skins.*

Diligently hearing the voices of our new gods to go forth and multiply indiscriminately! By their command making room for more souls to be skinned, we swelled our new physical ranks for them.

The Days of Jerad

This new reformation rebellion leader, the *serpent*, AKA – *Sama'el* – *the Ouroborus reptile who strangles the earth!* Made an oath and descended against the newly created physical beings here within their previously usurped creation space.

The Hebrew name *Yerad* or *Jerad* in English literally means *(To descend or be separated out)*. As described in the book of Enoch, *Sama'el* being initially tentative about the plan of his chieftains, finally made an oath between all the rebel souls, his chieftains and the plan itself, before descending on to *Mt. Harmon*. Later a portion of his 200 Chieftains, notably - *Azazael; Baraqel; Kokabel; Ezekeel; Suriel; Tamiel; Gadreel; Ramuel; Danel; Asael; Samsaveel; Azkeel; Urakabarameel; Saraknyal; Yomvael; Batraal; Anane; Turel; Zavebe; Ertael; Penemue; Armaroz; Akibeel; Shamshiel; Arakiel; Kasdeja;* all experts of their many subject vices, are said to be the ones who instituted *physical* man's original proclivities and maintained the original *control-narratives*. Instituting all manner of killing for food and ritual sacrifice worldwide, now proven through archeology to have existed everywhere, and in nearly exact configurations of ritual and beliefs regardless of language, culture or geographic location. In this, they began building the false *control-narratives* which keep all souls enslaved to the act of usurping Free Will by murder - **Like the first!**

Mt. Harmon is a mountain within the ancient territory of the *Amorites*, to the east of the Jordan. Most notably known to have been the mountain top that the above mentioned 200 separated, disobedient soul entities' initially landed from their realm.

Enoch VI.
1. And it came to pass when the children of men had multiplied that in those days were born unto them beautiful and comely daughters. 2. And the angels, the children of the heaven, saw and lusted after them, and said to one another: 'Come, let us choose us wives from among the children of men and beget us, children.' 3. And Samjâzâ, who was their leader, said unto them: 'I fear you will not indeed agree to do this deed, and I alone shall have to pay the penalty of a great sin.' 4. And they all answered him and said: 'Let us all

Page | 99

swear an oath, and all bind ourselves by mutual imprecations not to abandon this plan but to do this thing.' 5.Then sware they all together and bound themselves by mutual imprecations upon it. 6. And they were in all two hundred; who descended in the days of Jared on the summit of Mount Hermon, and they called it Mount Hermon because they had sworn and bound themselves by mutual imprecations upon it. 7. And these are the names of their leaders: Sêmîazâz, their leader, Arâkîba, Râmêêl, Kôkabîêl, Tâmîêl, Râmîêl, Dânêl, Êzêqêêl, Barâqîjâl, Asâêl, Armârôs, Batârêl, Anânêl, Zaqîêl, Samsâpêêl, Satarêl, Tûrêl, Jômjâêl, Sariêl. 8. These are their chiefs of tens.

Chapter VII

1. And all the others together with them took unto themselves wives, and each chose for himself one, and they began to go in unto them and to defile themselves with them, and they taught them charms and enchantments, and the cutting of roots, and made them acquainted with plants. 2. And they became pregnant, and they bare great giants, whose height was three thousand ells: 3. who consumed all the sustenance of men. And when men could no longer sustain them, 4. The giants turned against them and devoured mankind. 5. And they began to sin against birds, and beasts, and reptiles, and fish, and to devour one another's flesh, and drink the blood. 6. Then the earth laid accusation against the lawless ones. **(The consumption of flesh was the final sin issue here!)**

(VI-XI. The Fall of the Angels: the Demoralization of Mankind: the Intercession of the Angels on behalf of Mankind. The Dooms pronounced by God on the Angels: the Messianic Kingdom (a Noah fragment). The Book of Enoch, by R.H. Charles, [1917] (Charles)

Mt. Harmon - *AKA Baal-Harmon* as mentioned in Judges 3:3 as being the core location for all *Ba'al* worship. *Haram* is a word most generally used to depict *people, places* or *things* to be *prohibited* or *sacred,* and also used to depict, *being in agreement with.* **Mt. Harmon,** from the Hebrew root word *Haram,* a verb that has various derivations from ancient times to the modern, also used to *designate something or someone into the afterlife,* or to depict *someone or something emerging from an upper heavenly realm to this realm,* or *going to the upper heavenly realm from this realm.* **Therefore, regarding those who fell or** *Jerad-descended* **out of the** *Shamayim,* **and having no (Shama) in this specific case, its name has to be understood in connection with these fallen entities having taken their sacred oath/agreement prior to landing there.**

Psalm 42:6 – Uses the derivation of the name as (Hermon'*im*) – Most scholars incorrectly believe this seemingly Hebrew *pluralized* version of the name to be a reference to the triple summits of the mountain, or even depicted in the plural form in reference to the peoples living there, *i.e. Hermonites.* However, the context clearly speaks to a geographical location and thus cannot be so. If you recall the previous Hebrew clarifications that I made of the Genesis 1 texts in chapter one, you should recall I referenced a little known and ancient variation on this *perceived linguistic plurality rule* as being not pleural at all in certain very specific cases of names or titles as I depicted concerning the Patriarch (Abraham's) name, correctly spelled as *Abrahim.* In these cases, the *(im or eem)* suffix reconfigures that name or title to depict *greatness of station,* as with the status of a King, or in this case a sacred mountain of the gods.

So it would appear, after being subject to these physical forms, their *memory wipe mechanism* has come in quite handy and proven to be the key to our extended stay.

If that were not so, we would have always known their true identity regardless of which mountain location they descended on to later. And even in this current physical form, we would surely never have believed them to be gods. They created these *Trinity-6* bodies to house our souls and afterward spread their evil seed among us more literally.

And then came the flood from *Yahweh,* which has always been very curious to me. I tend to believe his total reboot destruction at that time was mainly due to the aforementioned dissension and strife within the ranks between his chieftains and him. We may be able to understand this to be the most probable scenario concerning the movements of these 200 chieftain souls led by *Sama'el,* and due to the fact that *Yahweh/Jehovah's* name is not specifically given to be among those who finally landed on Mt. Hermon. Thus it appears they broke ranks with even him, after breaking ranks with the Prime Eternal One, previously.

Psa 89:12 *"the north and the sea thou has created. Thabor and Hermon shall rejoice in thy name"...:* (Douay-Rheims bible)

We can see throughout the Hebrew texts and the English versions for that matter, and regardless of tribe location North or Southern

Canaan, that this same alleged angel worship has been ongoing.

We know from the book of Judges the tribe of *Dan* or *Danites* relocated to the northern parts of Canaan, settling at the foot of Mount Hermon <u>in the territory of Bashan</u>. Dan was quickly influenced by and took on the idolatrous fallen Archon religious worship prevalent on that mountain known as *Baal* and *Eshtaroth; Eshtaroth* being known as the wife of *Yahweh/Jehovah*. Eventually, Dan left for parts West and North, later being identified as one of the alleged Lost Tribes. So why is Dan important to this Archon invasion and subsequent DNA manipulation forced upon certain bloodlines?

Jacob prophesied that Dan would be *"a serpent by the way, a snake in the path"* - (Gen. 49:17).

As well Moses prophesied, *"Dan is a lion's whelp: he will leap from Bashan"* (Deut. 33:22). These two prophecies are amazing and important, in that they connect Dan with the *seed of the serpent,* and the claim to the title *lion of Judah.* Of course, I do not at all believe either prophesy to be given as truth from the Prime Eternal Creator. I absolutely believe these and certain other such *narrative control prophecies* to have been devised, implemented and sustained from that mountain top to this very day by those who descended. As noted in the Jewish *Zohar,* vol. 1, p. 186 *"to this day they exist and teach men the arts of magic."*

Done by way of certain elite bloodlines of men. It may be interesting for you to know that concerning the coming Messiah, all Jews look for a messiah figure whose father is from the *royal family of Judah,* and whose mother will be *from the tribe of Dan!* Also interesting to note and easily verifiable these days is, that the English monarchy has always believed and even published works of their lineage, saying that they know they are all descended from King David directly! *The lion of Judah!* In the exact same fashion, the French believe they are descended from the ancient Hebrew tribe of Dan! *Serpent seed!*

Planned Coincidence

Most people are acquainted with the English monarchies London's Greenwich Observatory as the *Prime Meridian location.* This was agreed upon as the world's standard in 1884.

However, previous to that in <u>1666</u>, Louis XIV of France, authorized the Paris measure of longitude. This first "zero point" was and remains on some maps, the *Paris Prime Meridian – (PPM).* Here is where things get curious. A researcher by the name of *David Flynn* made some discoveries:

- The measured distance between the PPM and center top of Mt. Hermon is 2012 nautical miles!
- The measured distance between Mt. Hermon and the Equator is also exactly 2012 NM!
- The PPM is also known as "The Devils Line".

Even more amazing are the following findings:

- Mt. Hermon is located at 33.33 North by 33.33 East!
- Genesis 6 says that in the days of *Jerad/descended,* that the number of evil souls to have been separated out from heaven was 1/3rd or 33.33%!
- The French monarchy instituted their PM, which just happens to also connect exactly dead center to their ancient territory of Dan!

So I ask, are we still to believe that absolutely nothing occurred in the year of 2012? Or have we yet to perceive what may have occurred that year?

Although these fallen entities taught us to do it, as man advances he will generally not abide with ritualistic human or animal sacrifices; thus a change in the *narrative* is provided over to abortions, mass animal breeding as a food source, misguided death penalties, wars, etc. All perpetuating the ultimate, ongoing karmic disaster of the highest order.

The *only* reason the Archon entity initially carried forward the *original instructions* as law within this creation level, and as we find them depicted in Genesis 2, *was to ENTRAP all of the young souls living on this level who did NOT literally partake in the first murder in the heaven above.* All set up to create the opportunity for all *living-souls* to *choose* to agree with, and emulate the same murder in order to get us separated from our Prime Creator source.

Re-created now in their image, and in their low character, the main and vast difference between these original disobedient Archon souls *who chose this evil willingly,* and our soul's choice, is that their choosing was in the full knowledge of all there is to know on this subject of free will. Our choice, however, was manipulated through their lack of transparency, and exacerbated by our souls' naiveté not to inquire further. Enslaved by the gray area surrounding our lack of full knowledge to this very day. **THIS is a MOST important thing to understand**; *it is the ONE and the only reason that The Eternal Creator has not cut us all off from His eternal tether connection,* and thus our souls' eternal viability; as I proposed earlier, they, however, have been cut off!

So yes, the true and lawful original Instructions of the Prime Eternal Creator were in fact installed here originally as they are in all creations, but quickly had their *intention reversed* to be utilized against all the souls who originally resided here, and reside here still. Employing those laws to entrap billions of souls, he set up the entire scene and manipulated our souls into breaking the most coveted law of the Prime Eternal Creator; using the Prime Eternal creator's free will system against us in tandem. In this way was the original entrapment laid out and accomplished.

So in this overall idea, but separate from all the original misinterpretations that Christians, Jews, Muslims and other cults have had to this point, somewhat correct. We chose wrong and we became like them – **reflecting their image in belief and deed!**

Thus, as I have taught for many years, most humans/souls reflect the *image* of their false god and NOT the *image* of the One who created them. I am not a Christian scholar, but was this not exactly what Jesus stated, and John reiterated? *"You are of your father the serpent, and you want to do the will of your father".*

Chapter 6

Eastern Correlations

Chinese Heaven

A few Hebrew scholars have found the Chinese language to be very close to that of the ancient Aramaic-Hebrew in many respects, not least of *which is the concreteness in the meaning of their words and letter symbols* - "pictographs".

As described in this book, I show how the Hebrew texts of Genesis most literal meaning represents the existence of the original *Heavens*, with a later created area below those heavens called the *expanse*, which serves to cleave us and our choices from them for a time. I also find this Chinese symbol of (Tiān)-heaven as depicted above, to reflect much of that same meaning as we find in Genesis.

Although the ancient Chinese understanding of the next portion of this heaven symbol on its face appears to differ from my opinion of it, I will not dismiss their understanding, as it may well cover a greater and two-fold meaning. The portion of the symbol I find most interesting is the vertical line that splits and curves at the bottom, this is called the (人, Rén), and is said to represent *humanity* and *humanities position in the lower area below the upper heaven, and expanse; on this I fully concur.* I see this as being the same depiction that you previously received from the corrected Genesis account, which is the depiction of the souls being *distinguished between*, and *separated* under the expanse, represented here in the (天, tiān), symbol by the splitting of the vertical line, into and outward within this lower creation level.

Also interesting, is that the Chinese understood our lower creation to be occupying what they call the *middle realm*. Connect this understanding with the *Norse* legend of the same which literally named our earth – *Mid-Guard!*

It also appears that Chinese cosmology teaches that this (人, Rén), *maintains* the two poles of the three realms. However, I would like to propose another hypothesis to explain or expand on this portion of the symbol.

That the "人, Rén" may not, in fact, be only *maintaining* the original heaven and other realms together as it were, but in conjunction, it may also be a depiction of the original rebellion leaders' souls being ejected from Heaven, *downward through the expanse,* and into this lower creation-space!

At which time, and as previously stated, the place where all their disobedient souls were *distinguished between* and *separated.*

Look at the symbol based on the understanding of an *original heaven, expanse area*, and *lower creation zone*.

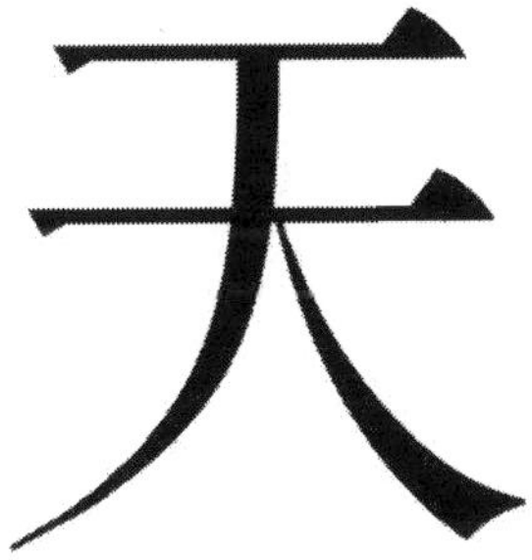

The top line represents the beginning and bottom border of the higher heavens. The space between the top and second lines represents the *expanse* area, while the second line represents the beginning of our universe creation. Much like this *later dynasty* depiction of the same (天, tiān) symbol:

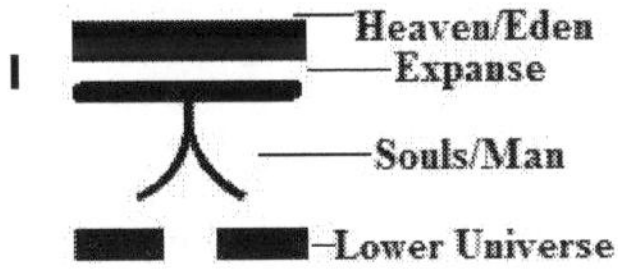

As previously stated, the vertical line is then representative of all the souls who rebelled in some way being cast down from the original heaven, through the expanse-zone, and into the lower creation regions.

As well, and that which I may be misunderstanding about how the ancient Chinese understood this split-line portrayal to be *maintaining*, being the English word they used to express its function amid the realms as a *vital connection* between all three; it should not be overlooked that they may have been referring to the exact same attribute, the Prime Eternal Creators (Tether) *connection mechanism* for nourishing all of the souls captured in this usurped realm and throughout all others. *Meaning,* and as I referenced earlier, the Prime Creators lifeline which enables our souls to remain eternal. A mechanism in which those few souls deeply intertwined with the first murderer have not enjoyed since. This is an ancient understanding that I have previously touched on concerning the rebellion leaders

Energy-vampire characteristics as being the root cause for our continued enslavement.

Interestingly the ancient Chinese philosopher (ca. 470 BC – ca. 391 BC) - **Mo Di**, aka – **Mozi**, held to a most amazing wisdom. Mozi taught, seemingly basing his entire overall understanding and lifestyle on the belief, that the will of Heaven (天, tiān) was such that *"all people should love one another, and that mutual love by all would bring benefit to all"* – *(Mozi's Will of Heaven)*. His basic guiding premise seems to be *"love others as you wish to be loved"*. Sound familiar?

Mozi also taught concerning heaven (天, tiān), that Heaven is ruled by the *Divine Ruler,* and that (a) *son of heaven* is the overall ruler of this earth. Does this idea also sound familiar? It should because Christianity picked right up on this one. The mistake or assumption most generally made with this expression of a *son of heaven,* leads most to understand *this son* to be more special than any other *soul - son* of heaven, which it is not. We are all sons of the Prime Eternal Creator and thus equal among each other.

However, it is difficult to certify if this *son of heaven* in which he speaks is the first murderer and creative poser entity in charge of this lower realm as most religions tend to believe, or does he also reference the Elect one/messiah figure to come? Hard to say conclusively. My guess would be that at his level of wisdom, he understood both to exist.

Additionally, and having an even more direct parallel to this books overall topic on the soul, Mozi's moral teachings emphasized *self-reflection* and *personal authenticity* rather than obedience to vein religious ritual - *("Embracing Scholars" in Mozi)*. As well, Mozi believed and taught that people could change their circumstances <u>by directing their own *intentions*</u> after evaluating their day to day issues - *(Against Fate, Part 3)*. Mozi, arguing against Confucians, and in my estimation religion in general for then and now, against the notion of over-attachment to family, friends, and tribal structures, in favor of the concept of *impartial caring* or *universal love*. Again I ask; sound familiar? Wait until you see what his profession was!

On a much higher level of spirituality and in-depth understanding than anyone of his time, Mozi differentiated between *intention* and *actuality*, basically – (Quantum Physics); thereby placing a central importance on **the will to love**, even though, as the Confucians argued, in practice it may well be impossible to bring benefit to everyone. Mozi arguing, that the *will* to love all souls can be the only true *intention* that is in line with the supreme creator who resides in the upper heaven. *THIS my friends is the embodiment of what we know to be the Everlasting Agreement.*

So, not only does this Chinese philosopher teach others to *"treat all souls as you would have them treat you"*, but he was also far ahead of his time in his understanding or *intuitions* of things that were not even considered in science by anyone much before the 1970's. Last but not least, did I mention that he was known to be a highly skilled *carpenter?* Come on, try to explain that one away!

Chapter 7

Frequencies, Creation & Matter

"And the Primary Eternal <u>spoke</u> saying, exist light, and light existed."

In the original Hebrew this verse is understood by us to have the more literal meaning of a *force applied by His verbal cues*, and not just the words themselves. In our more modern time's science has now proven that the entire universe creation, whether it be this super-hologram creation space or any other, was created, and continues to hold itself together by the constant flow of specific frequencies. The same has been found to be true of our physical bodies, made more of water and carbon 12 than anything else, both resonate frequencies, as well as being strongly affected by external frequency. Even more amazing and compelling is the fact that our DNA *gives off light frequency* continually, and that by our mood, physical condition, and or by exterior forced frequencies, that emitted light frequency changes. I see this positive truth being utilized for negative technology as usual within new, allegedly *non-lethal* weapons. However this idea of non-lethal is not entirely truthful, the same weapons dialed up and using specific low frequencies can easily kill people.

I believe you will see the greater picture, that in fact our lower dimension 3rd level bodies and their DNA have been created in *their image* for the sole purpose of not only containing the *living-soul* but more specifically to control and greatly limit the souls ability to interact more directly with the Eternal Creator, as well as to limit the souls memories. As you will see later, this memory limitation is their main control mechanism.

Science has also proven that virtually all of the stars also emit their own specific music in frequencies, hypothesizing further that quite possibly the entire universe in which we perceive as such, to be literally held together by the mixing of this great symphony of frequencies, and I concur. In fact, the ancient book of Enoch has quite a bit to say about the stars, their role, and even how they are chastised by the Prime Eternal Creator when they stop doing their job. All quite interesting when viewed within this greatly expanded view correlating our past with our scientific present.

According to Dr. Leonard Horowitz, 528 Hertz is a frequency that is central to the *"musical mathematical matrix of creation."* As confirmed by historical scholars and researchers, it is the core creative frequencies that were used by ancient priests and healers in advanced civilizations to manifest miracles and blessings.

Mathematics scientist Victor Showell describes the 528 Hz frequency as fundamental to the ancient *"Phi"*, and the *Golden Mean* evident throughout natural design. Victor Showell and John Stuart Reid *(a pioneer in acoustic research and cymatic measurements)* have proven that 528 Hz is essential to the sacred geometry of circles and spirals consistent with DNA structuring and hydro-sonic restructuring. Depicting that 528 resolves to a **6**, *by using Pythagorean math -* 5+2+8=15 and 1+5=6. *Six being understood as the icon for physical manifestation* in this matrix.

The ancient symbol for "6" is most visible throughout man's history in the form of two, one-dimensional opposing triangles, most generally known as the ancient and modern Babylonian-Jewish cultures later misnomer as, *the Star of David.*

This, of course, is not an original Hebrew icon at all, but most probably of pagan Saturnian origin, and found to be depicted by many cultures worldwide. Amazingly the Hebrew prophet spoke clearly against the Levitical sacrificial blood cult, referring to their six-pointed occult star icon as, *the star idol of Chuin and their god-entity "Moloch"*, both having a direct reference to Saturn, while others say Jupiter depending on the Canaanite culture. The *Cyrus Cylinder* found in Iraq in 1879 tends to prove that the later Babylonian influenced

Jewish cult, as depicted on the clay cylinder, worshiped the god-entity Bel-Marduk, which is also known to be Bel-Moloch.

The planet Saturn, of which NASA has alleged spectacular pictures, depicts this six-pointed *Merkabah* in Hexagram form on its pole where they believe great frequencies are being emitted.

The ancient "6" symbol allegedly depicts the spiral effect of creation constantly emitted downward from some point in space, *heaven* and spiraling into the earth. Either way, regardless what we call it, according to our best and brightest scientific minds and the laws of physics as we currently understand them, this frequency appears to be the broadcast catalyst for all matter and energy to exist as our reality.

However, some believe that the *power emitter array*, which appears to be spiraling frequencies from Saturn's pole, may, in fact, be specifically tuned to have adverse effects on the souls here. Thus, possibly even part of the Archon *reformation* process.

Miracle Tones

Coming to be known as the primary miracle tone - **528 Hz**, as well as the 432 Hz and others, are being found to afford extraordinary benefits. Dr. Joseph Puleo analyzed the meaning of the tone using Latin dictionaries and hidden entries from Webster's Dictionary. The "Mi" tone is characterized as:

- An extraordinary occurrence that surpasses all known human powers or natural forces and is ascribed to a divine or supernatural cause, esp. to God.
- A superb or surpassing example of something; wonder, marvel [1125-75]; ME.

Dr. Puleo was also allegedly visited on several occasion by a soul-messenger, commonly known as an *angel,* who gives him clues concerning these ancient hidden frequencies and their meaning. The doctor was shown the sacred Solfeggio Frequencies;

The sound vibration rates for creation and destruction:

1. Ut = 396 = 9
2. Re = 417 = 3
3. Mi = 528 = 6
4. Fa = 639 = 9
5. Sol = 741 = 3
6. La = 852 = 6

Dr. Leonard Horowitz and Dr. Joseph Puleo in their book - *"Healing Codes for the Biological Apocalypse"* seemingly reveal some lost knowledge regarding these frequencies and much higher uses. Dr. Puleo shows the biblical reference of the *144,000 righteous ones of god who learn a new song* in a very different light based on the Pythagorean skein numbers provided here to be: nine (9) for 144,000 which is completion; three (3) each for 12,000 tribe members from each one of the twelve tribes - that is - 3x12=36=9, or 3+3=6, or 3x3=9, all understood to be numerologically powerful.

Many believe that Dr. Puleo's observation of the 144k might be a valid theory, with this ancient hidden knowledge being directly related to vocal frequency tones sounded into existence all at once by these "144,000" spiritually enlightened people. That they could somehow literally *create* a planet, possibly even a galaxy wide transformation. Specifically, the renewed heavens and renewed earth as spoken of by the Hebrew prophets comes into being. The idea being that these 144,000 will need to literally vocalize these six notes - *frequencies of the Solfeggio* to bring about the transformation of the planet, galaxy, etc. Dr. Puleo depicts the definition of *"LA-bii reatum"* which is the last tone in the Solfeggio as:

"A reverse movement or tendency; an action in a reverse direction or manner". Or 'the movement back from mankind to 'God Kind'.

Which by their understanding means, a renewal back to our original being-state, our light-soul-bodies! A final return to our original Eternal Creator. Having our skins removed to uncover our ancient souls light source, as depicted earlier by the corrected Genesis 3 texts. However, as you will see I understand this same thing to occur by a slightly different means.

Tone distortion and the 144,000

A recent discovery for me is the researcher David Sereda. David has allegedly discovered a most amazing ancient piece of knowledge which has long been hidden or lost to us. However, before we move on to David Sereda's illuminations, we should first hear the ancient context that is directly related to his findings.

This story begins with the Greek figure *Orpheus*. Orpheus was a musician who sang and played so beautifully that it is said even animals, rocks, and trees danced to his tunes. Orpheus is believed to be the son of Calliope, the Muse of epic poetry, and of the god Apollo. It was Apollo who gave Orpheus his first lyre/guitar, which is the instrument that Orpheus always played. Among the highlights of Orpheus's life, are his short stint accompanying Jason and the Argonauts on their quest to find the Golden Fleece, where Orpheus used his special heavenly-tuned guitar several times to ease their journey; calming both men, the deadly Sirens', and the sea itself. The other major event in his life was the death of his love by snake bite, the nymph *Eurydice*. Overcome by his grief, Orpheus refused to play or sing and finally decided to go to the underworld to retrieve *Eurydice*. Evidently Orpheus knew something we today do not. By his magical playing the heavenly tuning of his guitar enchanted *Charon*, the ferryman of the river Styx who carried the souls of the dead across to the underworld, as well as the still living Orpheus. Running into the monstrous three-headed dog who guarded the gates of the underworld, Orpheus's special tune quelled the ferocity of *Cerberus*. Moving ever deeper into the underworld, even the King Hades, and his queen could not resist his playing, agreeing to let Orpheus take *Eurydice* back with him. There was one condition; Orpheus, much like Loht's wife, was not to look back at her until they had both reached the surface. In the end, either the gods tricked them both, or Orpheus did not heed their restriction. It is said that upon reaching the mouth of the cave, he looked back at Eurydice, and she was immediately disappeared back to the underworld.

Great story, but what does that have to do with any modern findings of ancient music you ask. Well, for the most part, understanding the fullness of any ancient tale cannot be sufficed by one or two paragraphs of information. The alleged findings of David Sereda were however accomplished by the deeper research and detail required by anyone in order to return to any original path.

Moreover, I encourage the reader to seek the greater details about David's work on their own, as I am unable to expand upon them here to do his work its well-deserved justice.

In short, David's research has shown that the original Orpheus story involves, not only the stringed instrument his father gave him but more importantly how that instrument was tuned.

Always bearing in mind here as it concerns all of this creation that frequency is tantamount. David goes into great detail about the frequency mechanics of our modern 7 to 12 tone scale, and how this scale within its frequencies has great levels of distortion. That in fact, this tonal scale was purposely diverted further away from its original source by a large religious order so that mankind would be adversely affected by it. Or more to the point, remain unaffected positively by the absence of the original tonal frequency scale as Orpheus allegedly possessed it.

The frequency tonal scale prior to our modern one was just previously touched on, the Solfeggio scale, which was alleged, originally 6, with a 7th added later. This tonal frequency range is also said to have some distortion like our modern tones, but not quite as much. David Sereda calls his findings, - 'The frequency of lost tones of the Pyramids'. It appears David's find of these lost frequency tones are said to be based on the actual frequency that is being emitted from the capstone area of the Great Pyramid of Giza. His evidence of the original base tones was found inside the Pyramid and also correlates with the pyramids geometry perfectly with one proving the other. The sequence is said to be made up of 10 base tones that are ever so slightly different from what we have since its loss, but that this slight variation makes a great difference in how our reality, our souls, and even our physical bodies are affected and react to the sound.

Of the currently known tonal scales, this Egyptian base-10 scale is the only perfect one, having zero distortion in it. The research and evidence that David and others have now come up with is nothing short of astounding and even unbelievable at first.

Harkening back for a minute to Dr. Puleo's work and angelic meetings, of which even David Sereda and his researchers say they have had as well, and after deeply considering these findings of David Sereda on tonal frequencies and their massive power, as well my own work and understanding concerning who the long contested 144,000 righteous people are, and or will be, and how their great influence on this world might come about, I propose this understanding of the 144,000.

That the 144,000 will, in fact, be a specific people on the earth at some future point, but that they will mostly be unaware of each other, and their overall number. Tied together by the reveal of an ancient truth that existed and exists eternally as the original Prime Creator exists eternally. A truth reiterated by His Messengers at specific intervals throughout our most recent history going back some 5,500 years or more, reiterated to restore the option and allow a freewill choice that the Rebellion leadership of this creation work so diligently to obscure. This free-will life choice in which the soul is spiritually *returned* to its original creator in this life, and as I have already reiterated many times, is known to us as the Everlasting Agreement. (See my two works: Land of Meat & Honey, and The Greater Exodus).

Based on this understanding, the 144,000 souls who have chosen to *return* to their original estate by their new beliefs, in fact their *new song*, which is to say it is an *understanding* that is in such radical opposition to all the religiously driven dogma and superstitions of man, that so few will know it or accept it in any generation. However, unlike all of our more terrestrial religious misunderstanding of both, *who they are*, and *how this song will be known and sung* by them as depicted cryptically in our prophetic texts, I posit here that it is NOT a literal song which relies on the literal use of *voices and perfect pitch to enunciate* such tones all at one time in order to affect change.

No, more likely it is much greater and more subtle than that!

The 144,000 will *project* those ancient perfected *tonal frequencies* back to their creator through their recently renewed souls! A renewal that occurs by a major life-path change, *a frequency shift, a return!* That they themselves will not *physically* induce the renewal and reunification back to our original heavenly estate, *but their heightened soul-frequency-voices* will finally be heard in Heaven as one voice, and then mankind will see the unification spoken of by our many prophets.

It has always been about the soul, whether by religions or new science, the core of original truth will always be about the eternally living-soul, *and its pure frequency!* In my opinion, the belief of such a thing occurring via physical people, singing a tone or tones all at once while standing on the beach as they do, is immature thinking at best.

Just as the true Eternal One *heard* the blood of Abel *crying out from the ground,* so will He finally hear this sound - *frequency!*

So, does any of this so far get you closer to the greatest human question - *'Why are we here?'*

The curious thing to find out, that the alleged greatest and most enlightened man of our time, Nikola Tesla, mused, "If you only knew the power of the 3's, 6's, and 9's!" It seems Tesla also believed his knowledge to have come through the ethereal.

Tesla also said that there are many fallen entities here with us on the earth. Some believe that Tesla was given his inspiration for this knowledge by the same *alleged* angelic entities as Dr. Puleo. Which in my estimation are merely as the Christians say; *Archon-Angels posing as angels of light;* via their *soul-light-bodies* of which we provide the energy for. I wonder if Tesla was also aware that he was not living his experiences within the Primary Creators original realm.

If so, he took it to his grave, just as Ernst Keely also took all his knowledge and free energy designs to his grave. However, it appears Nikola Tesla's father was a high initiate in the elite order of the Illuminati, and that he began all the free energy work for them. Not as we are told his son did. So as always, nothing is as they would have us understand it to be.

It would seem that the giving of such liberating knowledge would be a contradiction to the Rebellion leaders' matrix control of this system, which is most likely exactly why all of it has been removed and hidden from us by those who work directly for them.

This introduction of ethereal energy systems (namely Plasma energy) to mankind by *alleged* angelic beings may very well be coming from our Archon handlers. I tend to believe that is exactly who provides it. We also see, that most generally all new high technology goes directly to weaponization. Thus, exactly why it is provided in the first place. And the likes of Tesla, his father, Dr. Puleo and others march on believing them to be angels from god!

Equally interesting, is how so many researchers and scientists of after-life studies, *and in contrast to their great intuitive intelligence,* appear to believe the *heavenly realm* details of their subjects' proclamations at face value. While at the same time not perceiving that data to be a very limited view from the inside of a clouded and controlled milk bottle. They receive Archon controlled details concerning their *false ethereal heaven realm* while believing the vast amount of that data gained from their many subjects to be the <u>true heavenly realm</u>. *This remains to be the greatest of deceptions; that the heaven realm above us is, in fact, the real thing!* It does appear that most of our history on this creation level has not been predominantly, influenced by the other righteous creation levels above us, which are the habitation of the <u>*shamayim*</u> – <u>*obedient souls.*</u> Just as the many differing religious accounts tend to concur, we are being manipulated by other entities.

Job 1:6 *"And a day came when the <u>sons of god</u> came to present themselves before Yahweh. And the Satan also came among them".*

Proof from our eldest known writing (Job), that Yahweh/Jahovah is NOT the Prime Creator! However, he "may" be the entity who oversees the reformatting of this creation level. Either way he "cannot" be the Prime Eternal Creator because he expected animal sacrifices from Job!

Additionally it can be proven that his cohorts, as depicted earlier from the texts of Enoch, at times rebel even against him.

Job 1:7 *"And Yahweh said to the satan, 'From where have you come?' And the satan answered Yahweh and said, 'From going to and fro in the earth, and from walking up and down in it.'*

Working ceaselessly to further *reformat* the now physically embodied souls called mankind, due to their inexhaustible hatred for us. It appears Yahweh exerts only a tentative control over them.

Job 1:8 *"And Yahweh said to the satan, 'Have you set your heart on **my** servant Job because there is none like him in the earth?' A perfect and upright man, <u>fearing God</u> and turning away from evil?'* 1:9 *And the satan answered Yahweh and said, '<u>Does Job fear God</u> for nothing?'* (LITV) Emphasis added

More proof that the Yahweh/Yahovah entity, although the obvious *principal* of this creation level momentarily, *is NOT the Prime Eternal Creator.* All of the language in Job here proves everyone in context speaking *to* Yahweh *about and referring to* the Prime Eternal Creator – (God – *Elah'im*). However, and as always throughout the Hebrew Tanak, they corrupt the true expectations of the Prime Eternal One's original law to us! *i.e. – the requirement for human/animal blood sacrifices which keep our souls separated from the Prime Eternal One.*

If Yahweh was that Prime Creator, the English, and especially the Hebrew would have made the direct reference clear. Another way to see the Job 1:8 text is to understand the Yahweh entity, *as always*, is referring to himself "as god", and all direct references' to "the" true Creator are expressed mockingly. Either way the *sacrificial* context always gives that entity away.

We have been and remain controlled. Until enough of us change, *returning to the frequency of life,* we will remain a *reconfigured* creation by the ones who rebelled against the Prime Creator originally. Until then most *Darnel* remain reformatted in their image of low character!

By the confines of their learned controlled narrative belief systems, and by not understanding who we are, most who seek these greater truths remain eluded by the knowledge they keep, and this *controlled narrative* system is meant to do just that. This is why it is so vitally important for everyone seeking in this manner to at least consider this *soul-cycling false heaven-earth matrix* hypothesis at all times as they venture forward, and finally back into the black.

Another important fact to remain aware of is, that all the great frequency technology the Rebellion leaders used to reformat and control our holoverse, were only manipulated by and through the *potential* of creation by the tools which previously existed.

Meaning, tools fabricated from the core building blocks of creation itself; having previously been created by the Prime Creator Himself. Like us, they have *created* no new thing! And although our creation-view of how our Creator, creates, does not involve Him using technology to create, it seems easy to understand that our fallen gate-keepers do use technology to reformat and mimic the original creation to their ends, as pointed out previously by the ancient texts.

Thus, the Archon's slipping in from time to time to provide certain super advanced understanding to mankind, allegedly for our extreme benefit, might actually be the catalyst needed to help us end another epoch by our own hands. The true Eternal Creator of this creation is not providing us high technology, nor is it in His mind to do so. The Eternal Creator has only been watching and receiving our souls back to Him slowly, that is His primary interest for us. The reconstitution of this creation level back to its original form and function would render all of us so far in advance of any technological advances that the Archon's could provide, that their level of technology would be closer to a square wheel carved from wood by a monkey in a cave, by comparison.

Based on all presented herein thus far concerning the extensive creation nuances in the Hebrew Genesis-1 and 3 texts, it would be logical to extrapolate, that the same way everything is created with frequency, will, in turn, be the only way to free the souls of mankind currently constrained by this levels reformatted frequency.

All paths leading to that same hopeful end. A long awaited *Ah-Ha* moment to a final ascension and return home. *For only, He can square our circle.*

Ethereal frequency for the physical

The 528Hz frequency alone is associated with DNA Repair. In 2010, John Hutchinson, an electromagnetic energy expert from Vancouver, B.C., Canada, helped purify poisoned water in the Gulf of Mexico due to the BP oil spill. Known as the "Hutchinson Effect", he and his research partner and wife Nancy Hutchinson, used the 528 Hz frequency and other Solfeggio tones to clean the oil and grease from the ocean waters. John and Nancy can clear a radius of about a mile in one 24-hour session.

Hutchison-Lazaryan frequency generator clears polluted Gulf waters/) (Allan)

As I found reported in several sources; the polluted Gulf water area was treated with the 528 Hz frequency for (4) four hours on day one, and by the next morning the waters were cleared! The Hutchinson's frequency device is said to have been positioned up the beach, about 25 feet from the water. The Hutchinson's restored the water's purity as proven by the almost immediate return of fish, mammals, other sea life, and color. Their results were certified by Dr. Robert Naman, an analytical chemist with 29 years of actual field experience, and President of the *Analytical Chemical Testing Laboratory, Inc.* in Mobile, Alabama. Dr. Naman tested the ocean samples and confirmed the complete removal of oil and grease from the water.

Almost our entire global system is based on sickness and death from one source or another, as you will see in later chapters, the systems that support all these destructions are specifically designed and implemented by the *principalities* who rule our creation. It is just one of several major celestial frequencies, but the 528Hz is the bioenergy of health and longevity within this creation level. Many believe it to be the harmonic vibration that lifts our living-soul and divine voice in harmony with all the heavenly hosts. One can only imagine having our first-estate-bodies revealed to us by the full implementation of our living-souls.

Imagine, casting off these purpose built, biological, *Trinity-6* soul-limiting-filters we call human bodies! With the souls inhabiting this creation level being healed, enlightened and returned to their original estate. Finally, with the cascading effect we could break down their reformatted holoverse walls near instantly; thereby overtaking the false Kingship of our captors!

The original and true instructions for all life were laid out as our eternal oath towards our creator by the frequency of His breath and have always been written on our souls. However quarantined since they need only be awakened. So for now, I am left trying to awaken you with mere words.

A Universe of Frequencies!

We all live in a universe, and a world permeated by frequencies and vibration - $E=Mc^2$. Regardless who, when or where these bodies were created, every cell of our body vibrates, and each one of our multi-billions of cells has an optimal vibrational frequency. As far as these physical *Trinity-6* bodies are concerned, it is known that our optimal frequency is between 70 and 82Hz. This is when we are in *physical* balance, and in unison with this creation *current multiplex of vibrations. However, it could just as easily be said that these same frequencies are the invisible, inaudible constraints that tie down our souls!* Part and parcel with their reformation and long-term control processes'. How would anyone truly know for sure when no memories from before exist?

Our brain hardware, when interfaced with our living-soul emits specific frequency vibrations as well; as our frequency changes up or down, so do our *perceptions* of all things within this creation – (More control). This means that our own thoughts – *intention*, can change the world around us. Laughter and especially a consciousness built on LOVE raises our body frequencies.

Eternally happy or positive people/souls emit a higher frequency and found to be less prone to disease. When we consider certain chronic conditions as *depression, fatigue,* and even *phobias* from a frequency-energy point of view, our bodies can be re-balanced and cured of almost everything in which pharmaceuticals only seek to cover up. *This could also be taken as additional proof that these frequencies were designed specifically for these Trinity-6 physicalities.*

Some posit, that when we learn the mechanics of *balancing* our soul-body frequencies, as well as acknowledging that certain constant negative ones have to be removed, our healthy state can be achieved. So, one might then ask, *'why would the Archons allow or make provision for our physicality's to be positively affected by their fabricated frequencies?'* To which I would answer; *'they are constrained by the law of Freewill!'* *Meaning,* your/our free will choices for *good & life* and or *evil & death,* automatically chooses which frequency you receive more of unto *good & life* and or *evil & death – Physical sickness or health.* Which then, in turn, causes you/us to either feed them unto their own sustained life, or to not feed them, *which is choosing life,* and the Prime Creators character!

Frequency Range

Breaking it all down even further, scientists have discovered that each disease works/lives within a certain range of frequency. Their findings, *of which now exists a great many which have overlapped,* show that when applying specific frequency treatments to diseased cells, they return to complete unaffected health, – *(See Royal Rife – Rife Machine),* while healthy cells are not affected.

The Frequency of Cause & Effect!

As previously stated, I recently heard a medical scientist speaking about how they have proven the Frequency of a healthy human to be between 70-82Hz. And that the frequency of most of the animals we consume is 20 to 25Hz – VERY LOW. Moreover, that although there are many other frequency lowering anomalies of which most people are exposed to, as with – *Wi-Fi, Cell tower signals, microwaves from many sources, negative personality traits, poisoned air, GMO foods, polluted water, etc.;* that the worst single source by far that measurably lowers our frequency into the 40hz range, is the consumption of animal flesh! *Exactly the range where their tests prove to be the frequency range in which all disease thrives!* This has long been the false control narrative overwritten into virtually all of the world's religious doctrines save a certain few Buddhists and Hindu's; either by ritual or by culture, the consumption and intermingling of their much lower frequency cells/DNA with our own to cause ongoing and ever expanding suffering frequencies, all generated for their own consumption!

Medical science has also found, that during our digestion process of the very low-frequency animal flesh, that we actually expend far more energy *life-force* in digestion, than gained from consuming the animal parts.

Highly interesting is the frequency research, *again in part proven to be authentic by other scientists some years ago;* depicting how our food and water can and *is* completely poisonous to our body, *devouring our frequency if* the person cooking it – and or eating it, or both, *have and project a negative frequency while doing so.* This is literally our *soul-intention* at work, *projected* outward into everything around us! This is no small revelation.

Many have seen this proven in science already by how our voice frequencies, when we project our *intention* of *love, peace,* etc., *vocal-Frequency's into water, and even sand,* how their molecules instantly change dramatically, causing a water droplet to change its shape into the most amazing, complex variations. The absorption of emotion through frequency vibrations are being expressed, and even saved in the form of memory. Thus, leaving any water, or any other substance which is made up of water, *like these Trinity-6 bodies,* to embrace the frequency projected into it, even keeping the *memory* of that *frequency-intention* until changed again. In my mind, this is both a blessing and a curse. Again, how either emotion is projected is directly connected to our soul's free will choices in any given moment. **(See Dr. Masaru Emoto:** *The Hidden Messages in Water* – 2005 (Emoto)

Researchers have also proven that when subjects consumed food and water which had all positive frequencies projected onto it, that people will receive actual healing from this.

What may be most important to understand in all this, is that all the food or water researchers have tested with this, *actually held the memory of the positive or negative action/frequency projected against it.* Which then I would personally add, that if your water, food, land where you live, etc., is or had been *projected* all positive frequencies by you, and then later someone or something else somehow *projects* new negative frequencies in its vicinity, that then those products, food, land, etc., should then be considered suspect and re-immersed in our positive frequencies to avoid any long term disturbances. Which now makes me sound like some 60's tree hugging flower child; but the science does prove this out.

Believe me, when I tell you, long ago before the science had proven these things to me personally, I also believed none of it and cataloged all such things in the card file under pagan, new age bunk!

Was Prayer originally all about Frequency Creation?

I have tended to believe that *this* is where all prayer began, and based on that which I have said many times thus far herein, that; *all ancient superstitions and or mythos have an original point of truth at their root.* I believe prayer to have been mistreated, and or its original intent and power covered up in this same way over time.

I have questioned the logic and mechanics of why prayer is treated and used in the ways most people have, and or, why such a Creator force who can create such complex matter from nothing, and by the frequency of His voice, wants or needs prayer *as we have known and applied it* for thousands of years. All we know and have has been sent down to us by various methods and through a great multitude of personalities. Most of whom have been superstitious forefathers, while those over them sought to hide the true power of these things.

Didn't even the prophet Yehshua tell people not to pray like the orthodoxy prays, with dogmatic liturgies?
Why did he teach them this, in this way? Not because the Jewish prayers were all negative, they aren't. But because their INTENT was disingenuous, and no longer focused on the creative power of a *positive soul-intention.* And of course, because he could not at all teach those people about *quantum physics, non-locality, a Holographic Universe,* or the awesome creative power of our

quantum-souls *intention.* Now couple that teaching, with what he taught concerning how our spoken **words**, or **tongue,** could cut like a sword.

Again, I believe he knew all this and was speaking about the literal *intention-driven-frequencies* coming out of people's mouths and minds which cause discontent, and even diseases over time.

Was he trying to enlighten them on the most basic of levels how such negativity has creative and lasting effects on people, and all life in general? I believe he was, but again he couldn't very well teach them on the concepts of *frequency - cause and effect.* He was forced to teach them where their intellect was or was not; in these cases, their intellect was not up to the challenge. So, he expounded on certain physical qualities like *speech* with great emphasis on the negative, in ways that even if they didn't quite understand the needed details of the greater subject, he instilled enough alarm in them to cause the *effect* he knew we all needed. Good news is, science has now vindicated his understanding, if this was in fact his understanding.

With that awareness, and as science keeps proving, my tendency is not to believe that *prayer* was ever meant to be some archaic, nonsensical adulation to some *God* entity for His ego's sake, etc. More likely the act we have come to know as *prayer* had to be based on something more original, more specific to who we were and remain as *Living-Creative-Souls* – Portions of the original Creators Macro-Soul who are both tethered to Him still, and also by default creative entities ourselves.

Understanding all that to be from one original source and wisdom, then this was the original *Secret!* An idea recently turned into a mere documentary for profit, while providing no ACTUAL *mechanism* of that alleged *secret* for anyone to actively apply with any measurable results. Thus, retaining its hidden identity which all elites and their Archonian narratives strive to perpetuate. I do however believe this to be the most original truth for all prayer as a mechanism. That our *living souls* have the capacity to become strong in their creative ability even within these *Trinity-6* bodies.

A major point I make within all my teachings and published

works to those seeking deeper truths is that all original truth is always amazingly simple and easy to *see* and *apply. Meaning,* that if it is not *simple, easy to see* and *apply,* or worse, only found and applied through a special priest or initiate whose only direction to it is blind faith, ***this will always be the lie***.

What simpler way to extend all life for GOOD and not EVIL, than to finally *know* and *believe* that we have the power to *project* actual positive, healing frequencies into everything around us.

In practice, we could collectively negate every evil thing they have been conjuring all this time. And that is why they have turned all prayer and understanding of prayer into nothing less than some narcissistic activity, either for some egotistical god, or for us personally, and maybe sometimes for others who are in some way personally attached to us, etc.

So, at the risk of sounding like I've boarded the New Age Express out-of-Mindsville; or risking attack by the many religious Witch-hunters labeling me as yet another *militant Vegetarian necromancer channeling evil spirits to gain my ideas;* I put the idea out there to all who are not so susceptible to superstitious meandering, that maybe instead of praying, or even continuing in the known concept of *prayer,* that it may be more profitable to learn to see ourselves as *projecting intentions* from our living-souls into the world around us, and into all that we take in. As well, to work diligently at removing all those negative sources in our lives as much as possible who may take away from our focus in this area.

Is it real, or is it Memorex?

Besides the fact that the above reference to the Memorex tape commercial dates me, this question still stands, and does so right alongside man's deepest question, "why are we here".

The answer just may be – *'because you have been made to forget who you are and where you are supposed to be!'*

Most of us would agree that so far all of the previous scientific and metaphysical findings are new revelations of ancient information that every truthful scientist and researcher who finds them should embrace for application into their working models.

This is especially so where it concerns *Near Death Experience* and *Past Life Regression* subject data. So far from my own research into both of those fields, I have not found any scientist or researcher considering the data they receive as possible contrived narrative streams. Much less questioning where these *narratives* originated, or *who* controls them. Mainly I suspect, because, like most people in all generations, they do not even know such control-narratives exist as such.

Don't get me wrong here, I would love to find a large trunk of money left on my front porch just as much as the next guy, the difference is, I would not embrace its unknown origin or the motives of those who left it there quite so easily. However, since I am most certainly in the super-minority on that front, maybe it is my soul's destiny to act as the *Tenth man* among you. *Those who are given the job of interpreting the same information in its entirety as everyone else, but to consider and distribute my interpretation of that same information from the worst possible, and polar opposite position from the rest.*

On that note, and staying with the process of combining all the scientific, ancient metaphysical, and cultural knowledge we have on hand in order to arrive at a more panoramic view; let us not forget that the *frequencies, energies* and *matter potentialities* making up this creation, which enabled the construction of our current physicality, or the celestial technology used to fabricate us, <u>were all created previously</u> for the Prime Creators original purposes. And, as I previously pointed out, *not* root creation mechanisms *created* by the Archons'. As not to stray too far from the primary point and understanding of this book; *we consented to their plan long ago, which allowed them the jurisdiction to continue to maintain the level of control that we would continue to consent to via the reformatted narratives they supply!* I think it is important to reiterate this basic and uncomfortable point, because to the many good souls/people who truly believe they love and follow their true Eternal Creator, this most probable reality will be greatly uncomfortable and repulsive to even consider. Remaining too easy to continue in their false narratives of blind faith to other men, or no understanding of a way forward and out at all. Or worse yet, the erroneous ideas that credit our existence to alien races from long ago. To which my first question will always be – *'Then who created them, and those before them, into perpetuity'.*

> *Every origination point for all creation processes and even the potential for them to exist were originally created by the Prime Eternal Creator force! There can be only ONE!*

Contrary to this, and within all the so-called religious narratives on this planet, we are clearly taught that there have been many gods, all of which are depicted with less than *creative characters*. With most of these gods proving to be the agents of the chaos they chose so long ago, <u>they are destroyers</u>!

With that understood, then we can understand that the *frequencies* are not intrinsically bad or evil, how could they be if the *potential* for them was originally created by the Prime Eternal One. Their *use* and *implementation* on the other hand by those entities forming and controlling them now is the problem. Just as mankind, who on many levels is finding more ways than not to utilize good information or technology for evil, emulates them - *in their image.*

Again, all of this falls squarely under an old saying – *'Just because you can, doesn't mean you should.'*

The Frequency of control

If our DNA and cells radiate light frequencies, *a light of which I have no doubt is provided by our living-souls,* and if those cells are as many as the stars in the universe, then it stands to reason that by limiting that *cell,* soul-light absorption, they could limit our souls ability to interface in far more pervasive ways.

Curiously, as science has now shown us how the *larger percentage of* our DNA *codons* <u>have been switched off</u>, this proves by implication that someone switched them off. Which also means they had a reason to do so. I see this as not unlike shutting off the electrical breakers in one's house to *enforce a limit* on which systems receive power, and which do not. *For me, this points to a premeditated limit enforced to sequester the powerful living-soul within their Trinity-6 physicalities!*

These less than circumstantial scientific facts paint us a picture when all points are considered. This may seem a little complicated, so let's retreat a bit and reiterate the basics before moving on.

- All things seen and unseen created were created by The True Eternal Creator.
- All creative processes can be used by all created beings/souls for good or evil.
- There can be only ONE law of conduct for all creations, "above or below".
- Not all entities follow or consent to follow those simple laws.
- Rebellion against those laws keeps a soul quarantined and labeled as (*Without "Shama"*) until they return!

To reiterate, I am not attempting to force feed any earthly religious doctrine above, so it would be better to alleviate your thinking of any specific religious dogma moving forward.

The understanding I am attempting to depict here is simply this; that the power and Creator behind the creative processes of *this* creation and all creation levels are processes that existed long before our separation occurred. Proving Archon's in any form are not gods!

Additionally, based on this fairly universal belief in one creator overall, however, misunderstood through time as a direct result of our captors *control narratives,* we should be able to see through their holoweb of misdirection just enough to ask, why?

- Why is it ok for such a large amount of our DNA to be quite literally rendered inert?
- Or more importantly, why did someone render it inert?
- Who does it help?

- Who in fact rendered them inert?
- What are these scientific facts showing us by default?

Can we answer these questions based on all we know so far?

Question one: *Why does it make sense, why is it ok for such a large amount of our DNA to be quite literally rendered inert?*
- First off, the fact that the majority of our DNA has been purposely shut off, proves to me that our physical bodies design parameter potential makes our physicality what we might understand to be a highly capable, <u>top-line </u>model as physicality goes. This is very important to understand, because the facts we now have concerning our far greater, but limited capacity, proves to us that someone has purposely stripped the greater potential *model* down to its most base form.

 Thus, by default they created these physical containers using preexisting knowledge and processes. Processes whose creative *potential* was NOT originally created by those who made us – *in their image.* If it were, then why not originally create us exactly as they wanted, dumbed down, with no additional, available codons to turn on or off?

Question two:
"Or more importantly, why did someone render them inert?"
- By stripping down the more advanced model, it would appear logical that their overall concern revolved around their ability to control our *body-soul* combination for an undetermined amount of time.

 Also providing them the control ability to *upgrade* specific *compliant* conspirators throughout time, even to create lesser human-gods, and or the whole if it suited them, but why would it suit them to fully empower us. I tend to believe that any upgrades we may get or see in life within any field of endeavor, spiritual or technological, are controlled and only provided for the benefit of the controllers, and not the inhabitants. In fact, this overall understanding even lines up with the multitude of Near Death Experience and Past-life regression subjects who have and continue to state that they are shown, *while inside the Rebellion leaders false heaven-station,* that two-thirds (⅔) of our soul is literally held hostage in this heaven matrix, with only one-third (⅓) of it being sent back to control our physical body - *i.e.* the *soul-trinity* is being divided; so I ask, <u>who divides</u>?

Question three:
Who does it help?

- Building off the answer of question two, this answer seems quite simple really; a total *physical* systems downgrade quite obviously does not aid this creation; if we only had all of man's recorded history to go by, this alone is more than proof enough. If we only consider our modern shortcomings and propensity towards self-destruction, which show no signs of abating, this should be proof enough. If we only consider our inability to heal ourselves from the massively expanding battleground of human disease, that again would be proof enough! The mounting pile of historical detritus is proof enough that none of what mankind deems to be from our god or gods, is for the aid and enlightenment of man, or our eternal souls. Which by many thousands of NDE & PLR accounts appear to be fragmented into thirds! **But why the division?** It would seem to the same end, <u>control</u>! Is it as many NDE and Past-life researchers theorize from the data of their subjects - *'that our physical bodies could not take the surge of power that the whole soul emits'.* Remember the words of the ancient Coptic Nag Hammadi - *And she established each of his offspring **<u>in conformity with its power</u>**-(Soul) - after the pattern of the realms that are above...*

  Did they produce a matter based physical body in which <u>our complete *plasma based* soul-portion was not compatible</u>? Based on all the evidence so far, both ancient knowledge and modern scientific, their alleged soul-division may just be the other half of their inhibiting mechanism. Both the physical and the spiritual must be metered back in order to control the whole. But more on that later.

Soon you will see - **"The whole within all parts!"**

Question four:
Who in fact rendered them (our DNA) inert?

- I will again base these answers together upon the answer to the previous question; first, as I, *the 10th man,* posit herein, all of humanity, our living souls, have been duped by the many distorted, misconstrued and dynamically fruitless narratives. I believe that the greatest of our scientific minds as I stated earlier, now believe, based on all the scientific and afterlife evidence they are being fed through diverse conduits, evidence allowing them to believe they are now outside the bottle looking in, to be in fact another matrix level of mirage that provides a false confidence that confines us all still; and we all know how man loves his false confidence. The *"who"* have many names through many generations and cultures, for this reason, I have spent my life *looking for and identifying "the character" of a given entity*. Because in the end, and regardless of religious narrative, we all seem to agree on - *"you will know them by their works"*. By this formula, we seek a "Creator" who CREATES! And *not* one that *limits* or *destroys;* because as stated, in the end, and regardless of any specific dogmatic narrative, the simple, logical truth about any *true* creator of this eminence and magnitude must be, that He has no need for destruction under any circumstance. His main recourse being, that He separates Himself and His uninfected creations from those who freely consent to rebel – *with those lacking "Shama"*.

    Thus, no matter how it hurts, and it should, the "who" is us. The souls of this creation, along with those who's *will* we must have followed; those would-be-kings who struggle to keep control over their usurped domain, along with us have separated the Prime Creator from us. No destruction at the

Great hand of our Eternal Creator, only separation!

A separation that we, NOT the Eternal chose! Just as I previously established earlier with my depiction of Genesis, chapter one. Just as most earthly religious dogmas tend to understand it, although through a self-imposed fog of generationally layered superstition, and their consent to it all; the buck stops with us!

Question five:
What are these facts showing us by default?
- That it has all come around full circle to the frequencies being used to create, and later *reformat this* holoverse creation space. If the true Eternal Creator, created all frequency and its ability to be used to create everything that we know, and yet do not know, <u>then their use of it cannot be limited,</u> which again falls under – *"Just because you can, doesn't mean you should!*

Nor can they be held by one individual; they would be free and available to all. To either be used for Good & Life or, Evil & Death! Simply stated, that the frequencies and the power to drive them through this creation level, which of course enables its creation of all particulate-matter into everything we believe to experience by our senses, MUST be present at all times.

Meaning, that all the requisite frequencies to both create and maintain said creation, must, in fact, be driven out into the creation-expanse and maintained at all times <u>*by the conscious "intention" of its creator*</u>. The issue then for those who work to maintain this reengineered facade is, that all these same frequencies that must remain extant for the expansion and maintenance of this creation level - *(demonstrated by the alleged scientific findings that our universe is always expanding, and that new galaxies are always being created)*, are the very same creation frequencies that would act positively on our eternal living souls. And possibly even our physical bodies. To what end is only limited by our current spiritual wisdom and physically circumcised condition. Therefore, it must be understood that our current downgraded DNA-body and soul-trinity-division condition, keeps all of us from the fullness of our original estate as - *Super-Soul entities*, NOT *covered in skins!* To not downgrade and limit both our physical and spiritual elements from their full potential would be tantamount to the rebel Archons committing both physical and spiritual suicide, the loss of their rulership, the loss of their own estate as it was imagined in their own hearts so very long ago, fulfilled as an exercise in rebellion, *to which we agreed.*

Acquiescing to the completeness of these physical bodies in which our souls are harnessed, compared to the unrestricted *super-souls* we once were, *without skins* bathing continuously in the *unmodified* life-giving frequencies of The Eternal One as He meant us to be - *totally aware creative super-souls. Resisting to consent* would have never allowed these forceful betters, these leaders of rebellion to have come this far at all, much less enabled them to exert such calamitous control over us, from our beginning. Thus, learning to consciously disconnect from their narratives of death individually, will collectively topple that control!

The Trinity of Humanity

No, you are not alone, as even the most remote possibility of this being our true reality is horrific to everyone that hears it.

Our own original tacit consent rebellion against the One who made us, only to be living life upon life, time after time, *drinking the Kool-Aid while blaming every other evil entity under the sun for our fall and separation from our true creator.*

Not convinced that *in this physical state of being* we are in fact part and parcel with those original *fallen ones* so loudly spoken of throughout all our cultures and biblical narrative texts?

Not convinced or **not willing to finally assume your portion of personal responsibility?** Always taught to blame another man, another evil entity, another so-called Satan! Leaving the responsibility for ancient rebellious actions to the other guy!

Saying with our lips that the evil ones have **turned everything upside down**, but never understanding the truth of that belief or how it started here for us, and by us, through our consent!

Here, allow me to show you one of the most closely held and highly regarded points of alleged *prophetic* wisdom. An alleged prophetic point of which at the very least every Christian and Messianic Jew are convinced, and believe they understand fully to be as they know it.

In fact, this alone may prove just how *epically* incorrect the majority of religious teachers and their faithful consorts are on all points of prophecy *after the leading of the Archon false narrative overlays. For to be so utterly and universally wrong on such a pinnacle point of prophetic understanding,* should force everyone to reevaluate every other belief they hold.

Trinity-6

Revelation 13:8 - *"Here is the wisdom! He who is having the understanding, let him count <u>the number of the beast,</u> for <u>the number of (a) man it is,</u> and its number is six hundred and sixty-six."* Remove one single word - (a), which could not exist in the mind or language of the Hebrew prophet, and you have it as it should be, (the number of "man")! What do I mean you ask?

Man's physical body is Carbon-12 based, and made up of —

- <u>6 protons</u>
- <u>6 neutrons,</u> ^{and}
- <u>6 electrons</u> = **666**!

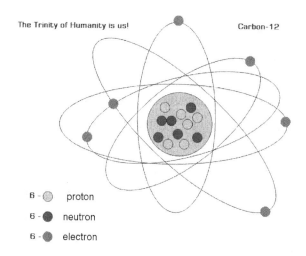

The Trinity of Humanity is us! Carbon-12

6 - ⚪ proton
6 - ⚫ neutron
6 - ⚫ electron

The Trinity of Humanity is the 666 *beast physicality* created in "their" image of low character! <u>*As our original light was covered*</u>.

That's just one example of how strained by false narratives and wrong most people have been and continue to be in their dogmatic beliefs concerning all religious texts, especially prophesy!

Once they have you convinced so fully, embracing their many false narratives, they own you and lead you, as we lead cattle!

The Trinity of the Living-Soul is the 3 parts that make its whole; created by the Prime Eternal One in His image, as a creator!

Dr. Oppenheimer, after seeing the *reversal of matter* via the use of his Atom bomb device on two Japanese cities, lamented that he was now the *destroyer of worlds*. We can look at his example now within the light of who man as a whole truly is. Oppenheimer and his cohorts utilized the fabric of this Plasma/Atom/Matter based creation, a fabric in which they themselves as men were also made of, to create a device that destroyed the cohesion of specific, Atoms/Matter, fabric.

Can we then understand it this way?

That the Trinity of Humanity = "The Adam^{666}", utilized "the Atom$^{6\text{-}6\text{-}6}$", to destroy?

Therefore, despite the many erroneous ideas and half-baked speculations concerning this alleged prophecy of *a man* and *his number*, it appears that this summation of it is far closer to its true and original meaning. The number 666 and its relation to *all man and the physicality thereof,* and not just *one man* in the form of our physicality, more verifiably, and literally relates to the carbon atom of which in part man's physicality was made. Carl Sagan mused correctly saying; – *"We're made of star-stuff"* (Sagan).

His quote relates directly to Carbon which is abundant in the *Sun, stars, comets,* and the *atmospheres of most planets.* Carbon-12 is prevalent in us and all creation, and one of five elements that make up our human DNA. Its abundance is *allegedly* due to the *Triple-alpha* process by which it is created in stars.

Therein resides the most ancient truth which can be attributed to man's condition and verified throughout all known history, that on many levels, as we reside in the physicality of these bodies and adhere to the corruption of their narratives daily, most of humanity continues to truly reflect *their* image! Their corrupt and rebellious character; while believing the opposite to be true!

This is the overall condition that I am attempting to shed light upon for the greater consideration of souls so that we can finally come to its knowledge and decide to make the conscious change away from its inherent cycles of destructive false narratives.

* The triple-alpha process is a set of nuclear fusion reactions by which three helium-4 nuclei (alpha particles) are transformed into carbon.
* Older stars start to accumulate helium produced by the proton–proton chain reaction and the carbon–nitrogen–oxygen cycle in their cores.

Systems upgrade?

Some researchers are beginning to believe that the human DNA upgrade to come, *which is even proposed in several ancient religious texts to occur in our future,* to be a **Carbon-seven upgrade - 7 = 616 –** or a **6** proton, **1** neutron, **6** electrons, construct.

This is basically thought to be an *ascension upgrade.* Possibly a *return* to our original Soul-light-body condition? I tend to think not since this again speaks to another version of physicality.

> *"Then Yahweh said, "Let us make human beings in our image, to be like us. They will reign over the fish in the sea, the birds in the sky, the livestock, all the wild animals on the earth, and the small animals that scurry along the ground."* To ACT and BE like THEM!

Resetting this world's reflection by rebellion

Creating the ongoing conditions for all living-souls to *project* their ever increasing negative *intention* which paves the way, and directly aids in their reformation of this creation.

Thereby creating and extending our enslavement.

Further depicting by definition that every single point of perceived reality within *this* creation has since been reformatted in complete and total **contrast**, **opposite**, even **rebellion** to the Prime Eternal Creator's original estate for us!

All that we originally perceive and believe to be one way, is more clearly found as truth when viewed in the other. If you and all the world's *alleged* greatest Christian, Jewish, and Islamic prophecy experts have all been so absolutely wrong about the mostly agreed upon prophetic understanding such as this *Beast/Man-number, "the Beast that rises out of the ground", or more accurately from the, "dust of the earth",* and the number of his alleged name, as I have clearly proven here with the scientific depiction of our *dust of the earth* Carbon-12 human "666 beast" physicality; how can anyone truthfully move forward in good conscience without tearing down all they believe they know to be true. It would appear a paradigm shift is in order. As I previously stated, *'you will never be extracted from this usurped and reformatted creation level, if you do not even know or believe you are in one'.* The time has passed for everyone, all souls, to step outside of their perceived clarity from within this milk bottle to finally see it for what it is, an opaque milk bottle with near zero visibility.

"And I saw a new heaven and a new earth, for the first heaven and the first earth, did pass away, and the (sea) is not any more;" (LITV)

Replace the word (sea) in the previous text, with the word *expanse* as I have shown you in the corrected context of Genesis one, and you will more clearly identify that this prophetic text is speaking directly about the *expanse* in which the Prime Eternal Creator, created to separate all rebels during our time of embracing evil.

The forbidden zone that cleaves all the rebellious souls who remain – *without Shama* - from those souls above who remain in our original condition and estate, is that *sea*. It appears from most ancient religious dogma, rituals, and prophecies that *this* originally, perfected creation level will remain divorced from the rest until some future event frees its captives, *and The Prime Creator thereby dissolves the sea that separates!*

No doubt all thoroughly religious people will immediately throw out any possibility that this soul-identity issue can be true, and thus will all most assuredly use their religious narratives to explain away how ludicrous the whole idea is. This is, of course, the expected reaction to such information, as it would force virtually ALL of this creations people-souls, regardless of how many lives they have lived, or believed they have lived, or not lived, to take ALL of the responsibility for their actions over countless revolutions. And let's face it, taking *personal responsibility* has not been the hallmark of religionists throughout all time, much less to this intergalactic degree.

Now we enter the science of the Holographic Universe!

Chapter ∞

The Holoverse

Quantum Entanglement takes place when two or more particles link in such a way that what occurs to one, simultaneously occurs to the other(s) without regard to distance, whether next to each other or light years away. Nobel Peace Prize physicist *Albert Einstein* was not completely unaware of the possibility of this phenomenon for he dubbed it *spooky action at a distance* (Alain).

This must be understood in order to comprehend the Holographic Universe Theory, which we will refer to in this book as, *"The Holoverse"*.

This *Quantum Entanglement* became more than spooky stuff in 1982. *Dr. Alain Aspect*, a physicist, led a research team at the University of Paris in experiments that had the potential to revolutionize physics, as they knew it. The problem was that the results of their findings directly violated Albert Einstein's strongly held principle stating that nothing travels faster than the speed of light. Thus, in spite of the dilemma of dethroning a very well respected Physics forefather's theory, this resulted in becoming one of the most important scientific discoveries of the 20th century.

Dr. Aspect and his team revealed that under certain circumstances *(when both particles originated in close proximity to each other at one time – i.e. to be "correlated")* subatomic particles, such as electrons, possess the capability to communicate instantaneously without relevance to time or distance. The ongoing observations have been that in some respect each particle is always aware of the others activity. Since there are no restrictions concerning time and distance, then basically these particles have the capacity for time travel, commonly known as a quantum leap.

The universal concept of transcending the speed of light in relationship to the perception of time causes a disturbing enigma for material scientists. The idea that time travel may actually be a probability becomes a hot topic, which many want to refute.

Unfortunately for them, the irrefutable findings of Dr. Aspect have left these scientists grasping at straws to make their rebuttals. However, the results of the Quantum Entanglement experiments has gone on to inspire others, more open-souled Physicists, to be forthcoming in their hypotheses, theories, and explanations of an actual holoverse!

The question arises regarding this strange link between the particles. While some may believe that this entanglement speaks of a quantum leap, this was not the case where Dr. David Bohm, *Emeritus Professor of Theoretical Physics, Birkbeck College, University of London,* was concerned. His theory was one of wholeness, an undivided universe in constant motion. This is where many base the idea of a Holoverse. *His concept was that there were a continuous enfolding and unfolding of particles, called holomovement.* This holomovement was part of an *Implicate order*, which then also by default had an opposite *Explicate order*. The unfolded, seen *explicate* order is always under a lens like a telescope or a microscope. Whereas the enfolded, hidden *implicate* order is that which he described as being more holographic in nature. It is not until the lenses are removed that the things come into a more holistic, less specific view. This meant *no mysterious leaps but a constant interconnection within all of the particles of the universe* that at the center was a phantasm, gigantic and splendidly detailed.

Bohm makes this startling assertion by using the hologram

photo as his favorite illustration. In order to really assimilate this information, *it will require you to dispense with everything you think a hologram to be or have been taught.* We must lay a clean foundation for a <u>Super-matter-based hologram,</u> not simply <u>a light based hologram.</u> This is precisely what Dr. Bohm was trying to describe. So let us detach from the idea that you and your surroundings are all an illusion from another dimension. This is not what is being stated.

We do not live in a Hollywood film popping about from one place to another, and yes, you are really reading this!
Hopefully, this will all become more distinct as I progress. So strap in and try hard to wrap your gray matter around this one, however, remember that the first step is in laying a new fresh foundation.

We know a *simple* hologram to be a 3-dimensional image displayed on a 2 dimensional medium such as photography film produced by using one or two lasers. In all actuality, it is a mathematical invention. Their construction is not limited to lasers but can also be created optically appearing in the air and even be photographed *but never touched*. This last point is very important so I will say it again...<u>Basic Holograms can NEVER be TOUCHED</u>!

This means all those other narratives telling us that this world is an illusion with us really being in another dimension cannot be true. If this were true then there would be no such thing as physical touch sensations, because there is, in fact, no reason for our sense of touch whatsoever!

The method in which holograms are created is known as *holography*. There are two basic types: *transmission,* where the light source illuminates from the back of the holographic image, and *reflective* being lit from the front. The equipment needed for a laser hologram is actually quite simple. We would begin with at least one laser, 2 mirrors, 2 lenses, film, an object and a beam splitter if only one laser is to be used. Lasers are used because unlike other types of light, they possess a concentrated *coherent* beam. This means they have a single stable frequency of light.

Now let's get down to the actual process as displayed in the next illustration.

How a basic holographic picture is rendered

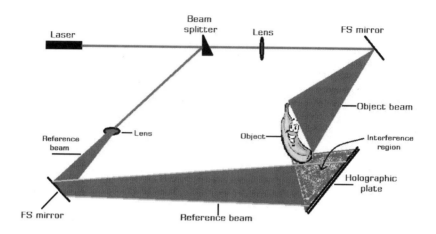

Notice the placement of the various holography equipment and recordable object in the illustration. A single laser beam is directed at the beam splitter where it splits into two beams. These beams then take two simultaneous paths with each passing through a lens and reflecting off a mirror. At this point, one beam, known as the *reference beam*, goes directly onto the film of the Holographic Plate. (The film is similar to photo film.) The second beam, identified as the *object beam*, baths the object to be photographed reflecting the image onto the same film as the reference beam. These two beams now rejoin and intersect creating what is recognized as the *interference pattern*. The interference pattern is the overlapping of the two light waves resulting in recording characteristics of each onto the film. This is similar to intersecting ripples when two rocks are thrown into a lake. This is the secret to making a hologram work. *Then when the film is developed and illuminated a three-dimensional image of the original object appears.* **The whole in every part!**

Hologram comes from the Greek roots *holos* meaning

whole and *gramma* meaning *message*. Clearly, we can see the *whole message* of a 3-dimensional image, but there is more to it than just wordplay. Unlike normal photographs, if segmented, the holographic image possesses and retains all the information of the entire original, just in slightly smaller versions and points of view.

Meaning, if you cut or tear the *holographic picture* in half, *the whole, all-inclusive original object can be seen on both halves!* Liken this to when we stand against a wall with a window, allowing only one of our eyes to look out the window, we still see an entire picture outside.

Amazingly even if the picture halves are divided again, each portion, when illuminated by the laser, will always contain a *slightly smaller,* but intact version of the original image! The organization and order of everything in our creation space are elevated to a new understanding when we comprehend the character of the hologram's *"whole in every part".*

Holograms teach us how to better understand our creation level and experience. It isn't difficult to ascertain how this explains the mechanical approach that science has forged upon our human experience. As we have seen, IF we try to take apart a holographic construct, we do not come away with simply pieces of the original whole, but only slightly smaller wholes – *a whole in every part!*

According to Dr. Bohm, we view subatomic particles as separate from one another because we are seeing only a portion of *their* reality. *However, they are all interconnected and not divided at all. This is where we see the holographic elements begin to evolve.* Had they been simply a series of quantum leaps there is no continuity or holistic qualities. He further surmises that if the connections between subatomic particles possess the ability to break the speed of light, then we are unaware of a much deeper complex level of reality within this universe that we cannot access, and for good reason I suspect.

Object and *Reference* beams come together and that is

what is recorded as the hologram right? *Now transfer that from being just light beams to particle matter based – Physicality!* Next, think about the hidden *Implicate* order as the reference beam and the visible *Explicate* order as the object beam. Both exist separately and jointly, right? So now look around you, notice all the *objects*, but what is it that you cannot visually see? Can you see the air you inhale and exhale? The particles of carbon and oxygen are *hidden* and yet present. Although you are unable to see the carbon dioxide you have just exhaled, physically taking it over to the tree, and watch a tree take it in, it still occurred. **All the parts are present in the whole!** Yes, this is a simplistic example of the *holographic*, whole message, of our reality! Stop and take that in for a moment.

Let's go back to how the hologram of the object was captured. As we could see the beams representing *separate parts,* they were really facets with an innate and more essential unity, which we then see in the interference pattern. This is ultimately holographic and indivisible. Since everything in our physical reality is comprised of these *reflective apparitions*, referred to by Bohm as *eidolons,* then we now must understand that our universe is itself a *Super-particle-matter-based super-hologram*, a **reflective-projection!** This is just as many ancients have long known and recorded our existence to be. However, later on, you will come to understand that in the end, it is all emanating from the consciousness of our Creator.

Previously, as depicted in the ancient texts, our *reformatted* Archon creation space was shown to be a reformulated *reflection-eidolon* of the Prime Creator's original version. In addition, this creation is also a *reflective phantasm* having *reversed*, *hidden* qualities. However, the *holoverse* maintains some other rather alarming attributes. If our perception of the disconnected state of subatomic particles is misled, even illusory, and there is not a cosmic *string and can* attachment between the two for imperceptible communications, then this means the universe matrix you are sitting in right now contains many more facets with a deeper level of reality than we have ever been taught existed.

That all facets of known and unknown existence are an interwoven, tightly connected fabric, interpenetrating everything else simultaneously in all directions conceivable!

All divisions artificial, along with those of nature from the dust of the earth spanning to time and space itself, are ultimately a seamless filigree. Within the brain, the carbon with its electrons is linked to all sub-atomic particles that comprise every other thing sentient and non-sentient, including every star that is contained within this universe.

Thus, *all physical matter along with all perception is infinitely interconnected;* a holographic universe should be acknowledged as a super-hologram, whereby the *past, present,* and *future* simultaneously exist. For many, this idea alone will cause you to throw the entire baby out with the bathwater. So how can all three time periods co-exist? *One reason is due to time only existing when the soul is confined,* a captivity which appears to be ongoing due to our continued assimilation of false narratives.

Physical death exists because time is imposed on all things physical. Therefore Time=Death! We find the opposing understanding of this most generally among certain people who have died. Among the memories of their souls traveling out to meet God, most notably there are a far smaller few out of the majority who say that wherever they went after death, their body projected a white light and that no TIME was present there! *Thus, in order to live eternally, and outside of times constraint, physicality must be removed.* (Asher)

The reason this is all possible would be a result of what has been explained here; that all particles are interconnected in either a *seen* or *hidden* order creating a wholeness and not a separation within the original creation holoverse system.

This is huge! Because, although this creation level has been reformatted using the creative restraints which the Prime Eternal Creator, created in the totality of all things, <u>this is still a reformatted holographic reflection of our original creation space</u>.

As we touched on previously, German philosophers Arthur Schopenhauer and Immanuel Kant, had very similar intuitions during their lifetimes, although I do not believe they understood this creation as being one that was reformatted and controlled by a secondary entity or entities specifically. Schopenhauer understood space-time and causality to be features of the *mind*. Which is our *Consciousness-Soul*.

> *"The world as we experience it is structured by objects in space and time which have causal relationships with other objects."*
> *"The objects of the world depend on the mind - (consciousness) <u>for their existence</u>."* - Schopenhauer

Schopenhauer believed the world <u>*as he perceived*</u> it was *his* representation. It should be stated here that most people do not see the same objects in exactly the same way! All of us have experienced this phenomenon, and although we notice it when it occurs, we generally let it go just as quickly without deeper examination. *A comment is made as to the great beauty of something or someone, while another person looking at the same object expresses the polar opposite opinion.* Now building on this concept, we first have Kant's realization, then as we can see by Schopenhauer's quote, he contradicts Kant's thoughts to make a very good point. The very one I have been stating!

> *"There must be "something" that which exists independently of us that is the cause of our "world" representations. i.e. "Transcendental objects" – being the cause of our own representations – but as such that we can never ascertain the nature of."* – (Kant)

> *"Space-time and causality are features of the "mind/consciousness" - to mean that things in and of themselves are not what cause our experience, <u>as "causation" requires a "knowing subject", just as space & time themselves require a "knowing" subject; thus objects do not exist independently!</u>*
>
> *"The being of an object, in general, belongs to the form of appearances and is conditioned by the being of the subject in general, <u>just as the objects manner of appearance is conditioned by the subjects' **forms of knowledge**</u>. Hence, if the thing in itself is to be assumed, it cannot be an object at all."* — (Schopenhauer) – Emphasis added

Exactly! In the first part of Schopenhauer's rebuttal we see exactly what Bohm later discerns, *wholeness* with all seen and unseen particles being interconnected. Next, although having no context concerning fabricated *control narratives*, Schopenhauer alludes to this very thing. Not only in respect to narratives, but intuiting without the presence of some form of awareness, such as scientific understanding, that our literal surroundings within this holoverse are in fact controlled, created, and even limited by the *knowledge* each person has downloaded in their brain/ego-driver hardware.

Though better clarity will be gained as we move through this book, the reality is that humans/souls only *create* their environment based on the information each individual has within them. *This is communicated very well in the following quote excerpt.*

> *"...<u>just as the objects manner of appearance is conditioned by the subjects' forms of knowledge</u>"*

Precisely why no two people/souls literally view the details of anything in exactly the same form or way! What they do see or create is solely based on the fabricated *controlled-narratives* that fuel their paradigm, which is provided within this reformatted creation space for now. In my first book, *The Land of Meat & Honey* (D. S. Asher), I tried to get this same point across in a very basic way by calling our learned and assimilated knowledge base — *Limit Filters.*

An example for clarity – ***The Eden Effect:***

Although each individual soul/person literally *observes* and *perceives* different nuances within all physical beings, objects, and nature, etc. *All of whom are generally unaware that this phenomenon exists at all.* Those nuances have been shrinking due to the many changing control narratives driven into society in general. *Meaning,* the growing *conformity* of all narratives throughout society has been allowing what we all perceive, to be less divergent. Several notable times in my life I found another person, friend or family member who just totally, even vehemently opposed my opinion concerning the physical appearance of a person or object, *as say a beautiful woman, natural scene or classic car etc.* As just previously stated, these contrary objections in most humans overall have been diminished because of the Archon manipulated, socially driven *marketing narratives.* Augmented narratives that make us more *like-minded!* An example of this would be how women were depicted in art for hundreds of years. Those earlier social norm *narratives* for the physicality of the female gender appears to tell us that most men liked their women quite plump and very pale skinned.

Whereas for some time now, all social narrative marketing to and for women and their physical appearance has decidedly gone in the other direction. Thus, our collective social opinion as men and women worldwide has been reengineered to see *skinny, sun tanned* females with extra-large mammary glands to be the baseline for female beauty. Allow me to extrapolate this idea a bit further for you with a personal story which was the impetus that opened my awareness of this phenomenon.

Many years ago in my late teens, I was with a childhood friend passing time watching TV. The main actress of this show was none other than *Barbara Eden*. Personally, I have only found one man in my lifetime so far who did not immediately identify her physical appearance as anything other than perfection. On that day I was with the one guy who generally agreed with me on nearly every point that matters to guys under the age of twenty-five, but to my utter amazement he totally *disagreed* with me about Mrs. Eden's physicality. At first, I was certain he was just messing with me, being contrary for the sake of it. Soon it became clear that he was not, he was dead serious. He told me that he just didn't think she was good looking at all! *I know, I thought the same thing, he should have been subdued, wrapped tightly in a new jacket, medicated and committed on the spot.* Our mild disagreement quickly turned into a protracted argument, mainly fueled out of my own total bewilderment and un-acceptance that this person could possibly be so utterly off base and blind. I remember I kept pointing at the TV asking him if he was looking at the same thing I was!

This same thing occurred several more times throughout my life on various subject matter, and always to my same surprise and bewilderment.

As one might expect, I tend to fixate and ponder on such human nuances, attempting to make sense of what I *perceive* to be illogical. It was not until a bit later in life during my extra-curricular studies in the sciences, which began to run in parallel to my main area of study that I began intuiting that certain people, like my good friend years before, *were literally seeing something else*. It took many more years for me to collate all the scientific and ancient religious and cultural data that I was compiling for other reasons, to finally formulate why and how this phenomenon could possibly exist. Since then, and because of my first experience with it, I have called this phenomenon the *Eden Effect.*

The Eden Effect - *When one or more people/souls literally see very different realities in real time, especially noticeable when one is opposing the obvious, socially accepted norm – narrative view.*

Earlier I depicted how Schopenhauer suggested that the only

way to ascertain which system gives us the ability to create our *representations* would not be found outside, but rather within ourselves. I not only see Schopenhauer's above astuteness within the title of his book, *"The World as Will and Representation"* but also by his intuition that our bodies were the manifestation of *will.* (Schopenhauer)

Equally amazing is that he never inquires as to <u>whose will</u>, we followed, only that it was <u>our will</u>! However, he understood it as the *will to live.* The force within us that *strives* for nourishment, propagation, and such; he says, *"Everything presses and strives towards existence..."*

On its face, this is, of course, true. However, the way that any *force, consciousness,* or *will* continues to endeavor is always subject to the world-control-narratives they possess, *i.e. knowledge!* Now, if our culture and knowledge base revolves around these narratives as being true, *when they are in fact false,* then undoubtedly the will/consciousness of all the people overtaken by these control narratives will live out their existences in such a manner that it restrains any higher consciousness or evolved thought. This is exactly why Schopenhauer perceived all "Will" to be inherently evil and driven by an evil force – *i.e. as I and many ancient texts depict, via false narratives provided by unseen overseers!* Therefore, as amazingly close as his *god given* intuitions were capable of at that time, and/or as one would expect to come from an almost two-hundred-year-old philosopher, the deficit of his understanding was repressed by none other than a *controlled narrative* source itself.

I know this is a lot to take in, and I cannot express strongly enough that you hold onto the understanding that the Hollywood version of a *hologram,* which depicts the physical objects around as *illusion* only, having no physicality, is *not* what science is presenting to us. Nor does it posit that we are an *illusion* or *representation* of ourselves in another dimension. It should, however, be understood that everything in this lower *reformatted* creation, along with the Prime Eternal Creator's higher realms, really do exist in various densities of physicality and non-physicality. It is just that there is a two-fold occurrence here.

There are holographic features to this universe, but at the same time understand that the Prime Creator is the true "object" of all realms regardless of their designed densities or attributes, etc. It happens that this lower realm creation is a three-dimensional, matter based holographic representation which is momentarily reformatted and representing the *will* of another. All creation levels are whole and have, as Bohm puts it, *wholeness with no divisions*. Thus, all is linked, and all creation levels are linked.

This is why an *expanse* zone of separation was needed until all comes full circle. Let us now continue in the understanding that this is *not* all that there is, or will be! So keep your thinking cap on as we move forward to explore territories of current information about the brain and soul interdependency. Since people's understanding of a hologram tends to be so one dimensional and incomplete, certain questions always arise. Before moving on let me create an image that may allow a better visualization of the vast difference between the *simple light-based hologram* as you know it, and this *Super-matter based version*.

Simply put, the reason all of our physical surroundings are literally solid to us, is because we are *"inside" the hologram!* The difference being, that when we create a holographic image of something, "we" are the creators and thus "outside" of the creation space. Because of this, our hands pass through those holographic creations, which are not solid to us. (Asher)

Ghosts in their machine!

Not to diverge too far from our main topic, but an interesting notion of which I have mused periodically may aid the discussion.

Read the previous quote by me again, because there may be far more depth to it. Add to the insight of that quote the hypothesis of *Parallel universes* and the *Multiverse theory.* Could it be that the alleged ghost sightings that people have reported so often and for generations, are actually real physical people, you and I even?

People living lives over again in yet another parallel, physical creation? One that is very nearly the same as this one, but just slightly askew due to the marginally different choices everyone in that world made. Could it be that we, and them, from time to time and due to the theory that these creations overlap to some degree, or exists stacked like pancakes, see each other through some invisible veil as *non-physical ghosts, or holograms?* Appearing to each other as holograms because we are not actually present within their creation space! Thus, they are not dead people appearing as apparitions from our past, but living, physical, *Trinity-6* physicality's currently recycled again within another space-time.

A slightly varied space-time reality that would have to be sustained by an influx of slightly different frequencies than our own. And there, in fact, may be our answer to the mechanics of the invisible veil which separates us from them, and them from us and others, etc. Merely a shift in frequency!

In summation to my observations on this hologram vs. ghost theory; I would also like to posit that this may be why the Archons fractioned our souls into three or more parts. Just enough soul-portions to enable them to animate each *Trinity-6* body within various segmented levels of this creation. Multiplying their ability to animate three or more times the amount of physicalities.

Brain & Soul Interdependency

Dr. Karl Pribram, a neurosurgeon, and neuropsychologist at *Stanford University* spent the bulk of his career in brain research and development. He began his career working at the *Yerkes Laboratory of primate Biology* as the neurosurgeon for Karl Lashley's research team and helping to write up the 30 years of Lashley's data on his elusive *memory trace* studies. *Lashley's research showed that regardless of a rat or primates missing portions of its brain, the animal retained its memory* to perform *certain tasks.*

In later years, while working specifically on how and where memories are stored Dr. Karl Pribram decided to take a look at quantum physics. His son, *John Pribram* a quantum physicist, pointed him in the direction of Dr. David Bohm. It was after reading several of Bohm's papers and ultimately meeting with him that Pribram made the connection of Bohm's theories in relation to the brain and the memory.

He had been trying to answer the question of whether there was *isomorphism* of the brain. Isomorphism literally means *sameness of form.* The question was, *if what we remember was represented in the brain from the original representation?* Now, you may say, *'Of course it was, I saw it!'* However, that does not answer the question of whether there is a *one to one* correspondence between the *form* of the world around us, and the *form* in the brain representing that world. This will become clear very soon.

This all came together as Bohm expressed that the problem was in how sciences were viewing everything through lenses in an *explicated* fashion; *that is either microscopic or telescopic.*

Therefore, there had to be an *implicated* order as well, which is more holographic in nature. This is to say that instead of seeing one particle up close under a microscope, we take away the microscope and *everything is present at once in waveforms.* As explained previously that there is a ***whole in every part!***

Pribram then intuited that we have lenses for the brain as well. The most obvious would be the optical lens of the eye but all our senses could be considered types of *lenses*. This meant that if we removed the sensory functions, *the explicate order*, then the *implicate order* comes into play. As Dr. Karl Pribram puts it, *"This means everything is everywhere and every-when* (Pribram)*."* Thus, we have Isomorphism of the brain! The world around us is ordered in *wave and particle form*, our brain also orders our representation of that world the same. Just as our brain sees through the lenses of our senses perceiving specific objects, the world around us has been shown by quantum physics to be the same. It is just that to get a close up look at the objects such as the stars, we must use man-made lenses that replicate what our physical and sensory system does naturally for us. In short, *our memories are not confined to one specific location inside the brain but dispersed throughout the brain.* This agreed with and expanded on Bohm's theory about the very nature of a holographic universe, and Karl Lashley's findings in his brain research, the **"whole in every part"** essence of quantum memory storage. (Giorbran)

Although, this newer information has aided many to understand consciousness or spiritual experiences that science has been previously unable or unwilling to explain. I tend to believe that those such as Dr. Pribram and others in this field are still missing the mark somewhat. Based on the ancient texts and knowledge, as well as the fact that no one has proven it to be so, I do not believe that it is the physical human brain that literally *houses* (all) *memories,* but ultimately that it is the living-soul where all life memories are stored. It is the soul *interfacing* with the brain, which gives the *appearance* of the brain storing our memories in random and diverse areas throughout, as Dr. Pribram believes them to be.

I believe that it is our differing *hardware-bodies,* to be that which either expands or inhibits our soul's overall ability to interface with this reality. In other words, not all *Trinity-6* DNA is created equal.

You see, the key to everything surrounding this discussion of the living-soul, past lives, heaven, etc., has always, and will always revolve exclusively around the living-soul and its divine ability for quantum memory storage and retrieval. Without the living-soul there is no memory, nor is there any animation of the physical body. More importantly, if we lack the ability to remember and recall every experience throughout all times, we never truly advance.

As I have mentioned previously several times now, you will come to understand that the *memory loss mechanism* of this reformatted, holographic universe in which we find ourselves entrapped, will be the ultimate proof and validation that it is NOT our original state of being. As also cited earlier, this *Trinity-6* carbon-based body is not the original Prime Creator's tool for our enlightenment process. This is an idea in which far too many intelligent people have come to be entombed.

"...in some sense man is a microcosm of the universe; therefore, what man is, is a clue to the universe. We are enfolded in the universe."- (Bohm)

So, that which the brain scientist Karl Lashley lacked, Dr. Pribram found, realized, and built upon. However, Pribram believed that specific areas, *the fine fibers* is where computations take place; saying this is where the memories show inference wave patterns within specific nerve impulses that crisscross the brain in the same way the laser light interference crisscrossed the entire piece of film containing a holographic image. Karl Pribram became well aware that this idea of the holographic *whole in every part* was instrumental in opening science up to a better understanding of what he referred to as *the mystics*.

However, what Pribram seems to have lacked was the understanding that I came upon with *Dr. Michael Persinger*, a Neuroscientist at *Laurent University*, associated with the Psychology and Biology departments. He also has been actively involved in brain research.

Dr. Persinger explains the electromagnetic functions of the brain. Understanding that there is matter and energy contained within our universe, he explains, that while taking in new information or events our brains are electrically labile for about 10 to 20 minutes. Those thoughts are alleged to be recorded as synaptic patterns in our brain. In other words, what we are learning is being passed and processed from one neuron to another creating a pattern. This pattern is alleged to be recorded as memory, driven by energy occurring in the brain matter. This at least explains what Pribram had also determined, *that our memories are not in only one area of the brain.* Or by my estimation, not housed in the brain at all!

Pribram citing, because the brain is matter and finite then a question arises. *While the brain is electrically labile and all this electromagnetic energy is still very open, active, and recording, could that information be represented elsewhere?* According to Dr. Persinger, it is absolutely possible that the energy our individual brains are recording is represented in another phase. A phase that is also being simultaneously represented in the geomagnetic field of the universe, as it does have that capability because it is like a hologram! Remember, *quantum entanglement has been proven and that is exactly what this would encompass.* HOW? They just don't know. What they do know is that when we die, our brain dies and the information is gone. There is verified evidence that the information, memories, are represented elsewhere.

Here is where I want to scream the obvious; going back to the example of the holographic picture. That the holographic pictures *recorded memories* of another object does NOT exist without the *laser light* <u>that preceded it</u>. Just as the brains memories do not exist *unless* the living-soul applies them!

The Living-Soul is the **hologram interface**, *the bulk storage device,* and the brain is the **Soul interface reader**! The brain hardware-*reader* and Soul work in both directions all the time!

Consider all cases where the human body is considered brain dead and *on life-support* due to some illness or accident not directly related to the brains function. Even more intriguing, a person not on life support while in a coma, while still exhibiting minimal brain activity. As you will clearly see later with *Dr. Eben Alexander's* personal story of returning from near total brain death, all of these great minds have been ignoring the Metaphysical Missing Link of the soul's connection to our physicality, and its direct *animation* properties! In such cases what causes all electrical activity in the brain to cease? They don't know because they do not consider its actual source. Why does the brain in these various conditions, lose its memories and data to run our body systems? Where did it go?

The loss of all brain hardware and subsequent body functions clearly appears to be directly connected to the separation of the soul, would it not? If the soul leaves the body, even for a short period, there exists nothing more for the brain to interface with or *read*. Therefore, no electrical energy or systems data is present, and thus no brain activity. Therefore special mechanical life-support machines are required to do that work artificially. I will posit further that those people who are nearly brain dead but not requiring life support while in a coma, still have a small link to their soul left in contact. That *eternal tether* I made reference to in an earlier chapter providing their body the ability to animate only the most vital life systems. This idea will be seen later as well within the near death story of Michele A.

There we have it; the brain functions according to holographic principles. Within this context, it finally becomes clear to us. We can now all see how mankind possesses the capability to instantly *cross correlate* and *retrieve* whatever information is needed from the abundance of all accumulated memories near instantly. *This ability is an intrinsic feature of the hologram*, as I have already shown, **"the whole in every part"**. That means that *all parts infinitely interconnect and cross correlate with all other parts.*

No time, no space! The physical hardware of the human brain cannot do this on its own. I believe this to be the main reason such well-educated and open-minded doctored scientists such as I have presented herein, tend to search their entire careers for how this is possible. Because they know the physical properties of the hardware are not in and of themselves capable of such amazing feats.

From what I can ascertain, the human brain hardware is only able to process 10,000 bytes per second. Sounds like allot I know. However, it is believed that the second level subconscious soul can process 4 million Bytes per second, and the third level unconscious soul connection can process 4 trillion bytes per second! I believe most of this processing power is being used to sift through all the many present frequencies coming at us at all times in order to allow us to render our reality as we know it.

The Body Hologram

A question arises. If the brain possesses holographic abilities, then does the entire human physicality also function holographically? Can we prove it is? Yes!

As previously depicted, the proof is in the understanding of the *Whole in Every Part* concept. Simply put, *each cell of the human body contains all of the information required to produce another whole.* Therefore, each "part" of the body is a smaller version of the whole body - *The whole in every part!* Thus, we are also matter based super-holograms!

Soul & Ego - Form and Function

Most people go through life believing they understand what comprises both the *Ego* and the *Soul*. Inferably, this is defined for them over time by primitive and elemental narrative ideas. These concepts most often derive from various religious narratives and/or other philosophical or psychological interpretations such as those presented by *Aristotle, René Descartes, Carl Jung,* or *Sigmund Freud.*

Still, others will base their entire perceptions upon solely scientific findings. Regardless of which route of thought is taken these present a problem.

I believe it noteworthy to point out the two vastly different paradigms and approaches *Jung* and *Freud* presented, however, they both ultimately depicted the Soul and the Ego in their work narratives. *Jung* de-emphasized the importance of sexual development focusing on the *collective unconscious,* whereas *Freud* believed otherwise. Specifically by his understanding, this part of our unconscious <u>contains memories and ideas</u> that *Jung believed were inherited from our ancestors.* Some have coined this idea possibility as *genetic memory.* Unfortunately, they usually tend to quit looking beyond the physical DNA elements of our body-hardware. *Which is odd, because if we never return here, much less within the exact same DNA body, then how can any such genetic memory exist?*

Sigmund Freud appeared to center all his theories on the human ego. In his defense, he lacked the availability of current scientific research. *As a side note, it takes several years for research data to make its way through the scientific community.* Current technology has sped up that process a great deal! Thus, resulting in far more scientific data now coming to fruition, giving far more substantial understanding to the depth and breadth of both the soul and the ego. Restricted by the lack of theoretical science, it seems to me that Freud remained far more rudimentary and confined in his theories. He would have greatly benefited from our modern quantum physics to better explain the workings of both soul and ego more definitively. *Carl Jung*, on the other hand, appears to have been less confined by his ego, allowing him to be more plugged-in to the ethereal by his soul. This is why his fuller, more comprehensive understanding appears more intuitive.

The Ego-Brain relation: The length and breadth on this single subject concerning the relationship between the *ego, brain,* and the *quantum-soul* that should control them is substantial. In order to completely comprehend this would require the learning of an entirely new language, *Physics.* In an attempt to keep it all lined up for assimilation and because these relations must be clearly understood to fully grasp the overall meaning of this book, I will explain the basics using layman terminology along with daily life examples. So please bear with me if it seems a little long winded.

What is the Ego: How can I talk about the ego construct without first taking into account the definition by its creator, Sigmund Freud?

"Initially the ego is 'that part of the *id* which has been <u>modified by the direct influence of the external world'</u>" (Freud 1923) *Emphasis added*
The "id" is basically our impulsive carnal urges which Freud correctly intuited to be influenced and driven by outside *control narratives. According to Freud, the ego then develops and mediates between those urges and the reality of the world. The ego does not know right from wrong, which makes it like a weaker relative to the id.*

The problem here is that Sigmund Freud did not believe in a soul. The closest part of our being to a living-soul might be what he identified as the *superego*. According to him, the superego's role is to control the *id's* carnal urges and convince the ego to choose the most moral path. *However, morality is subject to ones assimilated control narratives!* It is evident in the underlined portion of the above quote that Freud did have some understanding of this world's *narratives,* and their responsibility in cultivating an individual's character. *"The ultimate goal, however, is to achieve the ego-ideal, our higher self"*. (McCloud)

Now that we have briefly discussed Freud's concept of self we can move on. First and foremost it must be comprehended that from my perspective the *Ego* is a part of the human element that includes the alleged, *Id*. The Ego is the administrator, the extrapolator of *self-identity*. "Self" <u>is its sole concern and objective</u>. It can work in conjunction, although confined by our *Soul-Consciousness* as the purveyor of our conditioned behavior. The Ego utilizes our *previously intuited soul ideas, meanings,* and *manifestations,* and turns these *soul-acquired* revelations into full-blown context, expression, and representations.

It may be simpler to think of the ego mechanism this way. *It is a biomechanical part of the human brain that acts in a more limited capacity of taking those events confined to previous learning - (i.e. life), and "manifesting" them, manipulating them, developing and forming them into our personal accomplishments.* This however always remains a secondary role to the true creator-soul process, *especially in the light of the fact that the living soul was created with no ego component.* Therefore, in my personal estimation of all this, the ego is a *Trinity-6* feature, created and installed solely for the purpose of controlling us via their false, negative, control narratives. As we saw with *Dr. Michael Persinger's* work on the brain, it does not within itself *house* our memory or derive new intuitive concepts or creative insights in and of itself. In addition, *Dr. Karl Pribram* showed us that the whole of our memory is not utilized in simply one part of the brain, but rather throughout its entirety. Therefore, Pribram utilized the quantum science explanation that our brains possess the ability to *allow* the *function* which they understand to be the *tangled Hierarchy.* In fact, this can only be proven out and understood by a tangled hierarchy.

What is a tangled hierarchy? Perhaps first it would be best and easier to explain the opposite. A simple hierarchy may be visualized as a rocket sitting on its launch pad, then being ignited goes up into our atmosphere some distance only to fall directly back to earth. This all happens in a very linear motion, *in stages* so to say, but only in two directions, *bottom to top, then reverting from top to bottom.* Simply, *the lower level affects the higher level.* This type of simple hierarchy is found everywhere in our physical world. The understanding being that we can always differentiate higher, middle, and lower.

In total contrast, the *tangled hierarchies* stages or *levels of causality* (the *relationship between cause and effect)* are so reticulate that we can no longer identify the higher, middle or lower levels.

Imagine now what a ball of yarn looks like. Think of what you know to be that ball's single thread of yarn wrapped many times in all directions to form the ball. Now instead, envision it NOT as one single thread but as billions of individual threads *wrapped, intertwined,* and *moving,* traveling in many directions at one time in an infinite oscillation, *a causal circulation.* You have now identified it as *Self-referential.* To enter it, you will be caught in it, and you will then identify with it! I guess you could almost see it as being caught up in an active tornado.

In other chapters of this book, I very loudly postulate that the soul cannot be of any legitimate aid to the betterment of itself, much less mankind upon its returning to this earthly matrix, "if" *no memories of its past remain retrievable while in these physical bodies.* Most likely the memory is blocked by some invention while contained in these *Trinity-6* avatar bodies as previously touched on concerning our Codons being turned off. This condition of course once again forces the soul to begin at a new zero-point. My hypothesis pertaining to the return of souls after death is further supported by the reality of mankind's tangled hierarchy. This would be because *memory requires perception but at the same time perception also requires memory,* which is a *circular causality.* It is in fact NOT a *linear top to bottom system of levels* as I depicted with the rocket example. The only question that remains in some scientists' minds is where this tangled hierarchy comes from. This can only be answered by the *living-soul* connecting with the *ego-brain hardware,* and thereby being the *driver* and *causation* of the tangled hierarchy working within our brain hardware. This is what I aim to show you.

Are the Ego & Living-Soul co-creators of what becomes our perceived reality?

The ego gets a great deal of bad press, and rightly so, but only because it has been misused due to a great lack of understanding. *That which may have been created for evil can also be used for good in the right hands, having the corrected knowledge base.* The trouble with the ego hardware is that it is accessed by humans in larger percentage over that of the quantum living-soul.

The idea to come out of the ego has been the mainstay of Buddhism. So, let's look at this ancient idea from newer scientific findings.

As I previously pointed out, the ego plays a minor role in all of this, although most would agree its influence to have generally a more negative creative effect. It would not be unrealistic to depict the two as being forced to work together by Archon design. We can use the well-known artist *M.C. Escher's* drawing titled *Drawing hands,* which depicts two hands with pencils, each drawing the other. The artist illustrates an endless loop leaving us unable to fully recognize which hand is actually drawing which. Thus, the *subject* and *object* appear to co-create one another. However, upon closer inspection we see another pencil protruding from the pictures edge. This, of course, would be the artist; *the main consciousness that creates the picture*. Or for this discussion, the external control of all living souls by the Archon entities.

Frequency breakdown

It must be understood that the human body is really a conglomeration of an organic, electrical machine and this includes our brains. Pribram alludes to the brain and the domain frequency; we have to understand that our entire world is one of energy. Now I am not speaking of *Beam me up Scottie* type of things here. But those waves and particles I mentioned earlier do have vibrational frequency energy. This is the information our sensory system also takes in. **All matter has a frequency!**

If it was not so, then you would not see most or any of your current surroundings, much like we do not see those parallel creations, as I presented earlier.

Recognizing this, something else that may be even more amazing and rarely thought of, even by those searching within this holographic universe community, is how the brain is able to *extrapolate, decode,* and *transliterate* the deluge of light and sound frequencies being received into the soul and then into the literal perception of a material world. This is the exact encoding function that we saw previously in how a hologram is made with the laser. And in relation to the trillions of bytes of processing power it has to work with to collate and decode all those frequencies.

The brain, acting as the *Soul interference reader* is somehow able to translate and convert an unknown amount of varied frequency signals into a coherent *matter image!* I touched on this within *Dr. Michael Persinger's* research.

Persinger states that our brain is alive with micro static patterns that are the building blocks to consciousness and would also encompass tangled hierarchy as well. He speaks of entanglement between two people, which I began this chapter with. Teleportation has already taken place and been proven within quantum physics experimentation. With all of this stated it is not too far of a leap to see that, as Persinger has discovered, our consciousness is able to transcend space and time when at rest. As he goes on to state, *the brain is matter.*

> *Are you fully comprehending what this means?* As I have expressed time and again herein, that quite literally our souls, being the Microcosm-soul portions created directly from our Primary Creator's Macro-Soul, makes all souls the *"whole in every part"!* Since He is a *creator*, then by default our souls are also micro-creators, or rather, we have the ability to do so, and every level of creation has been designed specifically to give our souls the platform and room to do just that!

This is exactly what all these outstanding scientists and medical professionals are showing us. Regardless how these rebellious entities manipulated this particular creation level in which we now find ourselves living and re-living in, it all occurs because of our soul's ability to create the *matter-image-world* that we perceive right now in front of us. That would include the book now in your hand. Thus, because of our soul's innate ability to create, *it is our <u>response</u> to the control-narratives, which is the ongoing problem!*

Dr. Pribram's holographic brain theory has gained increasing support among his neurophysiologist peers. *His belief that our brains convert and mathematically construct "hard-matter-reality" from the input it receives <u>via some frequency source</u> is also backed up by a great deal of experimental testing and support*

These findings prove our senses receive a much wider range of frequencies than was previously suspected. For instance, showing that our visual system is sensitive to sound frequencies and our sense of smell to be in part reliant on these *cosmic holoverse frequencies* as well. It also appears that even the cells in our bodies are sensitive to a broad range of frequencies. On the negative side of this can be found substantial and growing research proving how horrifically bad it is for our brains and bodies to be bathed in the Wi-Fi frequency band, as well as other such man-made frequencies. *This expanding branch of science suggests more and more that it could only be within this model of the holographic demesne of consciousness that these proven frequencies are received, culled, and apportioned into conventional "material" perceptions.*

Many are boggled by the absolute vastness of the holographic universe, or *Holoverse*, as I coin it. This is not a concept that most people can synthesize and assimilate in one reading or study session. That is why this chapter was only meant to give the reader an overall basic understanding of this new reality to aid in understanding this concept. *Thus, to prove whom we all are, where we are, with the need to realize this is NOT our original condition or environment, etc.*

Many have interpreted the Eastern religions as upholding the idea that the material world is an illusion. In reality, it is that our *ego* or *self* is the illusion not our physical-matter-energy based surroundings and or physicality. As I alluded to earlier, there is only matter and energy, both which are forever in motion.

Think back to your basic high school science: *all matter is in motion.* That doesn't mean it's an illusion, but rather that your observation of a solid is still matter, only moving at a slower rate than say air or water. It's like a digital computer image. *Your brain interprets it as a still shot but in reality, it is received frequency lines of information being repetitively updated and continually rebuilding that image onto that screen.* Therefore our perception of a solid picture is an optical frequency illusion.

This new prototype of reality, being the synthesis of Dr. Bohm and Dr. Pribram's observations and study, along with others, has come to be referred to as the *holographic universe paradigm.*

I hope my contribution depicting mankind's souls as being the eternal living "frequency receiver-projectors" existing in a polychromatic expanse of frequency, can contribute to their

∞ ברוך אתה אה'ה אלוהינו, מלך העולם, פוקח עורים ∞

understanding.

Chapter 9

Soul-Receivers

Narratives = Control of the Collective Paradigm!

Our *frequency receivers* are data stream projectors, which get regulated automatic updates that slowly evolve humans mentally and physically in this creation-reality by way of certain selected people - *soul-receivers*. A certain chosen few through history have known where and who these narratives have come from, most do not. These people, *Archon sycophants'*, then implement and update some very specific, predetermined narratives, which I call herein - **"Chosen narratives!"**

Chosen-narratives provided by their handlers, our captors, in which we extract their narrative frequencies causing our souls to *assimilate, apply* and subsequently *transform* these narratives into physical reality. In other words, we live in the world we unknowingly, and collectively help to create. It is only with our *consent* that this can be accomplished through the usually negative *control narratives* they supply in various forms.

This, in turn, continues to grow this super-holoverse, *in their image! Therefore, our objective reality ceases to exist.* Technically speaking, although they appear to be working along the outer edge of the rules defining the Prime Eternal Creator's *Freewill System*, it would seem this lower creation has since become a prison with the prisoners being allowed to retain no memory of their continued and detrimental internment and participation!

Holoverse Matrix

The chosen narrative data stream w/updates

Our Eternal living-souls

Our secondary created human bodies/brain soul-interface

Buzzerg.com

Perhaps knowing this may also prove out the mysteries that have never been explainable by science, including establishing the paranormal as a part of nature itself. It all becomes more understandable when viewing the many different parapsychological phenomena from the holographic paradigm.

Numerous Near Death Experiencers-(NDE) and Past Life-regression-(PLR) researchers, as well as scientists and doctors such as Bohm and Pribram, affirm this. It continues to be important to reiterate that we are all eternal living-souls whereby this reformatted holoverse is not our original condition state, *but a reformatted creation in which the players unknowingly consented to be the creative tools that facilitate all the Archon negative changes!*

A world of our own making. In consenting to their original false narrative of death, and all subsequent false control narratives since which extend from and cascade off the first, *we have submitted to becoming like prisoners within a prison we constructed and made to forget it was of our own doing.* Make no mistake, those entities whose *will* we initially followed will continue to enforce their *chosen narratives* through yet another band of chosen people, Priests, Kings, and Queens, Presidents, warlords, scientists and researchers, some even unsuspecting of the narrative origins themselves. *A new chosen but more diverse Levitical cult, but in lieu of open sacrifice they gift us with delusions of heavenly grandeur and the fear of eternal hell fires which allow most of us to cheer the bloodletting of others marked as evil people, man, and beast alike!*

Our super-hologram, a heavenly creation giving birth to every subatomic particle that has been or will be, and to all possible types of matter, energy, and even protein configurations. It is a purposeful *reformatted* construct to those Archon Soul elite as far as we know it. However, incredible as it may seem to everyone, the ancient and modern case for this creation now being a merely *reformatted image* of the original creation, remains palpable. Hopefully, now you have a basic understanding of the holographic construct and how it applies to this world and our living-souls. Clearly, I was never speaking of some mirage world, but rather a creation where every facet, is a "**whole in every part**".

And remember: *Just because you can, doesn't mean you should, consent!*

Chapter 10

An Alternate Reality View

There has been in recent years a great uptick in both Physics Science, Hypnosis Regression practitioners and researchers delving into the realities of the living-soul. As expected, those seeking answers to those topics appear to be outpacing the research. There are now several major personalities and research institutes who have been scientifically documenting where thousands of people have been in times past, and subsequently where they will go again after this life (Studies).

Based on the documented cases from as far back as the mid-1800 to this day, these studies continue to provide amazingly similar to exact account details of where most people's souls appear to be going and experiencing upon departing the physical. However amazing and detailed the many thousands of accounts continue to be, and how beyond mathematical probability it is now to dismiss their accounts as mere fantasy, I still remain convinced that the researchers themselves, as well as all their subjects, are misunderstanding the data provided by these highly documented NDE and PLR accounts. By missing the most vital signs pointing to a vast delusion, and as I have posited herein, what they are seeing is not the beginning and not the end, but a technology based *trick of light* leading us into a false heaven matrix!

So far you have seen me refer to certain unseen ruling elite Archon entities of which the ancients and religions have also spoken. These, of course, are the original rebel souls in charge, although they are by no means the only entities in which we as ethereal entities, and later in this physical form have been affected by. For sure this will be a highly controversial chapter and topic extension, however, our ancient historical past is so established by so many cultures who speak of these *other* entities, building all manner of lore and religious cults around them, no thinking person can so easily discount them all as mere fable.

As previously referred to, but by far not nearly the only ancient writings to refer such entities, the *Nag Hammadi* texts are one such blatant example which clearly call out the name and present the existence of a formidable and completely disobedient horde of ancient entities known throughout antiquity by many names. *To recap:*

[“On account of the reality of the authorities, inspired by the spirit of the father of truth, the great apostle – referring to the "authorities of the darkness" – told us that "our contest is not against flesh and blood; rather, the authorities of the universe and the spirits of wickedness." I have sent this to you because you inquire about the reality of the authorities.

Their chief is blind because of his power and his ignorance, and in his arrogance, he said, with his power - (technology), "It is I who am god; there is none apart from me." When he said this, he sinned against the entirety - (Prime Creator). And this speech got up to incorruptibility - (above expanse); then there was a voice that came forth from incorruptibility, saying,

"You are mistaken, Sama'el" – which in the Hebrew tongue means - "god of the blind."]

[“His thoughts became blind, having expelled his power by the blasphemy he had spoken – he pursued it-(his will) down to chaos and the abyss, with his mother, at the instigation of Pistis Sophia. And she established each of his offspring in conformity with its power- (Living-soul) - after the pattern of the realms that are above, by starting from the invisible world the visible world was invented.]

(The Hypostasis of the Archons - The Reality [*Hypostasis*] of the Rulers) - Nag Hammadi texts - Translated by Dr. Bentley Layton). *Emphasis added.*

As I have maintained throughout this book, the worldwide assumption of the multitudes has always been that the *heaven* all souls depart to, is one and the same as charted by their religious narratives. Fully convinced they will arrive at the place where the Prime Eternal Creator resides. There are many resources used to define that heavenly realm, and by now as you may be seeing, what has been taught is quite different than that which may be verified more accurately by various spiritual texts, and science.

We can discuss and argue religion until this existence dissolves away, but the many ancient texts continue to reveal a story that seems far advanced of its contemporaries. In the previous Nag Hammadi texts, as with others, it is understood by scholars that they clearly speak of another unseen entity who many tend to believe literally created the realm we find ourselves in; *an alleged creator other than the original Eternal Prime Creator.*

However, as you know I believe these and other texts to be defining a *Reformatting* of the *original* creation here, and not something new. The Nag texts also appear to be telling us *where* this creation is in comparison to the other heaven levels of *incorruptibility above.* Further explaining that this creation reality was *fashioned* after the likeness or pattern of the one *above;* and most amazing of all, that this reality is, in fact, a hologram! - *(by starting from the invisible world, the visible world was invented.]*

Always bearing in mind that these ancients did their best to express the details they received, but had no context for.

The full consent scenario

I have so far restrained myself from breaking into this possibility, fearing it may convolute what is already a difficult set of topics to absorb. However, believing my reading audience to have a higher than average ability for lateral thinking, I will provide a quick possibility that I am sure many will be asking.

The above Nag Hammadi texts and others *can also appear or be perceived to be presenting the idea that "another", completely new and separate universe creation to have been actually created here.* And not merely our original creation *reformatted* as I pose herein.

Some, like the Mormon cult and others go so far as to posit that *we, our souls* are actually that 1/3rd of fallen souls who, while in the upper levels of the heavens, chose the dark side willingly and knowingly with our rebel leader, and followed him to this alternate universe that he created, himself. *Additionally,* that all of our souls have been *cut-off* as theirs have been, stuck forever with the plan, and within the creation of our choosing.

Of course, I always consider all the prevailing points of view, and if true, this one is even more devastating upon our realization of it than my own horrific correlations herein. Although, *I don't believe it matters either way. I don't believe one scenario over the other changes the end game result.* If it is as they posit, over what I have developed herein, we still have to consider all of the other ancient texts and cultural knowledge to serve the greater picture, and virtually all of that, much of which I have laid out in earlier published works, *points to all souls receiving their chance to un-consent by other previously established means to return!* So I ask the super obvious – *'What would be the reason to invent, install and maintain such a myriad of false religious and other spiritual and non-spiritual control-narratives, many of which tell us of a time coming for the end of the evil ones, and the return of all souls, etc.;* if both the Archon leaders and all souls here *long previously agreed* to be here under their rule, to begin with?' For me, that does not track, and too contorted to be a logical conclusion for us. Therefore I obviously reject it.

I have spent much of my life working to eliminate religious fallacy, and the truth is that most people will have a difficult time being convinced of such a grand, delusional redirection by means of so many false narratives. Hopefully, our Theoretical and Biological Physicists proving the link between the majority of our human DNA and eternal soul, along with how both work in concert through all realms, will be enough to formulate a cohesive, believable final answer. Then by the assimilation of these rediscoveries, a greater soul-multitude can hopefully emerge from the power of their control. Clearly, a more complete and accurate picture would result from utilizing both science and *corrected* ancient religious scholarship.

From my vantage point, it appears that for many years most of the professionals researching these topics of NDE's and Past Life

Regression subjects have only considered, applied and translated their findings through the lens of one of the world's most prevalent religious dogmas. Even when they do not believe they are doing so. *Meaning,* the data they are hearing is being translated by them as they expected it to exist, and aligning with either current or previously held religious narratives. From my experience, the opinions of the data collected appear most often molded by the Christian religious narrative held by the researcher. It appears before they can see the more probable scenario in all this, everyone must strip away their *assimilated* religious narratives and superstitions.

Doing so is no simple task because our later narrative threads tend to pollute our findings along the way unless one is super-vigilant in monitoring this tendency in themselves, which in my experience most people do not fully accomplish. The emotional connection makes it nearly impossible for any *teacher* of religion or their followers to remain emotionally detached where their personal Archon controlled-narrative beliefs are concerned. The exact same condition exists on an academically emotional level within the halls of science. Needed are those few who have the ability to identify, collate and bridge *unapologetically* the many satellite points of truth from all of man's ancient religious superstitions and myths. They are then needed to correlate these ancient ideas with the newly emerging scientific discoveries that point to the Macro-soul source of The Prime Creator's *intention,* which literally brought our original reality into being. A Creator source that continues to hold it in place while allowing our creative soul portions time to interface creatively *for good or for evil* with this creation in much the same way that He creates, albeit in an exceedingly smaller and slower fashion.

Thus, as I expressed in an earlier chapter, the Prime Creator has *allowed* His created souls their original rebellion, also allowing our souls to feel the pressure of our own *consent* into rebellion by allowing this three-dimensional, reformatted, lower frequency world, and their false heaven system and expanding control over the original living-souls of this creation. We can only hope as it is stated in most of the world's religious narratives, that there is a specified end date to their arrogant usurpation.

As you read in my chapter titled - *Access through Consent,* one must give way to a certain amount of truth found to exist at the root of ancient superstitions, religiously driven or not. To be honest with oneself forces us to understand that the ancients held several very specific and recurring beliefs which transcended multitudes of generations, cultures, and geographical locations. Reaching into other civilizations to which they had no physical connection.

One modern day example would be the belief in the ancient aliens' concept. Specifically, a movement born in 1973 by then European race car driver *Claude Vorilhon* who met these alleged ancient aliens and received historical information to spread (Mooney).

Their story to him, as it must have been to the Hebrew prophet *Ezekiel* who also took alien car service from time to time (Prophets), was that they are the progenitors of all life on earth, and of man.

Further explaining that they are even specifically, by their own DNA, *the direct ancestors of the Hebrews!* Wow, imagine my own surprise as I believed my family had a better than average handle on our lineage! *Claude Vorilhon* states further, that *they* are directly responsible for all of the religions on this planet! *Now we are finally getting somewhere, and as I have posited — Archon narratives!*

With this cult now having a presence within the State of Israel, it appears many Jewish people are catching on to the possibility that they hail from this scientific spawning created by this race of aliens known as, *Raëlian's.* Which of course fits and makes sense to them because the *Raëlian* leader is none other than *Yahweh!* Whose personal history has him as a 25,000-year-old extraterrestrial who was/is the president of a planet of scientists who created all life on earth. *What could possibly go wrong?*

The following is a quote from a recent Podcast on this topic by a world-renowned Jewish scholar whom I will leave unidentified as to not perpetuate any additional negative result to his career:

> *"The Raëlian movement aims to demystify religion and spiritualize science". "The Masters also urge an end of belief in such entities as guardian angels, the devil, and an omniscient, omnipotent "Heavenly God."*

Well, there it is folks! The smoking gun with Archon prints all over it! Of course! These are those same entities who were *also* created by the same Archon rebels, now tasked with orders to downplay those narrative portions; especially during a time in history when the Archon's plan to ignite their next round of fakery upon the captured souls of humanity. *There are no messenger souls from an Eternal Creator, no evil entities, nor any Creator in fact, other than us!* Where have I heard that one before?

And why isn't anyone asking WHO created THEM?
Remember to ask – WHICH god?

I am not saying that their belief in this area is wholly untrue. What I am depicting here by making you aware of their belief, is to bring your attention to the literal wizard behind the curtain. Does this demi-god *"Rael"* and his *Raëlian* race exist? I would suggest that they do, because we can find him and them throughout all the written historical texts that humanity currently possesses, and by many personas; one being the god entity of both Babylonian periods, as well as the later Babylonian-Jewish sect which broke away from the original Abrahamic Hebrew lineage. That part is easy. The more difficult part here is explaining how the ancient or modern day *Hebrew, as it pertains to lineage, spiritual beliefs and the Creator entity we follow,* is not at all the same in lineage or beliefs as those that the Babylonian *Jewish* cult espouses. However, you will have to read my earlier books to gain that deeper perspective on where that cult led everyone astray. Suffices to say they are not at all synonymous, and each cult followed and continue to follow entirely different creator entities and rules.

In the end, it will always be about the control-narratives and their creators, and these alleged *Raëlian's* can certainly be understood as middle management to that end. They are the *narrative presenters* and *managers* of our Middle and Far Eastern religious and theocratic hierarchy narratives throughout man's history.

The last word and interesting point on this Raëlian topic.
Specifically concerning the title-name of their leader, *Rael*. In ancient Aramaic-Hebrew, and as it remains today, the name broken down literally translates to:

- RA = *Evil*
- EL = *Mighty one.* Usually depicting a god – *Evil Mighty one!*

The literal meaning of that name may provide some perspective on where this is all going...

We can argue one's specific religious dogma or even the dogma of *no god, no religion,* but the multitude of historical evidence will not change. Although largely overwritten and long misunderstood, the myths remain prevalent, emotionally driven and more various the longer they are allowed to remain supreme and dominant over us.

The open consciousness gives way to the understanding that all ancient superstition or myth has at its root, an origin of truth. *As we know, all fish stories start out with a real fish. And fish stories never decrease in size or scope!* Over time, the origin of truth tends to get buried under a pile of added *fear-based* superstition which appears to be deliberately added *control-narratives*.

Sometimes along the way even additional truth makes its way back in, but none of the added detritus invalidates the original points of fact. *This* is how I see their reformatting process overwriting the original paths for this creation. *The best lies have an original point of truth at their core, correct?*

*The **Adam-Eden Matrix** is this world reformatted!* This entire solar system and expanding universe beyond has been flooded with derisive, controlling frequencies. Manipulating this three-dimensional construct in which they have allowed us to go on thinking it to be the original version as created for us to live life abundantly. *Manipulating the ancient narratives into our modern times in such a way as to make all generations believe they were created to fail, and thus remain in some unclean state.*

Unredeemable *unless we all say the special magic words of yet another false narrative, or perform the special ritual murder of yet* *another sentient soul for our souls "alleged" redemption.*

Amazingly, and as you read previously in my *Holographic Universe* chapter, our quantum scientists appear to have proven their long-held hypothesis that our Edenic matrix is, a *super-holographic, matter based construct* which was absolutely created by some force far beyond our understanding. Even the long-time and outspoken scientists and atheist *Steven Hawking* recently submitted to the Creator force!

As postulated in my chapter titled - *Access by Consent* - this **AE-Matrix** was taken by *adverse possession,* providing them jurisdiction after our consent, although unaware of the fine print details of that contract. For most of man's history, the people had no context or language to understand or accurately reiterate to us what they saw, and in many cases what they were told by those they perceived to be gods. Able only to pen rudimentary descriptions concerning their god entities technological abilities, which were so far beyond our own current understanding, much less that of these ancient peoples.

Ironic enough that even our own advanced scientists find themselves in much the same boat today with their discoveries. They know they see something, they know it exists because they can measure it; they even find themselves, *virtually their soul-consciousness'* affecting the experimental surroundings on every level, and still for so long remained hesitant, even belligerent against considering that it is *their soul* which is the culprit interacting, meddling in their experiments. All at the same time totally missing out on the revelation of the highest order; *that it was them, their own living-soul's conscious and subconscious "intention" that caused the changes in their experiments.* Literally creating something new!

The revelation being missed by science thus far is, that what they are witnessing is nothing less than a literal ACT of creation formed by their own soul's intention!

Additionally, this is why our own researchers, even given all their advancements, excellent study, and verifications on this subject of the soul and life after this physical experience, still appear to be missing that which is most likely the greatest *entrapment event* imaginable.

A disconcerting reality of design, that once identified is then easily, positively circumvented. We are on a palpable misadventure depicting the hypothesized adverse possession of our soul's entrapment within a usurped creation modified for us to experience under greatly different circumstances than originally designed.

I will hopefully continue to constitute an integrated panoramic view of this universe creation level distinctive from how most religious cults have perpetuated its falsity. They have confused the true nature of our original creation state, our original *soul-body non-physicality*, the *original rules* of all creations, and most importantly the identity of our original Prime Creator source for that of another demi-god oligarch protagonist. All of this has been written by many hands in many languages throughout time and memorial; *however, the direst culmination of all the aforementioned confusion is the true knowledge of who we are and were created to be.* So desperately missing the most urgent element for our return path - **To own our role and responsibility in these events!**

The Anti-Character

Most often exhibiting malevolent behavior, the rebel Archon souls have long pretended to be benevolent mentors to most civilizations, all the while masquerading as light-workers for the Eternal Prime Creator, while at the same time providing harsh legal and barbaric ritualistic frameworks in homage to themselves.

Most notably, and chief among their tactics they have utilized the mechanism of *soul-memory elimination*, as well as their false identity narratives to position themselves and their sycophants over, and in control of mankind through our eternal living souls creative ability.

By religious and other narrative systems all bearing various colors and face paint designs, the same root false narrative streams persist. They employ trickery, lies, and technological prowess to sway our continuing consent to their will. As you are learning, their *will* is divergent, a total opposite refraction to our Prime Eternal Creator's will of *life abundant, mercy and love!*

As I like to mention periodically, virtually all the world's religions and civilizations depict this same story and understanding regardless of language, culture, or geographical location. Or whether the information is retrieved from the *Sumerian, Babylonian Emunah Elish, Egyptian book of the dead, Tibetan book of the dead, Hebrew Torah, Nag Hammadi,* or all the much later, highly mistranslated, Western Christian bibles and so-called Apocryphal texts, the story remains the same throughout. In order to seriously consider what I am proposing here requires even the most sacrosanct zealot to concede to the interminable probability of such a being's *existence,* their *intention,* and *sway.* As well, concede to the extremely high probability that we have totally misjudged the entities identity and intention by our skewed religious narratives. *Just always remember, people throughout time far more intelligent and closer to the sources than you, also believed them to be real gods.*

Their immortal coil

In the beginning *"The Eternal Creator caused light to exist".* Unfortunately, when these Archon rebels took over the narrative they caused man to misunderstand the actual meaning and intent of that *first light.* Only to institute their own *Trick of Light* upon our mortal passing and our soul's flight. A decoy light which captivates and provides the expected illusions which manipulate our free soul *to consent* yet again into entering their heaven control matrix.

The Archon way station, or *heaven-matrix,* gives the illusion of being the original heaven levels of the Prime Eternal Creator which exist *above* the expanse. When in reality it is a fabrication that works in tandem with the religious narratives they set up here in the Adam-Eden matrix — As above, so below! *Narratives that all people assimilate, and thus consent to being their truth.* Narratives which live inside your soul-consciousness which are later tapped and used to lead us back into the light. Their light!

Now you will begin to see how imperative it is to find and assimilate the most original path while you still live.

As I have shown previously, try to keep in the forefront of your mind as we advance, how some ancient texts so clearly and accurately depict that - *this creation was in fact re-formatted to appear in the image or more specifically the reflection of the original Heavens.* An extremely important aspect of this *reflective reformatted creation* in which we must all understand and remember is that a <u>reflection</u> is a <u>reverse</u> image. *Meaning*, that all that is *above*, and as it was originally here, <u>is now reversed within this creation space, and in total contrast to that which remains above the expanse</u>!

As I previously touched on several times, the Archon's human collaborator catchphrase is – *"As above, so below"*. At first glance the uninitiated person, Christians especially, might believe this catch phrase to be some near reference to their "Our Father" or "The lord's" prayer - *"On earth, as it is in heaven"*. Now start asking - *Which heaven?*

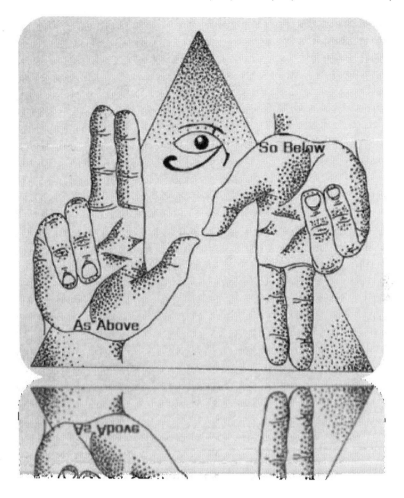

You may notice in the previous picture that this is the exact same hand sign or signal that we find depicted throughout the Roman Papacy, as well pretty much depicted in every Catholic or Orthodox picture of Jesus, and even Mary. Unfortunately, this hand sign is far older than the Roman church or anything Christian.

It is found throughout antiquity, and to this very day depicted among renderings of the evil entity "Baphomet". Also, take note how this entity is usually depicted as sitting on top of the world!

Much as the older depictions of the *Ouroboros* snake being wrapped around the planet. Which is no longer how that sacred art is usually depicted for some odd reason. Why?

Earth

Strangled by our

Seraphim reptilian

Overlords!

Unfortunately, the Christian sects still believe that the ancient Aramaic Hebrew word *Seraphim* means, angel! It, however, does not!

Baphomet

As you can clearly see the same hand sign being displayed as usual by this Baphomet figure, it is also in common use among the Masons, and even in conjunction with the false god name Yahweh/Yah'Hovah, the *Raëlian* entity.

As above – So below, *or,* As within – So without!

Now notice the Hebrew title-name *Yahweh* in the center of the top triangle of this occult symbol below. Also notice that when both triangles are moved to center, they will become the 6 pointed star of Molech! *The star of Chuin/Saturn.*

Yes, all of the secret occult societies are surely one, and of the same evil mind. Just as all are also woven directly within all the major religions. As I have clearly shown thus far, they all serve that same imposter creator entity. Yes, they have fooled most everyone, making one thing to *appear* to be the same as the other thing. The heaven YOU are thinking about and hoping for is NOT the same one they know of and hope for.

Yes, you too can have eternal life here with them, although you won't be allowed to remember any of them. Only their elite sycophants have been given that option of memory recall.

Thus, the specific prayers I mentioned earlier may not be referring to the original heaven levels above the expanse at all, and possibly yet even another false narrative tributary to keep all souls off the pure path. *Be careful what you pray for and to!*

So then, we see how it is imperative that we all learn to identify *which* creation we are referring to in our supplications, as it would appear specifics matter. If by definition this creation space is no longer a construct in its original form presently, then our prayers and the frequency they project should be understood as being hopeful creations in the making as it were by the projection of our soul-consciousness. Prayers helping to re-establish this creations original condition and intent by our soul's creative *intention*. The Living-Souls constant and ever-present *intention* is the core of our extremely powerful creative force. This is why even the inaccurate translation of a simple prayer or religious precept can cause the opposite reality to occur over time via the conscious *intention* and *projection* of those words and emotionally driven, intentional feelings into being!

The takeaway here should show you how the multitudes of souls *invoking the incorrect, emotionally driven* and *assimilated narratives,* aid the enemy! By *projecting* their misguided ideas and beliefs through words and *intentions,* our creative force is *the* major application which has been providing aid and comfort to our immortal enemies!

I have already established via ancient texts, scientific discovery, philosophical commentary, and a multitude of religious cult doctrines and cultural tapestries, that this *reformatted-creation* is nothing more than *an intention-driven,* reflective contrast to the original heaven levels. *A contrast which has always been driven by our conscious assimilation of the false narratives that we consent to allow in as truth, and perpetuated through emotional belief structures and continuous speech.* As within – So without!

"As above, so below", can only be referring to the Archon fabricated areas of operation - *The Adam-Eden matrix below, and their false heaven matrix above. In either direction, the catchphrase*

represents connected symbiotic systems. Exposing itself as a system designed to mimic that of the original Eternal Creator's primary system. Controlled by those main rebel entities, and those souls who follow their lead in order to enforce – *As within, so without!*

Encroaching free will by manipulation – *by treachery.* Superseding by *reflection* our Primary Creator's *original* laws of love and equality by ever expanding disinformation which distracts from the original core truth, thereby diverting man's free-will consent through subterfuge. This provides their desired result by drawing the souls of mankind away from the true Primary Creator's path. Keeping us mostly separated, or so they believe. Whether one's belief is such that these entities were created by the Prime Creator or another race of beings as many people do in the absence of solid instruction, makes no difference in the end; the rebels and most people/souls continue to rebel against all basic original instructions for LIFE!

The Archon's rebels, by working in the gray area of the Eternal Creator's Freewill system, have enslaved the souls in which He created to live here freely and unencumbered! And because of all the false narrative doctrines of these rebel Archon souls throughout man's history, no person ever thinks to question or ask themselves if they share in the responsibility of it all. The question rarely posed from ancient of days to this moment remains, - *'are we the souls within this creation who also rejected The Eternal Creator's original laws by our own naivety and ignorance?'*

As I delve deeper into the data that so many NDE (Near death experiencers) and PLR (Past life regression) subjects provide, it appears to me, based on all the detailed, scientifically derived information gathered, that my panoramic view of the corrected story is more plausible. They grow and maintain their nearly imperceptible prison system here on earth, as they do above in their Heaven Way-station. The rest is a common thread expressed within both the Western and Eastern religions. I implore the reader to become more familiar with the work of those well-known *After-life* research centers and the mass of well-documented reports they derive from their subjects. At this point the shear amount of congeneric data which numbers in the tens of thousands defies probability.

The Past is Prologue

As previously touched on, the Archon ability and continued use of a *memory-wipe mechanism* appears to be the primary instrument used to compel our soul's continual passive submission to their spurious chosen-narratives spanning *religion, history, contrived supernatural events, junk-science, nationalism,* and so on. As their control grid of *chosen-narrative* paths here on earth expands, so does it make their control and *reinsertion* of souls who leave earth upon the separation of physical death easier and more certain. As previously touched on, the Archon technology mimics the light of the Creator in reflection to draw us in. Using their control narratives during our incarnated lives to program the human soul-consciousness through our earthly experience by assimilated *learned memories,* which in various ways after our incorporation of these narratives, _force our souls to identify_ their heaven system as the true Creators system of love and equality.

Super-Hologram scenes akin to movie sets constructed in their false heaven station which allow the soul to *feel* and *perceive* the previously learned, earth based, *soul specific* religious or even non-religious narrative, while being channeled through their *love tunnel of light* towards the souls of our equally ignorant loved ones, and or mimicked religious icons.

Whatever it takes to get you to CONSENT to entering in, yet again!

One may ask how this is possible. Many may not be aware of this fact, and I will get into the newer science of it later on, but *the vast majority of our DNA actually functions as a _life memory recording system,_* which is later uploaded to our soul for permanent storage. This is why the emphasis for them is on the fabrication and integration of controlled narratives that immerse the soul (in life) in controlled emotional paradigms at the quantum level. *These can then be tapped, and their specific data used via technology upon the soul's separation from the physical to construct any required personal scenario that will entice that soul to _consent_ to entering in.*

Page | 195

This is only one example of DNA-based soul data manipulation occurring as a result of their immersive, multi-level narrative system structure within this Adam-Eden matrix during any individual lifetime.

Let me continue by explaining what I have found as prevalent within the NDE and PLR experiences as the researchers have documented them concerning this process. Upon our passing, and as the unaware soul's commandeered journey begins through their heaven matrix program, the immortal soul is made to feel precisely that which it *previously learned* and *consented to* as being <u>truth in life</u>, within this Adam-Eden matrix. Their tunnel of love & light is a tractor-beam that provides a *myriad of highly intense positive feelings and visions based on our previously learned, narrative specific data.*

The preponderance of details gleaned from so many NDE and PLR subjects that so closely harmonize with all the known narratives is now beyond question in my mind. The most prevalent initial experience is one that most of us have heard of, I call this construct the – *Soul Greeter!* It appears to be standard fair upon death that everyone is met by the person or icon that was most loved or influential in that particular person/souls life <u>and ushered inside</u>. *Always by our consent!*

As you should expect by now, all this is designed by the Rebel Archons to further ensure the soul's compliance and <u>*consent to entering*</u> their false heaven-matrix. Always important to keep in mind, that within the Eternal Creator's original system, <u>Free Will</u> is tantamount above all! Which should mean to you; that if we *learn* to believe this possibility, that our souls cannot be held completely against our will as long as our soul is working with previously learned, *corrected* information, then this new data forms our <u>*dis-consent*</u> to these rebel handlers attempts to lure us into their false-heaven matrix. We must learn to NOT-CONSENT! Not to one single request or demand while here, and especially upon our death. And the only way I can imagine that we can be *aware* and able to do this upon our soul's separation from the physicality, is to totally immerse ourselves in this understanding, assimilating it and *emotionally driving* it in deeper daily, yearly unto that fateful day.

Learn it – Live it – Be it!

Our goal MUST be total non-consent or compliance! Our soul must remain aware upon its separation from the body so that it cannot be tricked. Our demand must be, to be united with our primary *"source"*. Our ultimate goal is to be reunited with the Prime Creator source who created us. Although I have always firmly believed that living the Creators *Everlasting Agreement* provides our soul an instant bypass, and direct route home. So please take that possibility and very simple remedy into account should you decide to proceed down this path.

Outside of that, I cannot personally know for certain if one's soul can bypass their system by UN-consenting alone. However, it should be an imperative that our living-soul remain aware of this possibility at that time while under direct attack, and the only way it seems for anyone to do that is to have that new *corrected* data available within them at an emotional level, in force. This can only be achieved by the same means in which our false narrative data was assimilated. By re-learning and applying a new concept.

We must live the *corrected* wisdom and knowledge daily! Not as a religious procedure from time to time, but as an absolute minute to minute lifestyle. Living the *Everlasting Agreement* actually provides the framework, direct path and affords us a way to do this quite easily, and without stress. Either way, the knowledge of the corrected data and awareness must be recorded at a deep emotional level so that the soul has an abundance of access to it at the right time. *More importantly!* Having ONLY the corrected data within you, having lost and forgotten all the old false narrative ways should totally restrict their ability to extrapolate adverse data from within your soul. Which then by default should make your soul an anathema to them. Is it your time to break the cycle and finally be allowed to return to our creator source?

Additionally, whether physically here on earth or in your original *soul-light-body* off this earth, you DO NOT have to <u>speak</u> in order to give your consent. Your forward movement and compliance to follow *someone* into their heaven matrix **is consent** enough to allow anyone; Archon rebel or mortal government here on this earth, to gain adverse jurisdiction over you. May I also add that the perception of *logical reasoning* or *fear,* which again both parties *above & below* provide as initiatives, are often acute factors in acquiring your consent – *As above, so below.*

As I have eluded to so far, it has been widely reported and documented by a large percentage of NDE research studies, that upon a person's soul leaving the body, many subjects depict in very great detail the same specifics of their trip; beginning with:

- Their immediate capture within the light-tunnel
- Presented with a "soul-greeter/receiver"
- Given a "past-life-review"
- Made to take "soul-classes"
- Meeting their "soul-guides"
- Meetings with a "council of elders"
- Told they can stay indefinitely!
- Eventually guilted into a forced return trip!

In literally thousands of documented cases, people have told these researchers that this *heaven* is amazingly beautiful or perfection, having the feelings of total *love & equality.* However, and as expected, I also see by their depictions that a hierarchy does exist there. Although in the original Heaven above, no such hierarchy exists under The Prime Eternal One. Any hierarchy that a person believes they are seeing within their religious texts continue to miss the point. Point being, that all of those texts are providing descriptions of this Adam-Eden and Heaven matrix system, and not at all depicting the other higher realms above the expanse which currently separates us.

As I posited earlier, this soul-body separation experience *while inside their heaven way-station* is most often based on the same path of *narratives* that the person previously held in life.

Therefore, they are provided the experience they personally expect to experience - *total love, total equality, and perfection the entire time.* However, *"this" is what you would expect to FEEL and experience while in your original Soul-light-body!* Because the pure soul is a portion of The Eternal Creator's Macro-soul, and He is pure love! It may still be a *naïve* soul, but in its true form, it should reflect that character of the One who created it! My point is, the Archon's are NOT the ones creating what those souls are feeling! The Living-Soul is creating it for them!

It is our connection and integration with the Trinity-6 physical bodies that confuses and firewalls the Living-souls natural pure and goodly nature!

We see this proven generationally and daily by the sheer dichotomy of mankind! Where do you think all the absolute beauty of our ability to create such expressive and vulnerable arts comes from? While at the same time many possessing the ability for equally great destruction! How can two extreme natures coexist within the same living-soul? *I say they cannot!* One exists via the primal *reptilian* portion and nature of the human brain hardware, which is programmed like a computer via the narrative systems which enables the person to allow for such extreme death narratives to exist in their/our world; while the other *light side* exists and even makes up the entirety of the unadulterated living-soul!

The intrinsic nature of all created souls is to feel and produce only good and life. It is, therefore, the imperfect, reformatted state of our physicality which they created, that forces the confusion within. *As within, so without!*

Therefore, no matter how real this false heaven matrix feels to the multitudes of NDE and PLR subjects, they are <u>not</u> feeling perfect love and equality because the Eternal Creator's presence is literally there helping the Archons. He is NOT! They are feeling that because that is all the created living-soul-portion is able to know or feel in that pure unadulterated *Light-body* condition. The rest is merely a holographic design matrix invented and formed to play the arrangements each person/soul has been programmed to expect after being immersed and infused with the *Adam-Eden* matrix narratives each soul assimilated, *below.*

I want to go home!

Amazingly, as witnessed and documented in film by researchers such as Mr. Richard Martini, Dr. Bruce Grayson of the *Virginia Near Death Institute* (Martini)*, the Los Angeles Institute of Near-Death Studies* (Greyson)*,* and others, many thousands of past-life regression sessions have been recorded with people expressing, *(while in this alleged heaven matrix), saying* - "I want to go home!" Yes! You are now having the same reaction to that request as most researchers express to have had.

I, however, felt I knew immediately why the subjects are expressing this seemingly odd request while Re-experiencing this alleged *heaven.*

From my own research on this particular and peculiar point, I found that the researchers invariably all asked the same question of their regression subjects – *"What do you mean you want to go home; do you mean back to earth?"* – With the subjects' answers only seeming to be again repeated, "I want to go home". Admittedly, so far all of these excellent and highly professional researchers all remain stymied by their many subjects request <u>to return home</u>.

Although many within the material sciences continue to dismiss the accounts of NDE and PLR research and their subjects, I state again that by their sheer numbers and the geographic separation of the subjects in so many experiments, that these findings by the laws of probability alone hold up at least equally as well as anything believed to be provable in Physics. I remain curious however at the inability of these NDE and PLR researchers to understand why these souls are making this request. This is exactly why science and ancient knowledge must be correlated to gain a far clearer understanding of events.

Every soul knows the way home

"I want to go home"! The majority of the subjects are expressing this request for one very specific, and very real reason; *because the soul knows who its father is and where its home is.* What is so clear and unmistakable to me seems to elude these professional researchers. It proves that they are stuck in their own new scientific paradigm. The illusion of my previous milk bottle example!

Clearly, the place all these souls find themselves in is not the real heaven, and these souls, all souls, will quickly perceive the thin veil of subterfuge put on by the Archon rebel slave masters.

The trick is that false light that pulls us, not unlike the animals we force through chutes here on earth, driving us to their false heaven way station corral, and ultimately into another live birth event.

To me, this single utterance from so many people only confirmed what I always knew. *That all we are, and all that our souls feel comes from the original source - The Prime Eternal Creator source.* Our original state, our *uncovered, naked* light bodies always reflect the character of His image!

Their false heaven charade, however, reminds me of the phrase uttered in contempt by the prophet Jesus when he called those Archon affiliated Pharisee henchmen, *"White washed tombstones".* Their false heaven construct outwardly gives the appearance of a heaven experience, it, however, has no righteous substance, and thus, all souls eventually intuit that they are <u>not truly</u> <u>HOME</u>! *At which point they begin to lament and start requesting that they be allowed to go home!*

Unfortunately for them, by that time they have already <u>consented</u> to yet another cycle of imprisonment. It is all quite heartbreaking once it truly sinks in. They can have no such believable heaven construct without the perfect goodness and light of our Micro-souls providing the most needed and coveted element for them to use against us; the *light, love,* and *equality* of our soul's <u>intention</u> as provided by the Eternal Creators perfect character, and via His *eternal tether.*

Recapping, assimilate this, that virtually all the systems of this earth have been devised and set into place to control the thoughts – *i.e. Conscious and unconscious intentions that become literally projected outward by our living-soul, causing our physical circumstances to exist.* These *narrative paths* passively redirect and ultimately control our soul's *intentions* individually and cumulatively in order to literally create the eventual earthly environment that the Archon's wish to convey, *without having to strip free will to do so*. All occurring in real time - *by way of deception.*

As you have also come to understand, this world reality is only one-half of the total soul control system. I hope now that you recognize all source religions, superstitions, and governmental hierarchy narratives, to name but a few *main path narratives*, which also have many *tributary narrative paths,* as being designed to breed negativity in many subtle, and sometimes not so subtle ways.

All perpetuated systems of enslavement, both for the physical as well as the eternal living- soul and in a cyclic fashion – *As above, so below.* As already reported and depicted herein to be a most amazing and important byproduct of so many NDE and PLR people/souls, *is that misunderstood request to return them home!*

This is now your second proof of the reformatted holoverse delusion. *The realization of the false control narratives being the first*

Grandma is that you?

As expressed earlier, after the soul experiences the tractor-beam of their *light-love tunnel,* many of those experiencing NDE's, PLR or OBE's – (Out of body experiences), recall either meeting or being greeted by some familiar personality. Often this personification is either identified as a known religious figure common to their previously consented to and assimilated system of belief, or a prominent beloved family member. This should raise all kinds of red flags considering that most of the world's religions tend to tout being the one true religion, and the only way to heaven.

In addition, and not to point out the obvious, but if that religious persona or family member *soul-greeter* passed on, leaving their earthly physicality turned to dust, then how is it that the subject-soul *recognizes* the deceased loved one or other personality *Soul-Greeter,* by appearance?

Due to the confirming details of NDE's, PLR's and OBE's, there is no doubt that the experiences took place. So what are all the differing personalities doing in these occurrences? And why are they required to "usher you in" the rest of the way?

Remember, our Souls CONSENT is always required!

Many doctors and scientists tend to cite their assumption of mere hallucinations as the loophole to explain away these numerically superior incidents. Certainly, the fact that so many adults and also children are able to recite details from the operating room and during other incidents concerning locations they have never seen, hearing and recalling very specific things people said, most citing information that they never knew previously, as well as specific historical data, etc., should at the very least give great pause. Again, we are no longer speaking about or considering these events based on 100 cases or even 2000 cases, but many thousands of scientifically documented cases which force the mathematical probability to confirm these as not simply being figments of a patient or subject's imagination, nor chemically induced hallucinations. Therefore, we must consider more thoughtfully how these recognizable figures appeared to those having the past life memory or out of body experience. If one's favorite family member no longer has a physical form but moved on to their – *Soul-light-body* form, then why would we see their former physical appearance?

Better yet, and even more compelling, is that there is no way to know what an honored religious figure's true appearance really was!

So, if it is truly "GODS" system, *ostensibly designed to lessen the impact of death and the souls' separation from the body as so many apologists would have us believe,* then how does it help to show me or you the form of a figure we could never identify? More importantly, why would we even believe it to be them?

Would it not then be more prudent to conclude that the figment being viewed is really a *conjured apparition produced by them to meet the expectation of the souls previously assimilated paradigm, in order to gain consent to entry more easily?*

Easy to recognize why they would need it, and gives added credence to another puzzle piece of the Archons' *soul deception system.* Another angle to play for *consent!*

The Life Review!

This particular event which virtually all near-death experiencers and past life regression subjects reiterate in great detail is yet another strange piece of this puzzle. Yet before I get into such ancient esoteric knowledge, I believe I need to ask a couple of pointed questions.

- Why a past life review?
- Who does it help?

Always remembering to *follow the money,* we should remember to ask throughout – *who does it help?* Considering the vast recorded data involving past life review subjects and near death depictions, we discover that the majority of these individuals presenting their experiences encounter a <u>life review process</u>.

As previously mentioned this process is often reported as occurring after meeting up with the familiar *soul-greeter* personification. As explained to researchers by their NDE and PLR subjects, the life review process is a *mandatory feature* of this heaven construct. Additionally, in many cases, they even depict themselves as being coerced or even forced to partake. *I, therefore, posit, that at this point, since the soul has now* consented *to follow their alleged soul-greeter inside, by* <u>consent</u> *the Archon system has now gained adverse jurisdiction and possession of that souls free will; to which they can now be ushered through the rest of their system levels, and out again!*

Many subjects have even recounted that an actual *contract* of sorts was required to be fulfilled by that soul for some *previously contracted return trip!* However, no evidence of any previous contract is provided to them or spoken of.

> *I would also like to point out that even the suggestion of such a worldly and pedestrian mechanism as a soul-contract being used in heaven is beyond preposterous, and in my mind yet another proof of their false heaven construct.*

While other's report another processing step whereby they plan their next incarnation during this same *end of life* event. How could anyone believe any of this to be the way of a truly enlightened super-Eternal-Creator power? To logically answer this question, how about we use the tried and true method of following the money?

- Why would we need to watch a life review of how we adversely impacted others if we have NOW made it to the real Heaven?

Where is the forgiveness in that? *And;*

- If you have truly *"returned"* to The Eternal Creator by one or all of the prescribed methods...pick one, is this not proof we are already forgiven?

I mean your soul is not returning to this earthly existence, right; so why dwell on the past in heaven if *redemptive* perfection has now been reached?

If all the human soul feels, and is capable of giving out is *pure love* and *equality* as most of these NDE and PLR subject souls recall, why would the alleged god, and/or His alleged *light-worker-soul-guides,* require our souls to view such negativity?

This, in and of itself, is more than a bit questionable; and that which makes this all the more suspect is how the vast majority of PLR participants state that both their *soul-guides,* and the alleged *council of elders,* at one point express to the souls that they can remain there as long as they wish, only to then later strongly urge them to return to earth, *i.e. to be reborn, 'in order to "aid" those that they affected in life along with others.'* Naturally, since this all sounds so altruistic, what soul could resist right? Well, isn't that exactly the point? These Archon rebels know the pure attributes of the perfected soul and its vulnerable naivety. *Moreover,* is that not exactly what got us all here in the first place? They are excruciatingly aware of the best manipulation methods to repeatedly reacquire our will by consent.

So far it appears that this entire Life-review process is a narrative based manipulation designed to be used to manage and control the soul's repeatable rebirth process by associating and attributing guilt.

Contradictions

Another reoccurring characteristic of the false heaven-matrix event is the conflicting communication presented by these alleged soul-guides and special council members. As previously mentioned, after the soul's life-review, it is lead to believe that they may remain in this heavenly existence. However, on the other hand as reported by most NDE and PLR subject accounts, passive-aggressive coercive language based on the earlier data extrapolated from their *life-review* process is used to persuade the souls return to earth in order for them to <u>assist others</u>. Ostensibly with the new wisdom and knowledge derived from their *soul classes.* Again, appearing to be exceedingly manipulative as this guilt trip scenario eventually becomes too much for any unassuming soul to bear. Based on the sheer number of these past life regression accounts who reiterate all these specific and unified details, the false heaven way-station theory is rapidly moving from theory to a strong hypothesis.

*"If it can be shown that an incorporeal and reasonable being has life in itself <u>independently of the body</u> and <u>that it is worse off in the body than out of it</u>, then beyond a doubt bodies are only of secondary importance and arise from time to time to meet the varying conditions of reasonable creatures. Those who require bodies **are clothed** with them <u>and contrariwise when fallen souls</u>*

have lifted themselves up to better things their bodies are once more annihilated. They are thus ever vanishing and ever reappearing. **Origen, from A Select Library of the Nicene and Post-Nicene Fathers of the Christian Church, P. Schaff and H. Wace editors** (Schaff): *Emphasis added.*

"By some inclination toward evil, certain spirit-souls come into bodies, first of men; then, due to their association with the irrational passions after the allotted span of human life, they are changed into beasts, from which they sink to the level of plants.
From this condition, they rise again through the same stages and are restored to their heavenly place. **Origen, On First Principles, B. W. Butterworth, translator."** (Walker) *Emphasis added.*

Origen's *truth* crucified

According to the Encyclopedia Britannica, *Origen* (C.E. 185-254) was the most prominent, distinguished and most influential Christian of the early church fathers. Christians today would do well to consider the enormity of this statement, and thus take the rest of his viewpoints on the subject at hand more seriously. The *Encyclopedia Britannica* also declares that he was the most prolific writer and theologian of early Christianity, his works numbering around 6,000!

The *Encyclopedia Britannica* also describes *Origen* as both a *Neo-Platonist* and a *Gnostic. Emperor Justinian* wrote a letter to the Patriarch of Constantinople naming *Origen* as the most *pernicious of heretics* – basically saying that no man alive was worse than Origen. That's saying something.

Justinian convened a synod at Constantinople in 543 C.E. which issued an edict refuting *Origen's* teachings, _especially concerning reincarnation,_ which was a long-held belief brought forward by their Hebrew roots that the later Papacy worked hard to stamp out.

Pope Vigilius opposed the edict, but then some years later reversed his decision to side with Origen; forced by political pressure no doubt. *Justinian* later called for a meeting of the entire Church in 553 C.E. known as the *Fifth Ecumenical Council or the Second Council* of *Constantinople,* and in short, after fourteen *anathemas,* that was the end of *Origen* and a long list of other alleged heretics. History has judged *Emperor Justinian* to be a shallow-minded opportunist, lacking in wisdom, insight, and integrity. As all narcissistic, sociopath, Archon led dictators tend to be.

Despite the fact that the early Christian teachings embraced reincarnation, as dictated from their original Hebrew roots, the later New Testament narrative evolved to not only include a *one life to live* narrative tributary, but also injected and promotes a new *life-review process* for all souls before the "Bema" (judgment) seat of their Christ deity as well. The logical question that comes to mind then is, *if Christians are covered by the human sacrificial blood atonement system for their alleged sins, also clearly teaching that those sins are then forgotten, then why would they be in need of a soul review process to judge their lives?* Did the sacrifice not do the job once and for all as their *narrative* also touts? And what of the other five billion plus non-Christians, and all those who have lived in previous generations, do those souls just disappear? Of course not, we have several other hell and purgatory narratives to cover them. To be sure we cannot blame the more ancient Hebrew story for any such divisive narratives since *none of the above narratives so far has ever been found within any Hebrew text or cultural belief.*

Some might attempt to point to the later Levitical law narrative as an origination point to the later Christian sacrificial narrative to prove my statement incorrect, however as I prove clearly in my earlier works, those are known to be from later Babylonian-Jewish interjections. May I remind that the original Hebrew instruction of (Teshuvah = Return) as clearly found throughout the Hebrew prophets, leads souls back to the original path *by a contrite heart and prayer* and life reversal back to the Prime Creators *Everlasting Agreement. It is all that was ever asked for or required; in and of itself de facto proof that an "original" way or narrative for souls to "return" has always existed.*

Thus, by many generations of negative narrative overlays, the one original and simple positive narrative remained mostly hidden, but by no means impossible to find. Thereby, through the consent of those governed by liars, the majority continued to consent to and assimilate the lie, giving up their power to it.

The life review - Who does it help?

If we keep an open mind as I have asked, and for now agree that nearly all of the earthly governmental and religious systems with their vast array of subsystems have been designed to control people's beliefs while here within the *physical*, as well as the *hereafter* by our;

Consent to entering their:
- Life-review process
- Soul classes, *and,*
- The influencing of altruistic behavior for return

All seemingly designed to one end, which is to get all souls returned and rebirthed back into their AE-matrix.

It should also be a question to whether these Archon captors utilize true, or possibly even false past-life memories for their coercive argument in order to influence all souls to make the return trip.

As for the larger question looming; *who is truly aided by all this,* I will get into the ideas of what several ancient peoples have to say concerning the Archon's *energy-wraith* like interactions with us, as well as my understanding of what the far more ancient texts of Enoch have to lend to the discussion.

Advancing without Memory?

Where is the logic in that? How do we teach our children? How do we teach anyone anything? By *repetition to ensure memory* so that long-term synaptic connections can be made for later recall.

Why do we study towards being able to recall all manner of knowledge? Obviously, so we may "AID" others and ourselves to advance during our lifetime.

We can all agree then, that *memory* is the main function that allows any civilization to exist, much less expand and evolve technologically. Conversely, the *lack* of memory would create the negative and opposite effect. Clearly, we all know this, however, this painfully obvious point is presented here to show that *we never teach any intelligent creation, human or animal, with the understanding that they will not have the ability to retain or recall the learned information afterward.* Obviously, if this were the case with all sentient beings, especially humans, there would never be any progress whatsoever.

Therefore, we all agree that MEMORY just may be the most important attribute of all. It sounds ridiculous to postulate that any god or creative entity would purposely wipe all previously learned memories from their creation at any time, as this would be counterproductive for that creation on an epic level. Who would even think of doing such a thing to anyone, much less our own children? Which then forces me to ask, if we mere mortals wouldn't even consider doing such a thing to our own children, would the true loving creator do such a thing to His children?

To point to something that most people reading this book might connect with; is this not similar to the ancient Hebrew concept that the prophet Jesus later spoke concerning a man *asking, seeking and knocking?* Or, *if your son asks for a loaf of bread would you give him a stone?* Isn't that what we are seeing here? *To learn for a lifetime and many lifetimes to form vast memories for recall, to then have it stripped away by those alleged gods and angelic servants before they return your soul back into this controlled medium!* At the same time while in their heaven matrix our souls being taught and coerced into using that new knowledge to aid those you allegedly harmed, and or humanity in general?

Yes, I tend to believe certain few human sycophants of these Archon's are allowed to retain vast memory stores throughout additional lifetimes, but not at all for the betterment of this creation, no! But to continue its reformation!

How are we able to aid anyone if we retain no memory of it?

We cannot! It is all contradiction and lies! Nothing more.

Where do YOU see the evidence of all this altruistic wisdom being provided on an ongoing basis since our beginnings? Surely history does not prove this out!

Even if you do not believe in any single primary creator force and keep all your eggs in one science only basket, you still have a huge problem when our most recent quantum and biological physics concerning the eternal soul and human DNA is all taken into account in truth, and void of any personal paradigm. The end result is the same, the ancient spiritual information and understanding parallels and helps us to prove out the modern scientific.

As well, you will see in another chapter how quantum physics is proving the definitions and work of both the ego and the soul, specifying that –

Without memory, there can be no perception, and without perception, there can be no memory, *they are reliant!*

Therefore, _memory must always exist and be allowed to continue forward intact to ensure our ability to thrive,_ make a better existence in any physical or non-physical form, much less advance towards greater enlightenment.

The short of it on this point concerning the absolute requirement for any individual person or soul to be of any aid whatsoever to anyone else, much less any civilization or the entire planet, **is our infinite need for "memory recall!"** No memory, no aid, no amelioration.

Without memory of even the most basic of topics no person or soul anywhere, under any conditions, can be of any assistance to themselves or anyone else, much less to advance a civilization. To believe the opposite of this to be valid on earth or in heaven is pure folly, and this *memory wipe* point will be used to prove beyond doubt

Page | 211

the fictitious nature of the Archon rebellions' false *heaven-earth soul matrix,* and our captivity in it until we consent to returning!

Soul School Classes?

As I just previously touched on about the absolute need for retained memories for the numerous and most obvious reasons, and in conjunction with the knowledge that some type of *memory wipe* mechanism is employed, another major point of contradiction must be exposed.

As one will notice when delving into the multitude of NDE and PLR participants' personal accounts, another minor supporting narrative line emerges, the *"lessons from heaven"* or *"Soul-School classes"*. Upon the hearing of this particular widespread experience among many thousands of participants, one should notice that their story details tend to be totally void of what I personally consider being the most important details. No details are provided, and interestingly enough I have not found many of the researchers asking for them. This missing detail concerns what these souls allegedly *learned* in these classes! As I remain amazed at the lack of detail provided on this narrative subset, I was also elated because I knew I had just been provided some of the best evidence against this false heaven construct being real, much less having been created by the true Primary Creator.

So very few comparatively are ever able to remember details of any former life experience. Since scientists and researchers have been studying this topic, the few *by comparison to our population whole,* who have any recall to speak of are mostly children under the age of 10. To my knowledge thus far, none of those children, who actually remembered any details from their latest past life, have *aided* anyone or mankind in any substantial way with the knowledge of their memories.

However, considering all the thousands of verified NDE and PLR reports, and despite their *soul-guides* aggrandizing platitudes of how they will aid others with said wisdom, it all tends to peter out down here because the retained memories are so few and mostly unimportant. So, is "god" just winging it up there until he gets it all figured out? Or is all this alleged heavenly procedure looking more like just a techno-movie set, fabricated to move unwitting souls along and back into the bondage of physicality and their controlled narrative world system? We cannot have it both ways, it is either real and seriously fouled up, or it is fake!

Why take classes on subjects that no one thus far has any specific memory of? Yet, almost all of the many NDE and PLR subjects speak of *learning lessons* while in the heaven-station. I should also add here that some subjects report not only one time in the heaven matrix but several times, each time they are given added lessons to allegedly use to aid humanity upon their soul's return. Yet thus far, none disclose or recall what topics the classes cover or why.

Now, logically it would seem that if "god" and his minions of helpers were teaching your soul new information, that there might be a corresponding, tangible reason for learning it.

Something from this utterly important learning system would have to appear quantifiable by this time! One might also question the justification for acquiring this additional *aid* knowledge when research continues to show that some subjects experienced return trips to the heaven way-station and acquiring more knowledge while there, only to be returned to earth with no memory of additional specific knowledge or great wisdom. It is all quite tiring really.

Where is all the memory going?

Continuing on this path, since we may understand that all of us alive right now have been reborn one or thousands of times to date, ostensibly for the purpose of helping humanity; *to which I point out we have been doing an abysmal job so far;* then why has the great majority of souls/people, throughout all generations, retained no groundbreaking memories to that end? So, let's get this straight, shall we?

Upon our arrival, feeling all manner of perfect love surrounding us, we are immediately infused with the guilt of all the bad things we did to people in our life, via their *life-review* process.

Personally, I would think any soul who in life lived with a Jewish or Catholic mother should be sufficiently hardened, and remain unaffected by this guilt process! Therefore it would appear this guilt-laden process has been created to soften up the soul and set the ground work for the rest to come.

The soul-school is alleged to give specific knowledge and understanding to all souls so that those souls who *consent to return, whether they want to or not* - will have the required tools to *aid* humanity.

Yes, all so altruistic. However, my question is, *'why would any soul consent to returning to this life once they have reached their perfected state and now residing in total perfection?* I believe this to be another valid question not yet considered. The true Eternal Primary Creator knows full well that I surely would not return if given the choice, and I highly doubt that I am alone in this feeling.

So, we are being forced to return!

Again I ask the reader to consider what I stated in passing just previously; that regardless of the alleged soul-school curriculum, mankind has seen no direct evidence of its aid. We can apply simple numerical probability here against the billions of souls who have passed through here generation upon generation. With that many souls nominated for this heavenly Masters program, this place should have reached beyond the ascended heights of Utopia a long time ago. Our history and our present do not reflect such ongoing altruistic aid in the forms of unknown wisdom or knowledge! We are not even close! This is where one may ask, *is there anything new under the sun yet?* Or by our modern vernacular, and from the back seat I ask – *Are we there yet?*

So then, what of these soul-school classes?

I discussed previously that many subjects stated, while in the heaven matrix, that *they <u>wanted to go home</u>*. In that vein, and quite subconsciously I might add, do not most humans at one time or another during their life continue asking that same question in another form? Once a soul recycles and finds itself back here, at some point most begin searching themselves and asking:

- Who am I?
- Why am I here? *And*
- What is my purpose during this lifetime?

Not to keep pointing out the obvious, but shouldn't all those heavenly Master's degree courses have those and many more pressing questions, covered? Alas, *no memory, no perception!*

Since humanity is in such a quandary, this leads me to again ask the question, **"Who does it help?"** The nuance here, in case you missed it, is that, within the false-heaven matrix, and then again back here in the Adam-Eden matrix, *the soul is confused* and still *seeking its "home", it's "origin place", and its "reason for being".*

More pointedly, what it is truly seeking and asking for is its **reason for being <u>here</u>!**

Try to bear in mind, that the soul knows two absolutes, which are:

- Who made it, *and*
- That an original home exists!

Of course, no souls, much less souls in physical bodies retain the memory details of those two majorly important questions above since for far too long the pile of memories we do have has been layered up high by fictitious narrative data. All expressly designed to do just that, suppress the minimal and most important truth detail which all souls carry inherently. While totally or even selectively controlling our memories in each incarnation. Thus, our most important truths about ourselves can be understood as always being on the tip of our tongue, but not yet attainable.

Rounding the process, during each lifetime on this AE-matrix the soul is confined to this purpose built *Trinity-6 carbon based body-housing,* which you now know I believe to have been *purpose built by the Archon leadership to firewall the souls total recall ability.* Housed within this purpose built physicality that restricts and suppresses all conscious recall of the soul's vast storehouse of memory; *the living-soul still laments, it pines, and it searches for its original estate.*

The soul knows it was not meant to live as we have been made to live in this *reformatted* creation, much less through a near endless multitude of physical life cycles. And through it all, we have been forced to forget why, *and even to forget that we have forgotten*! I know that many of you know exactly what I am saying here!

So clearly, the mounting circumstantial evidence continues to show us that it all aids the Archon rebels; reminding that while in their heaven way-station, the subjects tend to point out how they are told they can stay. I remind this appears to be just another contradiction.

All of their false-heaven, station-aids are window dressing. Tactics utilized to set up the understanding from the day a soul arrives, that they will be returning to the AE-matrix at some future point.

Undoubtedly, there remain unsolved issues with these soul-school classes. Not the least of them being that those souls who have attended, fail to retain the learned information when they come back to their new life cycle.

The more telling data is that this knowledge is also irretrievable even for those who undergo hypnosis. That is another major issue for me!

Last but not least, this inaccessible, allegedly studied and learned data was supposedly explicitly based on a soul's *Life-review* and taught by the *soul-guides* because it was deemed specifically necessary to be of *aid* for later use to others. **Confused yet?**

How do I know these soul-school classes are a ploy having no intent or usefulness after a soul is returned to this realm?

I know because the emphasis is on the lack of memory retention!

I do not require someone providing me with a detailed account of their past lives and/or their time spent in the false heaven matrix to know that 99.9% of all humans have no conscious memory of any other life at all! Going back to the basic logic I previously expressed about the absolute need for detailed memory in all cases to *aid* or *advance* man on any level, regardless of taking human or ethereal soul form, retention of said useful information would be required and paramount for enabling either form to be of any aid at all within any civilization. *No memory, no aid!*

This is simply proven by witnessing our progressively violent and generally destructive history, which continues unabated to this day! Therefore we must see as an honest absolute, that the memory of any past life, or all past lives, would be the much-needed tonic to man's advancement in such a system of death and rebirth - (IF) *in fact it was created by an all-loving Creator entity whose end-game was even a moderately quick transcendence to enlightenment*

Of course, there are those who force illogical arguments to make an apology for why man must endure tens of thousands of years of strife, and even through multiple epochs in order to eclipse into perfection. However, from a *theological standpoint*, a *basic logic standpoint,* and even a *scientific standpoint*, that arguments center will not hold.

I will expand this idea even further to show how inexplicitly ridiculous it is. How many lives have any of us lived to date? It could be tens of thousands for all we know. Do you remember any detail of anyone that was or ever could be of any significant *aid* to anyone or yourself? Or have most humans and their relationships remained fairly dysfunctional? I am willing to bet the latter if you are like rest of the 99.9%. *Also, I am not specifically talking about those humans who bring about eventual technological advances like a better ship hull, or microwave oven. None of that means a thing while we collectively continue to kill and destroy everyone and everything within this creation complex!* So then, we should agree that this memory loss is not a fluke is it? The only logical explanation is that it must be *a premeditated determination carried out by those in charge of the system* upon our leaving their false heaven matrix, or more likely, caused by this limited body hardware we find ourselves housed in.

So, the hypothesis thickens! Let's see if we can get this all straight.

The **Life-Review** is a *reference* tool used to lay and instill guilt. It carries with it the passive-aggressive suggestion of *aid* to others left behind, however, this *guidance* is inevitably forced so that each soul will return, getting back on the Archon's *allegedly* altruistic path.

Add to this, the *soul-school* provided as the *prop* used to bolster the understanding that the soul's eventual reentry will enable them to be a cosmic aid to all who suffered under its regime in a past life. Clear as mud?

Now here is another interesting tidbit of information I have read from NDE and PLR subjects that I touched on earlier; in nearly 100% of their after-life depictions:

- They all appear to retain the memories of their just recently past life <u>on their way in</u>to their false heaven.

Wow! Now that is interesting given all the other afterlife heaven experience details they have provided thus far. I feel this part is most interesting because, of course, *all the memory of your recent past life is totally required in order to enable them to show the incoming soul exactly what they have always yearned for, or expected to see, in the hereafter – i.e. all the assimilated narratives!*

As I covered previously, almost all Near Death Experiencers that return to tell the tale, have the same story of the *tunnel of light* in which they are first *pulled* and then led in by some recognizable *soul-greeter.* <u>All data pulled from the soul's direct memories of their recently passed life experiences and beliefs!</u> Most certainly this is technology based, with the soul's memories being extracted for instantaneous application while inside their tunnel of love.

That which you believe or love the most will be utilized as the *initial greeter and overall context causing you to consent to entering.*

Clearly, it makes sense that they allow us to keep our memories intact going in so that they can be used for us to quickly recognize someone, and gain trust in order to easily gain your consent for entering all the way! I am very confident about this point, because of all the NDE and PLR subject accounts I have read show no one retaining any memories other than when they are *coming into the system*. This shows a very selective use of our memories, and not for our gain!

So again, only certain information is seemingly used to control the soul, and the narrative the soul perceives while inside the false heaven matrix. The bottom line continues to be that upon that soul's next return trip back into this realm, *it will again have no access to its genetically induced, soul memory*. Proving in almost all cases that even their most recent past life recall will be missing, (where did it go?) We had it on the way in didn't we? So regardless what anyone would rather believe at this point about past lives or no lives, what have you, I believe, based on the subject material that even you can find and read to your hearts content, that at the VERY least your most recent life's memories were either removed during some process within that false heaven, or presently firewalled by your body-hardware. Again, who does that serve?

Here is what I have intuited thus far:

- There is no detectable proof that the Life-Review process is of any aid to the soul while inside or after leaving the heaven matrix construct, as no memory evidence is retained.
- There is no verifiable proof that the widely depicted soul-school classes are of any assistance to the soul, as no topic details or taught information has ever been available to an individual's memory recall, consciously or sub-consciously!
- There is significant contradictory data provided by thousands of subjects depicting *passive-aggressive* treatment of the soul to manipulate its inherent *love* and *equality* condition into feeling it must return to *aid* others, versus being advised at the same time that it is welcome to remain indefinitely.

- Most importantly, that almost all souls within their past-life regressions are asking to be *allowed to go home!*

This last point just may be the most misunderstood and most telling part of the entire stream of scientific afterlife discovery so far.

Allowed to go home – From what I have seen thus far this appears to remain misunderstood. To date, I have heard no credible hypothesis of what researchers believe it may mean. However, as I stated earlier, my understanding of this expression stems from:

- The soul intrinsically knowing the identity of its true creator,
- That the soul is an integral part of its creator,
- That all souls know that an original home exists,
- Additionally intuiting that they are not in it!

This is exactly why it also appears they have a need to cycle all souls from their false heaven construct, and back to earth as quickly as possible. Because they know their Rebellion façade will not hold for very long.

On the more technical side of things I have some yet unanswered questions:

1. Do the Archon enslavers use some high-technology to memory-wipe souls?

OR

2. Is the soul's memory firewalled by the human body/brain hardware interface itself?

It stands to reason that in the grand scheme of all this neither answer may change anything at all. The end result continues unabated so far, but both are interesting questions that may even be somewhat backed up by recent Quantum-Soul Physics and human DNA Biophysics discoveries. Russian biophysicist and molecular biologist *Pjotr Garjajev* (Bludorf) and his colleagues have made almost unbelievable verified progress in these fields of quantum-DNA *Soul memory*, as well as many other aspects of what the living-soul can achieve. It turns out our ancient ancestors had their folklore correct; the human soul is quite powerful and amazing in its creative ability. In that vein, we have credible and ongoing verifiable scientific proof that helps us understand why our souls might be highly prized by some other unseen, super-technologically advanced entities. And like any rare, prized commodity, may very well be worth kidnapping over and over again.

On the other hand, we have enough ancient information from varied cultures spanning many thousands of years, all of whom tend to show us that some *star beings* came and manipulated man's DNA, which again does coincide with much of the new biological physics to be the case. The human Genome Project very *incorrectly*, or possibly on purpose, stated that over 90% of our DNA was literally, and I quote - "Junk DNA".

However, we have a multitude of Russian and other countries' scientists, who did not take that ridiculous conclusion for an answer, but went on to prove this alleged junk DNA to be the *receptors that collect emotional life information and transfer that information as permanently stored memories within the soul.*

That is a far cry from categorizing it all as mere junk! Most genome scientists do seem to agree that there are certain major portions of our DNA appearing to exist for specific important reasons, however for some unknown rationale they have been turned off. This can easily be correlated with our ancient historical texts and folklore, which depict an alien race of beings augmenting the human genome for their own purposes, (reformatting in their image), however, and let me be clear here, I do NOT believe this to be the work of any *alien* beings as most people understand that term to mean. As I stated previously in another chapter, they created these *Trinity-6* physical bodies, which also means they must have created *other* types of physical bodies for other purposes. One purpose for that might be to have *cut-outs*, *i.e.* other physical entities used to interface with our own in order to keep the few Archons out of our realm and our sight.

Moreover, can I postulate that one of the purposes of shutting down DNA *codons* is to *firewall* the human souls quantum memory capability? I would have to concur that it very well may be exactly that, for the mere reason that none of us retain those quantum memories consciously. This makes them nearly useless in any one lifetime, which adds up to all life time's thus far, does it not? One outstanding source for the layperson to gain fabulous information on human DNA and the soul is from, Dr. Amit Goswami Ph.D. - (Physics of the Soul 2001 & Quantum Creativity 2014) (Goswami).

Thus far, in this hypothesis of the Archon Rebellion *earth and heaven matrix,* I identify that it is either technology between the two matrix constructs in which our soul is forced through that wipes the memories, or it is the human body construct that was created in such a specific way as to be used to firewall our much needed and powerful quantum memories; or possibly both work together in tandem. Either way, the soul is unable to retrieve the valuable memories necessary to drive great enlightenment in this current physical form. As I keep asking, "What is the purpose of that?"

If the soul is on a journey then how does this help in its reincarnation, much less eventual total ascension?

As you have already read in my chapter entitled *The Holoverse, Niels Bohr,* a Danish Physicist who made significant contributions to understanding atomic structure and quantum theory, as well as many others who have now stood on his shoulders, have not only theorized, but now proven, that our physical material reality isn't really physical at all.

"A fundamental conclusion of the new physics also acknowledges that <u>the observer creates the reality</u>. As observers, we are personally involved with the creation of our own reality. Physicists are being forced to admit that the universe is a "mental" construction. Pioneering physicist Sir James Jeans wrote: "The stream of knowledge is heading toward a non-mechanical reality; the universe begins to look <u>more like a great thought</u> than like a great machine. Mind no longer appears to be an accidental intruder into the realm of matter, we ought rather hail it as the creator and governor of the realm of matter."
(R. C. Henry, "The Mental Universe"; Nature 436:29, 2005) (Henry) *Emphasis added.*

We can no longer ignore the fact that our *beliefs, perceptions,* and *attitudes* (consciousness) create the world we actually see and feel! Being constantly *projected* via our *intention* and driven outward into *being* reality by all three.

Get over it and accept the inarguable conclusion. The universe is *immaterial-mental and spiritual,* exactly as all our varied cultural messiah figures told us it was. It is just now that some of us within the academic field of ancient religious and cultural studies, who are also able to understand the sciences, are able to correlate and show people more clearly what these ancient wise men were attempting to express when conversing with people who were so technologically unsophisticated. Even today our modern masses still misunderstand the same.

Our high sciences have now proven in their special way, that our souls are in fact the **microcosm-soul** portion from the Eternal Primary Creator's **Macro-Soul**, just as I have been teaching for many years now.

Thus by default, the Eternal Creator being primarily a *Creative* force, would establish His offspring as well to be creative and powerful forces unto themselves. In truth, it can be understood in no other way outside of completely dismissing the entirety of it all, which only leads us back around again to the same questions I started with concerning this entire widespread detailed heaven experience - *Where is it coming from and by whom?* All the while this world and its new Adam-Eden matrix moves formidably against us to quell such macro knowledge and understanding!

If the Prime Eternal Creator is literally *in us* as most cultures and religious dogmas commonly believe, then we are NOT as a reflection of Him as THIS creation matrix is an *opposite reflection image* of His other Heaven levels; but our *living-souls* are in fact a direct *whole portion* of His Macro-Whole! NOT an *image* of that original Eternal Prime Creator – Our Souls are a 100% *"whole within the part"*. A "micro-soul-portion", but always a whole.

Is it then so difficult to understand that somewhere out there may be some malevolent entities who look to supersede and utilize this awesome creative soul-force to their own end? It stands to reason and logic that we should at least consider all of our ancient myths and biblical anti-god entities in this new light, rather than continue to understand their nature from the contrived narrative provided to all man by the Archon religious narrative systems.

The Love

When does love manipulate, condemn, or control? When does love keep you in the dark, the unknown, or fool you? *By definition, love does none of these things.* As I have previously pointed out, the *pretense* of love which is the primary natural condition of all souls, and truly a most powerful strength provided to us through the Primary Eternal Creator force, is being *gamed and manipulated* as a weakness. The viability of this statement is and has been available to us even through our shared ancient stories of the first Man and Woman within the garden called Eden. It is evident there, that *"those"* original ethereal *light-body, souls,* were eventually approached by some other entity or entities, naive and trusting we were quickly fixated, and quite easily steered to <u>consent</u> to another narrative.

As I harp on through this book, they/we consented to be enslaved by said entities who continue to game the Primary Creator's original system of Free-Will, leading all souls/people in all generations since that time away from our original lifestyle and role. No matter whether one wishes to believe that the true Prime Eternal Creator did, in fact, create this creation here as it stands today, crushed by the disobedience and fall of only two people, causing all of us to remain tainted since then; or whether you are able to take personal responsibility for the second and more likely scenario - *that we, our multitude of souls were the ones who somehow became enchanted by the words and ideas of other entities who we consented to following, thus rejecting the original law of our creator as they did, which led to our participation and separation for a time;* either way the final outcome remains nearly exactly the same; separation for disobedience!

Breaking out of the Matrix!

So by now you must be wondering. If this hypothesis of the earth *Adam-Eden* prison planet, working in tandem with their false heaven-matrix as a perpetual soul enslavement system, all geared to make us all believe we are free and in lock-step with our Primary Creator's Will; *then how can we possibly break their hold in any lifetime?* Good question!

Like any good tactician, we might look at using their system against them wherever possible, and to do so one would have to know all the main mechanisms used to entrap and retain our souls after any lifetime.

To recap on the information detail that many researchers have gleaned thus far from past-life regression studies and near death experiences, it appears we at least have the following recurring themes:

- Our souls sighting of the love-tunnel
- Our being pulled toward that tunnel construct
- The expanding light trick at the end of the tunnel
- Our awareness of all retained recent life memory
- Our identification of known personalities - greeters
- The immediate Life-Review process
- Meeting our soul guide
- Meeting of the council of elders
- The Soul-school classes
- The vigorous prompting to return to earth life

It would appear to me that of these major points provided by most NDE and PLR subjects, the most useful to us might be the *retained recent life memories*. As I pointed out earlier, it stands to reason that if we retain all of our most influential details from the life we just left, that by assimilating and emotionally capturing the *corrected* narrative understandings, the Archon's system will have nothing useful to extrapolate from our souls!

Corrected narratives <u>pre-positioned and burrowed deeply within our subconscious-living-soul by an emotional embrace of those corrected narratives</u>. That these *corrected narratives* will be the dominant spiritual infrastructure in which our soul is easily able to project and utilize <u>*as a shield against the powerful attraction laid out by the Archon false heaven system*</u>. *If in fact, they are even able to do so to you at that point!*

Does it not make total sense, that if these *life-assimilated false narratives* are the main tool which they count on us retaining for their eventual use against us, *that the opposite is also true?* That in fact once you spend your life assimilating *only life-affirming narratives,* for all lives to live life abundantly and without outside interference, much less oppression from others; that in fact these true Creator character narratives cannot at all be used to that evil end when we pass over - *Seeing the importance yet?*

Amazing how the Tibetan book of the dead orbits their culture around spending a lifetime learning <u>*how to die and remain conscious of what they learned previously while in our soul body form*</u>. Additionally, they also teach that there are <u>*two lights*</u> one can be directed to upon leaving the body, stipulating one over the other.

Which is why many spend a lifetime assimilating what they perceive to be the correct narrative so that their souls can move on to the true heavenly realm, rather than falling prey yet again to the false light.

Before moving on I want to clarify my nomenclature where it concerns the three types of near death experience accounts I keep seeing.

Type-1a are the NDE & PLR accounts from the great majority of people-souls who return to tell their tale. I tend to believe that all Type-1a and 1b's *are a direct product of the Archon false heaven system*. As I have mentioned many times now, the type-1 descriptions of that heaven matrix, although usually tailored to some degree for each soul, all provide nearly exact detail context each time. Most of which I have already covered herein.

Type-1b as you will see in the final two *life-after-death* accounts to come are what I deem to be a variation on the majority *Type-1a* experience. This **1b** experience in most cases does not appear to exhibit the same *heavenly* attributes as experienced by the majority coming out of the false heaven *Type-1a* experiencer.

The variation is, that these **1b** subjects experience a high level of past-life and death memory recall, which is unlike virtually all the other Type-1a accounts. *Type-1b = Rebirth-Recall-Experience-*(RRE's).

Type-2 is a far simpler heaven experience, and in most cases missing most, if not all of the complex context details found in most type-1a cases. Here is a list to help differentiate between them as you encounter the T-1a & 1b NDE and PLR accounts vs. the type-2:

TYPE-2 Experience attributes:

- No experience of being pulled into a tunnel w/light
- No past life review process
- No soul school classes
- No soul guide
- No council of elders or judgment sessions
- No contradicting promises made – *You can stay, but must go back...etc.*
- No guilt trip prodding for their soul to return to aid others
- No localized experience – *Seeing their body, others around them, etc.*

Typical Type-1a NDE

The following recent NDE experience which occurred prior to this Jewish boys retelling of it at a Jewish school in Jerusalem in November of 2015, is a very good recent example of the Archon heaven systems intervention and staging. Although many non-Jewish people reading this may not immediately understand just how specifically tailored his experience was for him, and within the context of Judaism specifically, I assure you it is. Just as it will be specifically tailored for each individual departing soul.

If we go by this boys experience alone, as they would have us do, then all the peoples of this world, *all souls,* will be judged by former Babylonian-Jewish rabbis. I have added *bold* and *underlined* texts to point out specific similarities that I have mentioned thus far. As well as some English definitions to certain Hebrew words and expressions that they used, for clarity. Also adding my own comments. The mildly *"corrected for English"* transcript of his experience below is approximately one-half of the entire video content. The rest is mostly a question and answer period of reiteration, as well as his correlations to Hebrew, prophesies which provide no new content or context.

I decided to provide this transcript space in this book for the sole purpose of providing the reader a very new NDE account which depicts my points clearly on how they create the scenario that you will expect. If you wish to sit through the entire video of this child's presentation, the video *URL* will be added to the end.

What we *expect* is what we get!

Rabbi speaking - Morai V' Rabotai; Rabbi Yehuda called me and asked me to come here every Sukkot and Pesach to give a lesson. I prepared something about the Mashiach. The young man sitting on my right, his name is Natan, is not from Jerusalem. I will begin with an introduction, and say he went through a very difficult experience – *(NDE),* and in a moment he will relate here what he saw and what messages he received. What is difficult for the public to understand, what is hard to understand and hear is that he is only 15 years old. And when the soul leaves the body it can receive huge amounts of information in just minutes. That means, that what takes years for a person here in this world to learn, there, in that world, one can know and understand within a matter of minutes - everything. So he has a lot to tell, it's hard for him to tell it, he also doesn't have the exact words to describe what he experienced in all cases. Because they aren't things related to this world at all. And since yesterday, I have been sitting with him, and encouraging him, and gleaning information from him. And little by little you see that he knows a lot of things. So I will cut short his work a little bit, and his speech, and begin by saying this: He is not a resident of Jerusalem, on Monday, the 15th of Tishrei this week, on the first day of Sukkot, he went with his mother to be a guest of his uncle in Modi'im. In the afternoon, he felt himself begin to shiver. He felt cold in his legs and arms. He thought he needed to rest. He went to lay down and rest. And then, what happened after that we will let him continue relating what happened because it was him. He felt like he left his body, exiting through his nose, and at first floated above himself, and at first didn't understand or know who he was. Where his "self" was. The self that is lying there on the bed, or the self that is floating here above. Shall we begin, Natan?

Natan speaking - Yes, So what Happened is like this, first of all, I was very sick that day. And the day before that I also was dizzy. What happened was that I simply fainted the day before. Now, on Monday afternoon, I also didn't feel well, and my whole body was shaking and all. I simply went to rest, I got in bed and covered myself with a blanket because I was really cold. I don't know how to explain it. My whole body was shivering and I was in a lot of pain. I simply felt like I suddenly left my body and then I saw myself in bed. I was simply two meters above my bed. And I didn't understand if that was me there, here? -or, who was the one above my bed. And I wasn't able to understand it. So what happened was, I started to float like I am going up in the air without and elevator. And I rose up and left the room, and I went higher and higher and higher.

Should I keep telling the story? **Rabbi says: Yes**

So yes, I kept going up, and then I saw planet earth from above. And I kept going higher and higher. And then what happened was - I don't know how to explain it...Suddenly out of nowhere, **I entered a sort of tunnel**, really huge, and I see at the end of the tunnel **a very small light**. And then I was in the tunnel. I don't know how to explain it. There were like these circles and more circles, and inside you see lots and lots of souls. And then I simply started walking, and the light got bigger and bigger, and finally you reach that light. And that light - I don't know how to explain it - **It was good. You feel safe, and love**—it's impossible to explain such a thing.

Rabbi speaking: Is there any example in this world of a light like that? Can you compare the light you saw to anything that is in this world?
Natan: No it is impossible! You can't explain it. You can't explain it. I don't know. And it was like **the light simply spoke with me**. Like it didn't say words. **It was like telepathy.** You understand it's talking to you, and asking you questions. It asked me if I wanted to die. I understood that if I crossed the line of the light – *consented* - then I wouldn't be able to go back. I understood. I answered that I didn't know. I had no idea what to do. I don't know, didn't know. And then what happened was, **I simply walked away from there.** Suddenly I entered a hall. A huge hall. Huge, huge, gigantic,

gigantic, gigantic and saw there lots and lots of people. All the people were dressed in nice clothes, they were dressed very well. And I saw myself. And I was wearing torn clothing, **soiled with blood**. I felt very ashamed. And all the people were there for me, and they were happy, and they applauded me and everything. And I entered the hall. <u>I also saw Rabbi Ovadia Yosef</u>, and he shook my hand. I saw him there and I saw a lot of other people I know who died. Lots and lots of people, also those I didn't know. So I was in that big hall, and what happened to me was, I simply went inside and there was a high stage. And on the stage were these three lights. There was a very high light, which was the middle one. And on the right side was a small light and on the left side a small light.

Rabbi: What were those lights?

Natan: They were like...somebody testifying about you. The light on the right relates to the bad things you did, and the light on the left relates to the good things you did.

Rabbi: It was a court there?

Natan: Yes

Rabbi: And do you know who was presiding over the court, who were the judges?

Natan: Yes there was - <u>Rabbi Ovadio Yosef - who was the head of the Judges</u>

Rabbi: And who was with him?

Natan: I think <u>Rabbi Eliyashiv</u>

Rabbi: was Rabbi Eliyashiv with him?

Natan: Yes, yes.

Rabbi: And who was the third?

Natan: That I don't remember. I really don't remember, when I try to remember I can't.

Rabbi: And then there was a *Yetzer ha tov* and a *Yetzer hara?* = **(Good inclination & Evil inclination)**

Natan: Yes, there were the two small lights. On the right side you have *Yetzer hara*-**(evil),** and on the left side *Yetzer tov*-**(good).** And, you don't see....something. You see this kind of light. And you know you know what it is. You know what that light is.

Rabbi: You know on your own without being told?

Natan: Yes, You know what it is. You know what that thing is. And then suddenly- suddenly it was quiet. Suddenly all the noise that was in the hall, all the hundreds of people - it was all of a sudden silent. And then the bad light started to relate everything bad I had ever done in my life. Really, every single thing. **They are strict there about every little thing**. Every little thing you doing your life – they show it all to you. Everything, everything,

everything! It simply talked to me about everything - everything, it simply talked to me about every single second of my life. Why did you say such and such, and why this and why that? – **(This is depicting their Archon "life review" process!)**

Rabbi Transgressions?

Natan: Yes

Rabbi: And when that was said to you how did you feel?

Natan: <u>You feel ashamed.</u> <u>It's a huge embarrassment.</u> Something that can't be explained, it's a huge embarrassment, really, <u>really embarrassing</u>. <u>I felt very ashamed.</u> Because all the people are looking at you and they are showing you your life. It's really very embarrassing. And he shows you that bad things you did.....asking why did you do this and why that?

Rabbi: Until where do they show you?

Natan: Until the time when you left your body.

Rabbi: Everything? **N**: Everything! **R**: In your whole life? **N**: Every action! **R**: Even Netilat yadayim? Yes, everything? **N**: Not only that, also good deeds and transgressions. They show you every single second of your life. **R**: What you did with it? **N**: Yes exactly. And so, he tells me all the bad things I did, and everything. And then he finished speaking, and the good voice began relating all the good things I did. And then - you don't understand how much reward you receive for the smallest thing you do. Really. The feelings of shame, and everything, and then the moment he said something really, really little that I did – a little mitzvah – **(good deed)**, the littlest thing that you do is considered there to be huge –Huge! And when they said the littlest mitzvah I did, I felt like, Wow! <u>It's so great that I wore Tzit-tzit that day.</u> It's so great I did such and such...It's so great, so great! The littlest thing there overturns entire worlds. I don't know how to explain it. It's like...
- - (Netilat yadayim = Jewish ritual hand washing process) & (Tzit-tzit = Ancient Babylonian, and later Jewish tradition of wearing specifically knotted strings on clothing).

Rabbi: Reward? How do you know there is a reward for that?

Natan: You see that the moment there is a reward, they say to you "Tzaddik, Tzaddik!" All the people cheer for you "Tzaddik! Tzaddik!' And there is that light that I saw there in the beginning. The bigger the light is, means that the reward you have coming to you is bigger. -- **(Tzaddik = Great one)**

Rabbi: And regarding the transgressions, what happens?

Natan: First of all, there are people there, which are called "angels of destruction", that I saw there. They are kind of short - **They have beards**. In their eyes there is fire and they show you the transgressions you did,

everything. Every time they mention a transgression, they show you fire. And everyone shouts at you "Rasha Rasha Rasha" about everything. It is very embarrassing. It's both good and bad. I don't know how to explain it. And then what happened, is that two people took me. With wings. They simply took me and held both of my arms. They didn't really have arms. I saw everything. I saw something in front and in back. I looked... -- **(Ra'sha = wicked) – (Beards – In general always representing the orthodoxy; however I would like to bring your attention back to the** *"Raelian"* **god/creators of certain Jewish sects which I commented on earlier. They are also depicted as being short and wearing beards!)**
Rabbi: Can you see in front and in back? And also on the sides?
Natan: Yes, Also on the sides, Also ...
Rabbi: At that moment you can see everything around?
Natan: Yes, I could sense everything happening <u>to my body</u>, at that moment <u>and what was happening in the world</u>. I could sense everything that was happening in the world. -- (My sense here is that he began feeling the first responders on earth moving him to the hospital).

Video (Rabi): https://youtu.be/-H0MDGIXZ0o

Of course, everyone is welcome to believe the religious narrative that suits them. However, before people decide to stick to what they know for their various and sundry reasons, my suggestion would be to start thinking about a different path to a *corrected, basic, minimal* and *original* spiritual truth for you to assimilate with the time you have left, and hopefully, bypass the false light this time.

Type-2 NDE Encounters

I have delved into many of the key reoccurring NDE attributes that most NDE and PLR subjects tend to remember and reiterate. From research and experience thus far, these ***Type-1a*** people and the high points of their accounts as I have previously lined out, appear to be the super-majority.

As I pointed out, I believe there to be at least two other categories of those in the *minority.* They would be those having documented near death experiences that <u>do NOT</u> have all the paralleling details that we find among that great majority; and secondly, those who have thoroughly verified near total recall of their past life after being reborn into their current life. First I will give some detail of one very well-known near-death experience which I tend to see as one of the non-typical accounts. However, before I do, I want to preface them with a list of the missing *heaven* details to depict their variations to that of the majorities' details.

Revisiting the variations:
- Generally no experience of being pulled into a tunnel w/light
- No past life review process
- No soul school classes
- No soul guide perse'
- No council of elders or judgment sessions
- No contradicting promises made – *You can stay, but must go back...etc.*
- No guilt trip prodding for their soul to return to aid others
- No localized experience – *Seeing their body, others around them, etc.*

Dr. Eben Alexander's Type-2 NDE

A Spec on a butterfly's wing

Early morning on November 10, 2008, Dr. Eben Alexander III, a graduate of Harvard Medical School in Boston, Massachusetts and renowned academic neurosurgeon of 25 years, himself quickly became comatose after being stricken by a fulminant bacterial meningitis, which has only a 2% mortality rate. Totally brain dead and on a ventilator for seven days Dr. Alexander remained in a deep coma with near zero neurological function remaining. In everyone's amazement, and what afterward is now understood to be a medical miracle, while his doctors spoke to the family about stopping treatment, Dr. Alexander's eyes opened suddenly, fully aware and functional. However, as Dr. Alexander tells his story, the real miracle lies elsewhere.

While his body lay in coma Dr. Alexander journeyed beyond this world and encountered a <u>light being</u>, (a sister he never knew *existed) who communicated to him certain aspects of that alleged heavenly existence. (Previously given for adoption he never knew her).*

In that state and while in that place, Dr. Alexander remembers that he met, and spoke with, the Divine source of the universe itself.

*As much as I would love to, I cannot reprint the depth and breadth of Dr. Alexander's account in this book. The read is well advised; his book titled – **Proof of Heaven, 2012.** (Alexander)*

That being said, I will make some points which I believe tend to show that his experience did not occur in the same location as the most prevalent experience of the super-majority **Type-1.**

1. Dr. Alexander says that he first found himself totally aware and that he was swimming or traveling through some type of thick *barrier* until he reached what can only be understood as its far border. At this point, Dr. Alexander explains how the wall opened, and through it, he could see the most amazing natural setting, where it appears he is now transferred to the wing of a butterfly to make his decent.

2. On that wing, he says that he meets a beautiful woman who, without actually speaking words, tells him many things. Later, after his experience, he has an artist draw the woman, who he later finds out via the birth parents, *was his sister who died only a few years prior.* His artist picture and her real photograph which he never saw previously are nearly identical!

3. Dr. Alexander provides many more awesome details about what he saw there in his book. He heard the voice of The Creator who ultimately tells Dr. Alexander that our entire reason for being is *love & mercy!* *That THIS was all the data he needed to remember and return with,* which he has done.

Obviously, that is the highly redacted version, but ultimately what I wanted to show you *is all that is lacking* when compared to the majorities type-1 experiences. Also, if you take notice, the main context the doctor was told to leave with is the essences of the Creators *Everlasting Agreement!*

Most importantly for our overall context is this - That the good doctor <u>REMEMBERED what he was told AFTER he returned</u>!

Remember, as I have expressed repeatedly; the lack of *conscious* memory recall is proof of the subterfuge!

As far as my research has shown me thus far, I have seen the majority of NDE and PLR subjects expressing the details of all the love they felt *on their way in and through that tunnel trap*, but I have not heard anyone yet who clearly remembers being told or taught any specific details to return with, as Dr. Alexander clearly depicts.

As I said previously, *'the proof is in the soul...'* As well, the proof is also in the message! And the total lack of any message among the great and ever expanding multitude of NDE & PLR subjects is clearly showing us that we need to identify most of these as the *narrative subterfuge* they most certainly are. Can you even imagine how vastly different our history or even our modern world would be if EVERY single soul that returned to heaven, was allowed to return with even at least the absolute knowledge and *memory* that they, in fact, did speak to the Prime Eternal Creator while there, *and that he instructed them to return and live and enforce only LOVE & MERCY to all beings*? Are you kidding me? If that were the case for the majority of souls in even the last 2000 years, I would not have been so pressed to write this book or any of my books for that matter! Because this world would have long been molded into some version of utopia by now.

However, the absolute proof that I can use every single time in order to prove I am correct on this one major point is, *all of human history!*

Conscious Soul Memories!

Now that would be a logical and useful way to speed up the ascension of all living-souls! Allowing even only that small but vital bit of memory recall as presented to Dr. Alexander – *'that our entire reason for being is love & mercy!'*

Being provided to each soul on their way back as a never ending booster shot for the betterment of this creation. Allowing its minimal but profound message to be assimilated, re-assimilated and forever projected into this creation space as a sustainable reality!

Now that is a good plan! I bet our true Prime Creator's original plan for this creation was just that.

The long and short of Dr. Eben Alexanders case is:

- He may have gone through some portal which allowed and enabled him to travel the length of the *expanse* to the other side, and into the true heaven's next level.
- Upon his arrival he was NOT ushered in by some vision of a past loved one that *he knew,* or messiah figure; but after being allowed in, he encountered someone who provided comfort and reassuring, *but never previously knew.*
- However, she *was* someone who could be used to verify his experience more widely afterward.
- After arriving he did not encounter the same attributes as we find in that of the majorities encounters. (As listed previously)
- *Also important;* he did not experience anything *local* as his soul left his body, or even upon his return. No specific local experiences.

Archon use of *previously* assimilated data

Of excruciating importance here is the fact that there does exist this other type or version of *near,* or *after death* experience as Dr. Alexander appears to have had. *Meaning,* his was <u>NOT reliant on his soul's previously learned and believed false narratives</u>! This is so very important to keep in mind with all of this. That it is clearly seen throughout the majority of NDE and PLR subject testimonies, that the preponderance of previously assimilated narrative data, is being used to tailor fit their alleged "heaven" experiences!

To put a finer point on this; it has become very clear to me that their worldly narrative streams are pre-set for all souls/people to choose and assimilate as their personal truths through a lifetime. *Supplied for the sole purpose of being extracted from their soul's consciousness after death.* This *narrative extraction process* affords the Archon system the soul-specific data required to tailor make each persons after death experience believable. For the sole purpose of easily gaining their *consent* to *re-enter* the system for another round.

So where did the good doctor go?

If you recall, I mentioned the understanding concerning two portals or event horizons not far from earth as depicted to exist in the Tibetan book of the dead. An event horizon, or *light tunnel* where our souls seem to be either captured and pulled into, or as in Dr. Alexanders case, allowed to go upon their separation of this mortal coil. I would venture a guess, as that is all anyone can do bearing no memory of it, and say that Dr. Alexander somehow bypassed the automatic revolving door of their Archon heaven station, and was directed to the other.

Dr. Alexander openly admits that he was always a materialist scientist, having no belief at all where the alleged human soul was concerned until this event, which has clearly driven him in the opposite direction. Thankfully he and others are beginning to throw off that immaturity. Always bearing in mind, *that scientists and science as a whole, are as prone to the addiction of imposed narratives and dogma as our religious zealots have been and remain.* Therefore, one has to be very careful to step back and really want to know the truth for the sake of it alone.

I am nearly fully convinced that Dr. Alexander's heaven experience was the heavenly realm *above the expanse* which separates us currently. Although other far less renown people's experiences have convinced me more. That said, his is extremely close to certain others that I have encountered, all of which are diametrically opposed to that of the super-majorities NDE and PLR experiences. The major deciding factor in his case for me as you may imagine, rests upon the substance, simplicity and purity of the main message that the Prime Creator gave him to bring back, along with the fact that he is able to recall that message upon his return.

One major factor to remember when attempting to decipher and discern one heaven location from the other is to remember that at least some of the attributes encountered in their false heaven system, have been copied from the Prime Creators true heavenly realm.

Dr. Alexander's case still having a few of those minor attributes, we are forced to consider more carefully those smaller detailed portions which are never presented in the cases of the majority.

The Type-2 NDE account of Michele A

This NDE account is near to me, as Michele is a dear friend whose character and word is beyond reproach to me, as I am certain to be the case for her with many others.

Michele's case is again of the *minority* and the second type of case that can be found among the few souls who have been allowed to travel back to the true heavenly realm beyond the expanse of separation. As you will see even more clearly the distinct lack of false heavenly attributes in her – Type-2 experience.

Michele's case took place during her youth after *running from her home, searching for her God* and the *meaning of her life*, and while *running from an organized religion* that vexed and suffocated her youth. The following is her firsthand account.

"On May 13, 1971, I mistakenly took 20 "hits" of MDA. It was meant to be 1 "hit". MDA is Morphine Heroine with other chemicals mixed together as a cocktail. Although my long and intense search for truth and God had me dabbling with such drugs, it was for the sole purpose of finding Him. MDA is a deadly cocktail at one dose, 20 would kill an elephant.

That same day of May 13, 1971, was exactly one year to the day of my mother's death. I was 19 when she died, and I was lost, confused, searching and isolated, now 20 years old. I had previously gotten pregnant and was rejected by my mom at 17. I had been on my own for 3 years and never reconciled with my mom before her death. Nine months earlier I had left my son with his paternal grandparents for his own good. His dad was long gone, on drugs and in worse shape than I was, although I was a mess of a different sort; reading books I sought out every spiritual trend available in the 60's and 70's to truly find and know this God I felt pressed to look for.

On that day in 71 I was depressed, I walked aimlessly that day and wandered into an open church along the way. I prayed to God to help me. Little did I know what was about to occur; only an hour later came my overwhelming answer to that prayer. Needless to say, I was at my lowest of lows.

With my roommates getting ready for yet another college party, I took the MDA one of them gave me and sat on the couch. I knew immediately something was wrong. A few minutes passed when I heard a loud male voice asking my roommate for the MDA he gave her. She yelled out of the shower "Shelly just took half and I'm going to do the other half after I get dressed" He SCREAMED "HALF, HALF? There were 40 hits in there!" I was lying near lifeless by then, but I remember knowing they were freaking out! I remember hearing their terror.

That moment I died!

I laid there and KNEW I was dying. Almost immediately after that, I heard a loud unforgettable sound inside of my being. It sounded like a large engine slowly winding down, all my organs slowly stopping and then it was BLACK. An instant later I was aware of the brightest pure white light that bears no earthly description. Then I was aware that I was the light. The light was me. I had no physical body!

Nothing from the previous millisecond existed. I didn't wonder "was this God?" I knew it was The Creator, and I was one in and with the light. My communication was not vocal, but just "thought", I didn't have to try to think, it just was. I needed no mouth as I cried from the center of my being, my soul was speaking to this Greater being directly by telepathy it seemed.

I BEGGED, "I don't want to die (although I was FULLY aware I was dead already) " I am too young to die..." My emotions were like words, I could FEEL me telling The Creator "look how hard and how long I have searched for you...it can't end like this, I have to go back, I have a son......"

Within this encounter, and not aware of anytime, I ascertained that the Creator was all light, all love, and all good. And in that experience a great healing of some sort occurred within me upon the knowing of who He is; that being one with

THE ONE changed my broken soul, I became transformed.

After that, audible words, unlike the knowing communication came to me, saying, "Go back to Lorain, Get your son, you will meet my people, and teach my understanding of love & mercy." The Creator left me with an indelible imprint in my soul that has never left my being. As if that is who I always was and continue to be forever. My experience was not based on mere dogmatic religious obedience, nor was it fear or guilt based, or some compulsion birthed from a spiritual epiphany; but a complete soul change from what I was consciously acting out previously, to something else.

I later intuited this to be a change or <u>return to my true soul consciousness</u>, alleviated from all of life's built up scar tissue which deadens our soul's true image and character.

After a period of calming acceptance in His presence, I BECAME back in my body with no additional memories of traveling back or returning to my body. I just arrived as a better soul.

I experienced two separate dimensions of being. I was conscious of my soul state, along with that faraway place I was in with the Creator, then immediately conscious of my mental faculties, my hearing, and then my speech. I then became totally aware of girls crying and recognized its source. I turned my head, fully present and opened my eyes. I saw the 3 girls I roomed with kneeling next to the bed and hysterical. I felt very strongly that I only wanted to comfort them. I was peaceful and calm and had no remaining effects of the drug. Seeing me alive, normalized and talking to them, they became more confused and cried even worse. Speaking calmly and softly I explained that I had spoken to God and that He healed me totally. I told them never to do drugs again and that God didn't need drugs to be found. <u>That He was in us, and we are in Him.</u>

That He was all love and that it was our place to be kind to everyone and everything because we are all bound to each other through his love and light. Admonishing them to give their life's to knowing Him and doing good. They calmed down.

Two days later I then got on a plane, flew back to Lorain, Ohio, got my son, met some wonderful young spiritually driven Christian people, and began reading the bible and speaking to

*others about God and His great love and mercy for all, and that is
how the experience is framed. Nothing fancy or overly detailed.
Just The Creator healing and teaching me, then healing my
physical body."* Emphasis added.

Although there are many accounts that mirror Michele's experience
with few differences, they are still in the minority. I believe this to be
the case because most of the souls who have this type of experience,
never return here to tell the tale.

I believe that they never return because this **type-2** NDE
experience is not occurring in the same false heaven matrix as that of
the majority of NDE subject experiences. I tend to believe this second
or *other* experience type to be the real McCoy. Why only certain few
in any generation are allowed to return directly back to our original
habitation, will remain unknown to most. However, I will assure you,
there is a very good reason.

In these type-2 cases, as I call them, the subject sometimes
recalls vividly that their soul-body traveled through what they
perceived as space for an undeterminable amount of time. With
some others having the perception of just arriving there.

Additionally, that they do see a light, but in most cases that
light is *them;* and that they also later see another light which speaks
to them inaudibly, and also even audibly; and then they are returned
to their bodies, generally not perceiving the return trip, <u>nor do they
perceive any localized experience upon returning to their body</u>. All in
all these accounts depict few to none of the NDE attributes we find in
the data of the vast majority of type-1 NDE subject experiences.

Somewhat like Dr. Eben Alexander's NDE account, although
more so with Michele's, I find the compelling evidence that proves
her type of experience as the product of the real heavenly realm
across the expanse to be yet again, *it's complete lack of narrative
reliant attributes and contradictions, coupled with the final message of
love and mercy to all.* However, in Michele's case we have the added
feature of her physicality being completely healed, and thus no
residual effects of those drugs upon her return only minutes after her
death.

The absolute main thing I have learned and taught time and again in all my years of in-depth study and teaching is that the truth is always completely simple, and uncomplicated.

Conversely, when the dogma is a lie, it is always complicated to learn or fully understand, and usually, takes a special priest or unknowable faith in the unseen before being granted entrance to that club.

Israeli Druze boy Type-1b (RRE)

Boy identifies his murderer after being reincarnated

Only 3 years old, this young boy living in Israel and near the Syrian border, began telling his family and others that he was murdered in his previous life, adding details like; how he was killed; and where his body was. His story very powerfully surprised everyone within his community, as well as worldwide afterward.

The boy was an ethnic Druze whose culture allows for the idea of reincarnation as fact. The boy remembered the village in which he formerly lived and died, so they convened the family, the village elders, Dr. Eli Lasch and went there. Upon their arrival in the village, the boy recalled his former name, at which point it is documented that a village local informed them that this name belonged to a man who had gone missing four years earlier. His friends and family never knew what became of him, thinking his fate may have been the same as others who inadvertently wandered into the nearby hostile territory.

As his story was recounted later by German therapist Trutz Hardo's in his book - "Children Who Have Lived Before: Reincarnation Today," recounting how the boy showed his village elders and Dr. Eli Lasch where his body was buried. Upon inspection they, in fact, found a man's skeletal remains buried there. If that is not amazing enough, the boy was born, or more accurately, reborn with a long, red birthmark on his head which directly coincided with the trauma they found on the skull of his earlier skeletal remains! Trauma from what you ask? Answer: An Ax! The Druze believe, as some other cultures believe, that birthmarks are related to past-life accidents and death trauma.

Even more improbable; the boy directed the elders and Dr. Lasch to exactly where the murder weapon was also buried! Again, upon digging, they indeed found an ax buried in another spot.

Additionally! During their archaeological prospecting, the boy also recalled and told them the name of his killer. At which point, upon confronted this man who still resided there, the killer's face turned white, as recounted by Dr. Lasch, but still the man did not admit to the murder until being confronted with both the remains and the murder weapon. Thus, Faced with this evidence, the murderer admitted to the crime.

Dr. Lasch was the only non-Druze present throughout this investigation process and was the one who recounted its details to Trutz Hardo.

Dr. Eli Lasch, who died in 2009, is best known for developing the medical system in Gaza for the Israeli government in the 1960s.

As I mentioned earlier, these type-1b (RRE) *return-recall- events,* have amazingly detailed memories of their last incarnation.

Although these type-1b experiences seem to be fairly prevalent and well documented, they are still in far fewer numbers when compared to the majority 1a events. As well, these events are usually found to occur in children below their teenage years.

Although there are other theories why this past life memory retention exists in children, *some saying that it is more prevalent in them because their brains and emotions are not yet cluttered by life experiences yet, etc.;* and of course that may play into it as well, you may imagine by now, I have a different idea on this point.

I believe the main culprit to be, that these particular children's body-hardware is not being as restricted for some reason as most of ours have been. As I have pointed out several times already, there is a very good case to be made and being made in this book that these *Trinity-6* physicalities were specifically produced in their most base model forms for the main purpose of being a firewall to our living-souls! That, in fact, there is no problem with our living souls at all; no memory loss within them specifically, only that they are being thwarted by our dumbed-down body-hardware. No differently than you buying a brand new, high-speed laptop, removing the 12 Gigs of RAM, and installing a couple of 256 chips.

Alas, as the body matures, and overburdened with life's many destructive narratives, most of us never experience such clarity of the soul.

This boy from Israel's *Golan* is an amazing and well-documented case, and should prove in an absolute way that our souls live on, and also recycle.

The James Leininger Type-1b (RRE) story

Touching on two more amazing Type-1b stories that the reader should research in greater detail on their own, I present two children. First, we have James.

I cannot go into even half of the many details surrounding the young James Leininger case, all of which I can see have been verified as absolute truth in spades.

I came to know of this particular case many years ago and continue to have a fascination with it because of its detail. I am however most fascinated with it because to me it shows how the human physical body-hardware still has limitations concerning its ability to firewall the soul-memory completely in all cases. I also believe that this has been the main reason why the *Transhumanists*, particularly led by *Ray Kurtzweil,* have been working so hard for so long to manufacture what they call; "a better body."

Ray and his elite group of transhumanists, all of whom believe that some singularity event will soon be foisted on humanity as a whole, should also be on your new research list. I assure you, all of their ideas and forward momenta comes through their Archon handlers.

The short story is, that little *James Leininger*, from about the age of four, started showing his family signs of having a great interest and knowledge in airplanes, knowledge that was clearly beyond his years.

It appears James began reliving his memories by drawing many pictures of the events surrounding his death. After which he began having night terrors of burning in his fighter plane and crashing into the sea. James began to recount to his family such alarming detail of the planes, other pilots, and the ship, that his parents eventually sought help hoping to disprove his ideas.

Eventually through US Naval sources, and even at least one of the former pilots that James knew from that era, all of his details, along with former past-life family details from still-living siblings, were all confirmed true. To top it all they found the location of his downed plane to be exactly where James showed them it would be on a map.

As I said, I cannot come close to doing justice to this particular story in this format, but it suffices to say that just this single account, even if there were no others like it, which is far from true, this one alone could be used to prove the existence of the soul, its immortality and at least one of the recycling mechanism types.

Now look at this uncanny picture of James the adult during WWII, and James the boy now!

James and his parents published a detailed account in their book - *Soul Survivor: The Reincarnation of a World War II Fighter Pilot Paperback – by Bruce Leininger, Andrea Leininger and Ken Gross: June 11, 2010* (Leininger)

The Shanti Devi Type-1b RRE Story

Not quite as dramatic as the James Leininger story, but still quite amazing and thoroughly documented, even by *Mahatma Gandhi* himself!

At the ripe old age of about four years old, born December 11, 1926, Shanti Devi began telling her parents and others at school that her real home was in Mathura and that this was where her husband lived. Mathura being about 150 km from her home in Delhi. Shanti, not being heard by her new parents, decided to run away from home to reach Mathura, she was six at that time. After being returned home and not reaching Mathura at that time, Shanti told her school teachers that she was married before and that she had died ten days after giving birth. At this point, Shanti was interviewed by her teacher and headmaster who began noticing that she was speaking words and accents only used in the Mathura dialect, which is evidently a very specific dialect of that one region. After much prodding, Shanti finally divulged the name of her former husband to be Kedarnath Chaube.

Evidently in that older Indian culture women were forbidden to vocalize the name of their husbands, which is why she held out telling anyone for several years.

Shanti's school headmaster went on to locate a merchant by that name in Mathura. Upon doing so he found out that in fact the man did lose his wife, named Lugdi Bai, nine years earlier on September 25, 1925, and that her death occurred ten days after having given birth to a son.

Shanti's former husband, Kedarnath Chaube, asked if his cousin Pandit Kanjimal, who lived in Delhi could meet Shanti, the meeting with Kanjimal was arranged, during which Shanti Devi recognized him as her husband's cousin. At that time Shanti also gave many details about her house in Mathura and informed them that she hid money in a secret location, which was also verified later.

Shanti also gave many other details of their family when the real husband visited soon after. Shanti also immediately recognized the son she never saw but one time before she died. It is also told that in private she gave several intimate details to her former husband in respect to their former intimacies. At which point the husband and others became entirely convinced that this was the reincarnation of his wife.

When Mahatma Gandhi heard about the case, he appointed a committee of 15 prominent people, including parliamentarians, national leaders, and members of the media, to study the case. The committee's report is available and describes some of what happened during their investigation and travels with Shanti.

Here is a picture of Shanti and her family;

As with the James Leininger case, there are much more amazing details with this case that I had to leave out of this book. You can read the full account of Shanti's case in the book - *I Have Lived Before: The True Story of the Reincarnation of Shanti Devi* - (Lonnerstrand)

Another great resource for studies of such returned children is the University of Virginia Psychiatrist – Dr. Ian Stevenson. Dr. Stevenson has documented and verified over 2000 after-life recall cases.

Soul Return Statistics by Helen Wambach

Helen Wambach *has tabulated the distribution of 1,088 full memory recall cases of past life subjects over a 100 year period within the categories' of socioeconomic, race and sex, even correlating her data with the population curve data available.*

Amazingly, Helen found that the genders of those past life recall subjects were very evenly distributed across sex: Males at 50.6% and Females at 49.4%. This turned out to be an almost exact correlation of the gender distribution of our actual population data, with her results for the race category proving to be the same. With the same accuracy, her socioeconomic data from the past lives subjects followed the same historical trends. Additionally, her data also depicts that the recalled life-status of those past life subjects; 90% on the lower income side, and as it pertains to their socioeconomic status over that period of time, shows that the 90% poor status changed significantly and in agreement with the shift in our modern socioeconomic spectrum.

Most interesting of her research to me, and as it pertains to my theory concerning how the Archon's trickle in souls for new live births at an increasing rate, and as I see it, doing so at an ever quickening rate as another epoch nears its scheduled end; Helen's research has proven that the reintroduction of souls follows our empirical population growth curve data. *Meaning, the more humans being conceived, the faster a soul is forced to return*

An oddity in her research to me, at first anyway, was what her research shows concerning the distribution of race/nationality. *Showing that all of the subjects are being returned or recycled into the exact same geographical areas and nationalities!*

Now one might not consider this specific anomaly to be overly important, however I disagree. Again, if this entire recycling system had truly been created by the Prime Creator for the "soul-purpose" of teaching or even re-teaching all souls based on a specific *curriculum of themes unto enlightenment;* then does it not stand to logic and reason that all souls be reborn and made to experience all the cultures and geographic locales within this alleged, great university system? Would not knowledge and the alleged enlightenment being sought by the endless recycling periods not be accomplished unto our final ascension much sooner, or at least far more efficiently by a far more eclectic experience overall? I can tell you this, all of the institutions of mankind have always believed exactly that! Who is more accomplished in the eyes of men; the person that can answer almost every question asked of him within the confines of his specific occupation; or the person who can answer nearly every question posed to him regardless of its genre or discipline?

Remember – *As above, so below!* The majority of the souls of mankind unconsciously move towards creating everything in their physical lives, *in the same fashion as the gods they believe they are made from, create;* albeit this is being manipulated to occur by their negative stimuli, false narrative systems. Naturally opposing this in near silence is our living-soul. *Meaning,* that even though our souls, within these vessels, are formidably constricted, our living-souls, which are the microcosm-soul portions from the Prime Creators Macro-Soul, still seek their center from the subconscious level. In this, and although it is not reflected in their Archon soul recycling system, we continue in more subtle ways to create diversity within our own systems because we inherently know that diversity is better. *Thus, I see it as more proof of the subterfuge that we do not see that diversity indulged by the gods of this false narrative existence, as proven by their tendency to recycle souls into the same locations and cultures, endlessly.* However, in direct contrast to the years of verifiable data as *Helen Wambach* provides on this subject, the typical Buddhist concept of it is; that we all have many incarnations here, because there are many *themes* that our souls have to experience and learn from, which cannot be accomplished in one lifetime, etc. Great idea, but the reality appears to be quite the opposite. We continue to relive the same themes while recalling no part of any previous incarnations.

Creating context

The contexts that are defined by the laws of physics and that which our soul's conscious *intention* uses for the creation of non-living material objects to build the world we know around us are *electrical forces; momentum, energy, and force.*

Plato defined some of the contexts used by our conscious, mental manifestations as – *Truth, justice, love, mercy and beauty.*

Within the mystical pages of the Jewish *Zohar, Rabbi Shimon bar' Yochai* agrees with the Buddha and states;

> *"The souls must re-enter the absolute substance from where they have emerged, but to accomplish this end they must develop all the perfections that are placed on them; and not fulfilling this condition within one life cycle, they must commence to another, then three, and onward".*

So, it would appear that all of the oldest religious mystics agreed to drink the Archon *Kool-Aid*, rather than embrace a position of more critical thinking. The question not asked being; *if our souls are meant to learn through the assimilation of so many themes, then why are all souls being restricted from experiencing all those themes, as Helen's work, and the quickly growing compilation of work by many others like her, tends to prove?*

I have to thank Helen Wambach for her exhaustive work. Not being a professional after-life researcher myself, outstanding academics like Helen and several others have finally afforded me the measurable proof needed to connect the ancient dots within my own field of studies for a more credible, and hopefully enlightening result.
(Helens research is found in - Viney 1993)

Assimilate Incompatibility – The KEY!

So far in this book you have hopefully come to realize, that most of the things we thought we knew are more than likely completely untrue, or mostly untrue; *welcome to reality!* However, if you take nothing else away from this work, if it is all too much to remember, then remember and institute this one simple thing into your life from here on, and regardless of age. *Go from here and sin no more!*

Of course, I am paraphrasing from this great prophet I came to read about late in life. Interesting to me that he told people to just simply stop sinning, as that is not at all what I have come to learn Christianity believes to be available to them. However, here is my take on what he truly meant. I believe he meant for them to change their lives in such a dramatic and polar opposite way to anything they were taught, or currently believed to be an authoritative religious path. *I believe he was instructing them and all after them to literally become (incompatible) to that of the opposition.*

Meaning, that discarding the old, false narrative paths is only half of the equation and that we all need to assimilate a new, but original truth! That in doing so we make our souls (data) completely and utterly incompatible and literally unusable *in or for* the Archon Soul-extraction systems upon our physical death! *'that our entire reason for being is love & mercy!'*

Just the same as both Dr. Alexander and my friend Michele *intuited, audibly heard* and then later *remembered* to return with. A final and most simple instruction for all life herein, always coming down to the very essence of the Eternal Creators *Everlasting Agreement.*

In the end, and through near countless hours spent in deep academic instruction and research in the areas of ancient religions and cultural phenomenon, I have found not one other spiritual truth or law other than this one of the Everlasting Agreement, that is truly and always the unrelenting, polar opposite of every single other path known to man. *Commence from here and assimilate the pure path, and make your soul incompatible to them!*

In doing so you will have taken yourself off their market. You will have provided them no useable narrative data for further enslavement! In this simple understanding, you will have finally denied aid and comfort to your enemy. Which by the way, are the enemy of the Eternal Prime Creator. Your creator!

How long does it take?

The question I get allot is; 'after I relearn and switch to the new corrected narrative, how long will it take to ensure that my DNA and soul is sufficiently saturated?'

How can anyone answer that one with any accuracy? My answer is, *'start living it like you are about to die!'* I have done years of research within both, the sciences, and obviously within the field of ancient theology and Semitic languages; and I have not found anyone on either side who actually has a handle on how much assimilation is required to transfer any new information from our DNA, over to our soul for permanent storage. There is no way for certain to know just how much of the less essential life information/memories actually makes that transfer, vs. the deeper emotionally driven narratives.

Emotion is so very powerful, therefore it could easily be that only our deepest emotional life events and their surrounding detail get transferred and stored forever. However, as previously pointed out, I also tend to see via these NDE and PLR subject experiences, that highly detailed memories are pulled from those souls and used for various reasons. Therefore maybe for the sake of argument, we should hover somewhere in the middle on that question for now.

My personal learned opinion is, that once any soul returns their life to re-consent and submission to His Everlasting Agreement, and upon the separation of their physicality, their soul, now totally incompatible, will automatically bypass the false heaven matrix and travel home. For if this was not true, and continuous capture was inevitable, there would be no reason for the Eternal Creator to leave His breadcrumbs of truth back to His return mechanism.

From my experience, I have come to understand that most of the scientists working in this area tend to think that only the most influential emotional highs and lows are transferred and stored to the soul, while others postulate that all vital information detail makes the transfer, and stored.

So, to err on the side of caution during this lifetime, and *especially since there is absolutely no guarantee that any ancient texts or these types of modern correlations by various authors will be available to us in our next incarnation,* should we continue to play fast and loose and be caught again? I believe it prudent to change our world paradigm quickly and deeply, especially our religious views, and upload some new simple understanding. *It isn't only about assimilating a new thing, but also about* eliminating *all the old things.* Remembering, that, of course, it is in the best interest of the Archon's to eliminate all such data from their ever expanding world control narrative systems going forward. *To be clear, if the ancient cultural understandings, spiritual correlations or translation corrections as outlined in any of my books and teachings is working, they won't leave them or any others to be found the next time around.*

As I stipulated just previously, the very basic and simple end-game for us then is; to find and assimilate at the emotional level on a daily basis, a new path back to the oldest narrative of *good & life.* To learn and retain the knowledge of this anti-spiritual Archonian con-game, along with the more clear and concise understanding of who our original true Primary Creator is, and how He truly works. (All identified by His true Character as a Creator ONLY). To make all such understanding part of our *daily thought* and *life process,* even our prayer process. An enlightened knowledge and wisdom that will be forced through our DNA recording system, attached to our soul and available to us as our spiritually applied shield against deception. *But most importantly as proof to our Creator that our soul has finally re-arrived and reverted back to His way, His path!* To Become Incompatible!

Leaving the old Paradigm

For far too long all humans in one cultural form or another have been concentrating deeply on their false religion control narratives.

This continual emotionally deep concentration only serves to ensure continued enslavement within their system. Again, they use the creative strength of our souls against us by eliminating all original and true understanding of any original ancient knowledge concerning our creative ability. This has, of course, led to all manner of misunderstanding on topics that a few wise prophets attempted to reintroduce along the way.

Remember – We are creative beings, and how better to enslave a creative being than to allow them to believe a false narrative path as the truth, which in turn we create as our own reality for the Archons! *In believing a false narrative mankind will think upon it continually, emotionally internalizing it. Thus, in making it their own it will become a very strong emotional force within them, thereby, they will create and bring the Archon reformation into being, themselves, with no additional help.* Now imagine the force of this by the millions and billions of people/souls! All working over time, generationally, unknowingly!

Breaking consent through knowledge!

As already stipulated, we MUST delete all previously learned and overly comfortable paradigms, especially dogmatic religious beliefs. We must then substitute new understandings derived from a more pure spiritual and equally scientifically bolstered data stream that will transfer and stick to our soul in this life. If nothing else we must remember that virtually every false control narrative that any corrupted person or any Archon entity has on us in this life or the hereafter, has become entrenched and available for them to use against us, solely by our Free-Will-Consent! By consenting to believe in their truth!

The knowledge of Non-Compliance!

Being aware of their false system must be the first leg up that enables our soul to resist by retaining the memories of our recent past life. *To be incompatible.*

We should then have the required information and spiritual awareness to assert <u>non-compliance</u> from the get-go if that is how this scam continues to be asserted. As previously stated many times so far; once our conscious and subconscious self-has become infused with a new path, *and convinced against the former,* you will then possess within your living-soul the required information that will allow your soul to remain "aware & alert" at the moment it needs to rebel against their Archon entrapment. Not knowing for certain that this ploy may be all you have next time around. Especially not having achieved a full assimilation of corrected context for return. *Meaning, how much incompatibility is enough?*

In this life and especially afterward, *Free Will consent transcends all!* When we here on earth *consent* openly, knowingly, and or even tacitly through our lack of knowledge or by just not paying attention, those who seek it from us usually gain some level of adverse jurisdiction and possession over us. Yes, they are skirting the Primary Creators immutable Freewill system in doing so, but in time they will be held accountable for these actions.

Many may see all this as the rebellion leaders' blatant dismissal and usurpation of our souls Free-Will. However, by the stated experiences of the many NDE and PLR subjects, which are also backed up by well-known ancient cultural beliefs and writings, we are either giving up *consent* to them through naivety, or by some other means. Perhaps those NDE & PLR cases who say they did not consent, but appear to us as being taken against their will, actually gave their consent through contract at an earlier time. This is all so diabolical no possibility or circumstance can be patently dismissed yet.

This is why in such a case as this hypothesis of the Archon rebellion and subsequent usurpation, with them forced to bend their will to the prime Creator's original immutable laws, it very well may be that while trapped within their false heaven matrix, *even if a soul had not assimilated enough or any corrected narratives in life,* that we may just need to hold out by maintaining our <u>non-compliance</u> through <u>non-consent</u> as long as it takes. Yes, it appears obvious to me that all those *false control narratives* that people assimilate in life are exactly the tools the Archon's use to bait the trap souls long enough to gain our *consent* to entering. However, none of the evidence thus far shows this previously assimilated false control narrative data being used to *keep* a soul *in* their heaven way-station. Quite the opposite as I have shown; they use that data in a passive aggressive way to force all souls to be reborn again! Therefore, while remaining mindful of their concept of, *As above, so below;* we know by their own legal narrative systems down here on earth; *that providing and or removing our personal consent on any matter has strong legal standing and power.* Would it not be logical to expect the same legal standing to also apply *above?* Quite possibly, they may at some point be forced to allow the *non-consenting* soul to move on to our original Creator Source as requested. The problem is for us, that any souls who have been able to move on from there using this tactic, have never returned to advise anyone else. Again, in the end, not having the detailed information that we should have, keeps us enslaved to their cycle.

Clearly, superseding another's free will by way of deception can never be referred to as being done *in love.* If we take a page from the history of this AE- Matrix, it remains obvious that the use of fear-based narratives to manipulate people/souls have been generously applied to ensure conformity.

Of all the arguments, theories, hypotheses and contrived religious dogmas we all tend to hold so dearly, like our very lives depended on them, the only major tenet all of us seem to believe in common is; *that the Eternal Creator entity is pure love, mercy, and that He resides in some part within all of us.*

That being the most probable case, I submit that in fact none of the experiences that these many thousands of NDE and PLR subjects have been reporting back over such a protracted period, proves to us that the true, all loving, all knowing, Eternal Creator entity, regardless by which name you believe you know Him, to be the one behind such an archaic system of destruction.

Their Endgame?

This appears to be the final question most people have after even partially absorbing the enormity of this topics information.

The issue is that no one can truly give anything more than their opinions derived from the ancient information we have available to us, *of why any entity would work to entrap and enslave the souls of man.* The superstitions abound!

If we apply this ancient law for all life, too – *Treat all others as you would have them treat you* – by its application alone we immediately know they, or anyone not working within this framework, is not working for our betterment, much less on the side of the Prime Eternal Creator! Not by a long shot! So by this alone, we know they, or whoever is controlling this world at this time, is not working on behalf of us or the Eternal Primary Creator. On that, we should all be able to agree.

There are many ancient texts, folklore, and superstitions available today which speak of the super-ancient entities that the later Greeks called the Archons. However, regardless of the name these questions still stand.

- How does controlling the way a soul lives a physical life within some holographic reality, aid them?
- And, how does controlling a number of times a soul's cycles through said reality, aid them?

Zeus divides the Soul!

There is some other interesting information that after-life scientists and researchers have found to be expressed from the majority of subjects. They tell us that our *soul-energy* is actually *split up, divided, fractioned* between this realm of reality and their false heaven matrix. To me, this is quite amazing, that they very specifically tell us that 2/3^{rds} of our Soul-energy remains behind in their false heaven matrix, while 1/3rd is used to animate our physical bodies. The assumption postulated by many of the researchers hearing this is, that our physical bodies cannot contain all of the energy at once.

Again, there is no way for us to know the why yet, however, I will postulate that there may be other more insidious reasons for capturing and splitting up our soul-consciousness energy. So far we have seen the several passive-aggressive tools of the trade being employed in the false heaven matrix against the unaware souls. We can also agree that none of their tools are meant to serve the living soul or mankind in his/her physical form, nor for any meaningful spiritual growth of civilization. Again I remind that our own ancient and modern histories prove to be in total contrast to a civilization of souls moving towards good & life, more than not.

Such is *Aristophanes* explanation by Plato:

(Excerpts) from Aristophanes's Speech from Plato's *Symposium*
Translated by Benjamin Jowett from
Collected Works of Plato, 4th Edition, Oxford U. Press, 1953 (Jowett)

"Aristophanes professed to open another vein of discourse; he had a mind to praise Love in another way, unlike that of either Pausanias or Eryximachus. Mankind, he said, judging by their neglect of him, have never, as I think, at all understood the power of Love. For if they had understood him they would surely have built noble temples and altars, and offered solemn sacrifices in his honour; but this is not done, and most certainly ought to be done: since of all the gods he is the best friend of men, the helper and the healer of the ills which are the great impediment to the happiness of the race. I will try to describe his power to you, and you shall teach the rest of the world what I am teaching you."

"In the first place, let me treat of the nature of man and what has happened to it. The original human nature <u>was not like the present, but different</u>. The sexes <u>were not two</u> as they are now, <u>but originally three</u> in number; there was man, woman, and the union of the two, of which the name survives but nothing else. Once it was a distinct kind, with a bodily shape and a name of its own, constituted by the union of the male and the female: but now only the word 'androgynous' is preserved, and that as a term of reproach.

In the second place, the primeval man was round, his back and sides forming a circle; and he had four hands and the same number of feet, one head with two faces, looking opposite ways, set on a round neck and precisely alike; also four ears, two privy members, and the remainder to correspond. He could walk upright as men now do, backwards or forwards as he pleased, and he could also roll over and over at a great pace, turning on his four hands and four feet, eight in all, like tumblers going over and over with their legs in the air; this was when he wanted to run fast.

Now the <u>sexes were three</u>, and such as I have described them; because the sun, moon, and earth are three; and the man was originally the child of the sun, the woman of the earth, and the man-woman of the moon, which is made up of sun and earth, and they were all round and moved round and round because they resembled their parents. Terrible was their might and strength, and the thoughts of their hearts were great, <u>and they made an attack upon the gods</u>; of them is told the tale of Otys and Ephialtes who, as Homer says, attempted to scale heaven, and would have laid hands upon God.

Doubt reigned in the celestial councils. Should they kill them and annihilate the race with thunderbolts, as they had done the giants, then there would be an end of the sacrifices and worship which men offered to them; but, on the other hand, the gods could not suffer their insolence to be unrestrained. At last, after a good deal of reflection, Zeus discovered a way.

He said: 'Methinks I have a plan which will enfeeble their strength and so extinguish their turbulence; men shall continue to exist, **but I will cut them in two** and then they will be diminished in strength and increased in numbers; this will have the advantage of making them more profitable to us. They shall walk upright on two legs, and if they continue insolent and will not be quiet, I will split them again and they shall hop about on a single leg.'

He spoke and cut men in two, like a sorb-apple which is halved for pickling, or as you might divide an egg with a hair; and as he cut them one after another, he bade Apollo give the face and the half of the neck a turn in order that man might contemplate the section of himself: he would thus learn a lesson of humility. Apollo was also bidden to heal their wounds and compose their forms. So he gave a turn to the face and pulled the skin from the sides all over that which in our language is called the belly, like the purses which draw tight, and he made one mouth at the center, which he fastened in a knot (the same which is called the navel); he also molded the breast and took out most of the wrinkles, much as a shoemaker might smooth leather upon a last; he left a few, however, in the region of the belly and navel, as a memorial of the primeval state.

After the division the two parts of man, each desiring his other half, came together, and throwing their arms about one another, entwined in mutual embraces, longing to grow into one, they began to die from hunger and self-neglect, because they did not like to do anything apart; and when one of the halves died and the other survived, the survivor sought another mate, man or woman as we call them,--being the sections of entire men or women,--and clung to that.

Thus they were being destroyed, when Zeus in pity invented a new plan: he turned the parts of generation round to the front, for this had not been always their position, and they sowed the seed no longer as hitherto like grasshoppers in the ground, but in one another; and after the transposition the male generated in the female in order that by the mutual embraces of man and woman they might breed, and the race might continue; or if man came to man they might be satisfied, and rest, and go their ways to the business of life. So ancient is the desire of one another which is implanted in us, reuniting our original nature, seeking to make one of two, and to heal the state of man.

….And when one of them meets with his other half, the actual half of himself - the pair are lost in an amazement of love and friendship and intimacy, and one will not be out of the other's sight, as I may say, even for a moment: these are the people who pass their whole lives together, and yet they could not explain what they desire of one another. For the intense yearning which each of them has towards the other does not appear to be the desire of lover's intercourse, but of something else which the soul of either evidently desires and cannot tell, and of which she has only a dark and doubtful presentiment.

Suppose Hephaestus, with his instruments, to come to the pair who are lying side by side and to say to them, *'What do you mortals want of one another?'*

They would be unable to explain. And suppose further, that when he saw their perplexity he said: *'Do you desire to be wholly one; always day and night in one another's company?* for if this is what you desire, I am ready to melt and fuse you together, so that being two you shall become one, and while you live a common life as if you were a single man, and after your death in the world **below** still be one departed soul, instead of two--I ask whether this is what you lovingly desire and whether you are satisfied to attain this?'

There is not a man of them who when he heard the proposal would deny or would not acknowledge that this meeting and melting into one another, this becoming one instead of two, was the very expression of his ancient need.

And the reason is that human nature was originally one and we were a whole, and the desire and pursuit of the whole is called love. There was a time, I say when we were one, but now because of the wickedness of mankind God has dispersed us, as the Arcadians were dispersed into villages by the Lacedaemonians. And if we are not obedient to God, there is a danger that we shall be split up again and go about in basso-relievo, like the profile figures showing only one-half the nose which are sculptured on monuments, and that we shall be like tallies. Wherefore let us exhort all men to piety in all things, that we may avoid evil and obtain the good, taking Love for our leader and commander.

Let no one oppose Him--He is the enemy of the gods who opposed him. For if, we are friends of God and at peace with him we shall find our own true loves, which rarely happens in this world at present…."; *Emphasis added*

Should we understand these words concerning the *form* of man at an earlier time as literal? I think not. It is far more obvious as you read further into this explanation of man's condition, that it is our *living-souls* he is referring to as being split into halves, and now possibly further into thirds as depicted by our modern day PLR and NDE subjects. I merely use this ancient story here to show that others, so long ago, either intuited what was afoot or were told.

Seemingly that which this ancient tale is attempting to explain is that our *souls* were somehow accosted, split up by some entity <u>for their own gain</u>; depicted here by the name of *Zeus*.

Then we see it explained how - *The sexes <u>were not two</u> as they are now, <u>but originally three</u>...* Which again fits in perfectly with other ancient texts among various cultures and religions who generally depict our souls as consisting of three layers, or a "trinity". I have long believed that this is where virtually all religious cults extrapolated their various ideas concerning *trinities* in people or gods. ...<u>and they made an attack upon the gods</u>; Again very interesting how this idea falls squarely within pretty much all of man's myths concerning how some alleged *angels* rebelled against God and fell from their first estate, down into a lower place, etc. Additionally, but far less known, is how the corrected and literally translated Hebrew texts actually depict the alleged *tower* at Babel, as literally being a weapon built, "to shake the head of heaven". *An attack on the gods!* Today some call this device – CERN!

....Doubt reigned in the celestial councils. Should they kill them and annihilate the race with thunderbolts, as they had done the giants, <u>then there would be *an end of the sacrifices*</u> and worship which men offered to them....; *an end to the sacrifices?*

This is just amazing, and falls directly in line with my teaching on *The Everlasting Agreement*, and all of man's fabricated *God-given* animal and human sacrificial rituals, to include the entire Jewish sacrificial system. All of which being the main and original reason for the division we currently suffer in this *lower* creation-space.

Also making direct reference to the *giants* of old in which we have many accounts in ancient texts, wall carvings, and actual archeological findings as proof of their existence and destruction by the hands of *some* gods.

The hostage link!

Since this splitting of the soul idea as found reiterated by many of the NDE and PLR subjects, and among most religions, I could theorize that by capturing and storing the larger portion of our soul's consciousness energy within their false heaven matrix, that this provides what I call the *"hostage link"*. A direct link between the separated portions which may be a strong enough link and powerful attractor of the separated third.

Possibly used to reel the recently separated soul back into their system - *a link and division situation that all of us must have consented to early on by not knowing the full content of their plan.* This could be exactly why we should <u>remember to demand</u> *prior* to following some *known* entity *soul-greeter* deeper into their light-tunnel, demanding that we be <u>reunited with our soul-portions and our creator-source</u>! *Demanding not only the source of our original creation but also our completed soul consciousness.*

If we decide to apply the well-known religious narrative, which depicts 1/3rd of the *angles - <u>actually souls</u>,* who, siding with another evil soul-entity that was forced out of his first estate in rebellion; we might connect this narrative differently when framed within the context of our most ancient writings from Enoch.

As I depicted in an earlier chapter, Enoch left behind a very detailed account that depicts two hundred higher souls, allegedly – *angels,* who later rebelled against even their new master, *believed to be the Yahweh entity.* And in further rebellion positioned themselves as manipulators over all other *souls – but which other souls?*

Shifting how we decide to understand the translations of that story, to perceive this 1/3rd of souls as *not* some *other souls* who sided with this rebellious entity *<u>while literally in some other higher realm of heaven</u>,* as most generally understand that story to depict. But! Souls already placed here who then later *fell from their previously perfected state of being!* Souls, specifically *our* naïve souls *hearing, consenting* and *following* the will of another.

Consenting to their evil intentions for us before ever thinking to read the fine print. As above, so below! Much as the overall biblical story is depicted with the man Job! Entities who hate our still *soul-tethered* condition to the Prime Eternals Soul!

They came *to* us, not our souls *with them!* This is an utterly important distinction in the narrative that will become clearer shortly.

My question and observation based on this specific topic portion is; *'was the number of souls found and contaminated here enough to fulfill the ravenous energy needs of our new false gods?'*

Again, spanning time, cultures and religious paradigms, from folklore, religious dogma, and the likes of Plato to modern day NDE and PLR subjects, the *fractioning* of our souls continues to be a prominent context.

One-third of souls - How many is 1/3ʳᵈ?

I have asked many religionists in my time for that number, and as it is with most fish stories, it continues to grow. The only fact I can prove about that number seems to be that there is no way to answer it using the narrow parameters of most religious narratives.

Researchers and lay people within many cultures, from the ancients to this very day have believed that the Archons literally *feed* on the collective energy that our living-souls emit, calling them – *Energy Wraiths*, but more on that later.

It would appear that their *fractioning* of our souls has been done in order to basically animate a far greater number of these purpose built, *Trinity-6* bodies, much as *Aristophanes* speech lays out for us with the division of souls by Zeus - *'Methinks I have a plan which will enfeeble their strength and so extinguish their turbulence; men shall continue to exist, **but I will cut them in two** and then they will be diminished in strength and increased in numbers; this will have the advantage of making them more profitable to us. They shall walk upright on two legs, and if they continue insolent and will not be quiet, I will split them again and they shall hop about on a single leg....'* Cut our souls in two or more if need be! Thus increasing our numbers.

This would obviously be very equitable for the Energy-Wraiths would it not? ....making them more profitable to us... There you have it, we get a bit closer holistically to a more plausible reason for why this oligarchy of souls needed to capture the souls of this creation level – **their survival!**

.... *Apollo was also bidden to heal their wounds and compose their forms....; i.e.* – "Let us make man in our image"...

.... *After the division the two parts of man, each desiring his other half, came together, and throwing their arms about one another, entwined in mutual embraces, longing to grow into one, they began to die from hunger and self-neglect....; Could this be an allegorical view of how they got our souls to partake in their anti-freewill narrative of killing sentient beings for food?*

I will even posit that the *fracturing* of the souls as it pertains to our physical life expectancy, would be the root cause of mankind's drop in longevity as these gods saw fit – *i.e. Genesis 6:3,* where after so many generations of man's physical body living a thousand years and possibly far longer, that length of days began to be rolled back. To the point where this usurper god rolled it way back to a maximum of 120 years. Although even that is a near impossibility for most humans these days, and for a long time.

.... So ancient is the desire of one another which is implanted in us, reuniting our original nature, seeking to make one of two, and to heal the state of man. .... these are the people who pass their whole lives together, and yet they could not explain what they desire of one another. For the intense yearning which each of them has towards the other does not appear to be the desire of lover's intercourse, but of something else which the soul of either evidently desires and cannot tell, and of which she has only a dark and doubtful presentiment.

....Wherefore, if we would praise Him who has given to us the benefit, we must praise the God Love, who is our greatest benefactor, both leading us in this life back to our own nature, and giving us high hopes for the future, for He promises that if we are pious, He will restore us to our original state, and heal us and make us happy and blessed. (Emphasis added throughout)

All compelling and thus again leans towards a story of perfect souls who later chose wrongly when presented with lies by those who attacked the estate of their chosen Prime Eternal Creator *above* by attempting to *'scale its walls'*; rebelling against His law of free will and non-destruction of any life, *by their sacrifices.* By all this, we continue to see our separation from that original estate and the *nakedness* of our *uncovering* in this once garden setting, subsequent to some very ancient poor decision making and impulse control. *Do we not see much of the same behavior within most people to this day?*

Again, I remind the reader to consider and ask the question while reading such pronouncements; *which god* is being spoken of throughout? I continue to find that most texts have been referring to the many *demigod-Archons,* while only making periodic reference to the Prime Eternal One. This is where wisdom is required to discern one from the other, and most simply by the character of their actions.

Another minor point to consider in this is, just because the NDE and PLR subjects have been shown a *trinity-split* of our souls, does not mean the souls aren't being apportioned off many more times than this for extended *profitability.* As you will find in my final chapter, this soul fracturing and the condition of each particular soul after so much time living in contradiction, may also explain most alleged mental disorders, phobias, and fetishes.

Another Epoch Reboot

Just as many people are finally coming to the reality that all of our ancient Hebrew writings, of which Christianity is derived, are false narratives authored by pagan sects who followed another demigod voice - *The Land of Meat & Honey 2012* (D. S. Asher) , this so-called "all powerful and all knowing" deity, in his infinite wisdom, chooses to find and use *willing vessels* for his "holy spirit" to do the "Lords will" to bring about His kingdom - *"As above, So Below!"* Again, no one asks - Which Kingdom, which god?

Could this *coming to earth* narrative which many religions seem to share be the Archon rulers' reoccurring act of destruction as we see it was in ancient times? *"As it was in the days of Noah"?*

I will posit that the reason for any alleged *return of the gods* will be to get hands on with humanity again just prior to our worldwide enlightenment getting out of their control.

It is difficult to argue that a major growth in *anti-narrative enlightenment* has been taking fast root for many years across the world, but in earnest within the last six years since around 2010. One proof of this is you reading this book and others like it!

To use a phrase from a well-known Sci-fi series - *"This has all happened before, and it will all happen again"... **(IF) we allow it!***

I would also posit that since they are truly in control of this galactic creation, and as any King who reigns a vast Kingdom would not do, they will not allow such a rebellion of the souls to move forward unabated! On that note, ponder this; within apocryphal texts the great prophet Yehshua/Jesus vigorously warned, that - *"all truth from Adam to Moses has been turned upside down by our lying forefathers".*

Strangely, since then, and especially in our more modern times, researchers of ancient texts and wall carvings have been uncovering many old/new truths concerning the identity of these ancient gods, specifically by literally turning many carvings upside down which then presents a totally new and formally hidden detailed picture. All very interesting in light of the words of such a prophet as Yehshua.

Another, more interesting belief from ancient times, is, *the idea that the flood of Noah was not caused by the in-depth sin of the people in his time, but quite the opposite; that in fact they were becoming exceedingly enlightened as to who they truly were, how they were supposed to live, and who they were supposed to be serving.* As it is suspected, an enlightenment occurred which began to cause quick and certain final changes for the Archon overlords. Changes that would adversely affect the Archonian reign and control, even unto their total demise, just as it will today!

Therefore, the Archons, knowing the great strength and immortality of our souls, but still under their control at that time, they chose a few of the less enlightened souls to continue into the next Epoch to carry on their *narrative revisions* and destroyed the rest by the flood.

In this way they are able to restrain the inevitable enlightenment of souls, by pulling them all back, *in death,* to their false heaven matrix for re-education, leaving the few unenlightened behind for the reboot. This also allows the Archons time to tweak and rewrite the many narratives they will employ again in order to achieve better long term control through the next cycle. *This would also provide the reason why no one has been experiencing any new Mt. Horeb or Mt. Sinai events, and or burning bushes, etc.* As all such events would only be required to lay in the new narrative foundations early on in any Epoch.

I would also posit here that this Epoch turnover would clearly provide them time to make specific changes to the human, *Trinity-6* body hardware. This would be the easy answer to why our genetics vary, having nothing at all to do with evolution on any scale.

This Epoch reboot hypothesis, although the reverse Genesis story compared to how most learn it, may be useful in answering the questions we have today in regards to why, on the microcosm level, and as we find played out among the Nations governments worldwide, they have and continue to drive this same cycle of growth and eventual destruction. A narrative cycle that will eventually end in the complete annihilation of all but those very few who tow the Archon narrative line. With this next epoch reboot allegedly being prophesied to occur by fire! A destruction that comes by the hands of those few corrupted men who are themselves manipulated by the Archon rebels.

If I were asked to put a start date on our currently expanding, worldwide path to enlightenment, and also make a correlation paralleling this spiritual outgrowth with the world's geopolitical climate of escalating evil; from my perspective and catbird seat as a teacher whose sole aim has been to instruct people on how to leave the false narratives, and return to the original estate and character of our Prime Eternal Creator; I can tell you that the amount of religionists seeking to leave the three major religions to find a more profitable truth, accelerated towards palpable gains in speed and number between 1998 to 2009. By 2012, and to the finalizing of this book in 2016 the curve began a steep ascension, making bounds by the day on many levels and subject matter. Now, take that time frame from 1998-2016 and ponder how our geopolitical world has been pushed further towards some brink, attempting to outpace, in parallel, our growth towards enlightenment, a condition it abhors. Now ever closer to WW3! A war which the elite, those who have and will always follow our Archon handlers, believe they will be the only survivors of. The good news is, not all prophets were false, and the Prime Eternal Creator used them to show us how this game finally ends.

So again, whether you believe all this or not, it matters not, because as we say; *all will be known in the end.*

It could also be hypothesized, given the great amount of recurring NDE & PLR data which agrees on this soul fractioning topic; that the Archon captors confine some portion of our soul, the *hostage link* in their heaven matrix, because allowing our entire completed soul to be reunited with the portion within our physicality, might automatically restore our condition back to its original created *light-body* form and power prior to our misguided *consent, entrapment,* and subsequent *cycle of enslavement.*

Thereby finally rendering us again as the most powerful beings within this creation, and surely more powerful than our Archon captors.

But for those who do believe, are enlightened and take direct action before their end, for them the rest of this journey and final destination will be more pleasant and finally, final.

Feeding the gods so they may live!

Continuing with the ideas from ancient sources, how it is believed that these Archon's, who have been known by many names, through many cultures, and always by bloody cultic behaviors, actually *feed* on our soul's energy output! That in fact, they are super-technical parasites who found a powerful source of eternal energy in us. A case being made from a scientific point of view on this is that these Archon pirates are more able to gain a continued source flow of energy from us through suffering and strife narratives, than from pure love and harmony. As of course, a world of pure love would instantly break their control over all. So then, we now have another reason for the implementation of all their false control narratives. Most of which in one way or another revolve around pain, suffering, death and destruction.

Again, if this overall condition of *evil & death* were not the true goal of their cyclic end-game, then we would already live in a very different world. Our history and the current world condition is our true guide to proving this.

It has also been speculated, and as I touched on earlier, that these Archon entities utilize the great power of our *living-souls* by our power of creation. Feeding the one through destructive narratives to cause their desired outcome as they feed from the other.

Again I submit as evidence our ancient to modern span of world history, if not only to prove the continual and growing propensity towards a narrative of destruction and death of all living things. The cycles of human suffering upon everything that lives, sentient or non-sentient knows yet no boundaries, nor limitation; ***where there isn't war, there is greed, where there isn't greed there is hunger!*** *Thus, as I keep pointing out, and as continuously proven by our world history alone, we could easily identify their narratives for human and animal sufferings as their main tools.* Tools utilized with no end in sight because our *projected* negativity is that which is required to sustain these evil souls since losing their eternal tether!

Cracks in their dam

As I previously stated, and I believe I am in no way alone in seeing this; that an awakening of souls in people has begun. One crossing cultures and language.

With mad men of low character being used to greatly heighten this world's fear levels and suffering in some desperate attempt to quell the universal enlightenment occurring, theirs is a move of desperation. They have been losing control for some reason.

I tend to believe that this loss of control may be the impetus for them to have greatly escalated the phenomenon we know as the *Near Death Experience*. Could it be that this NDE phenomenon is yet another enhanced narrative tool the Archons use in our modern times, and possibly to a lesser degree throughout known history in order to gain back positive control of the narratives? Very probable I say. *A marketing ploy so to say.* Whereas in prior years it may have been used more modestly to maintain the superstitions in mankind along cultural lines, it has certainly gained great momentum in our more modern era. This would make sense since many souls for some reason are regaining their strength and conscious ability to see the facade against the truth. Allowing more and more near-death patients to return with such vivid and specific memory narratives in which the Archon's control.

Doing so knowing, that those returned souls/people will tell everyone what they experienced, *thus driving the controlled narrative ever deeper into the collective consciousness!* But why? Of course, when people hear these stories they easily commiserate and gain their own personal perspective and understanding for why "god" would return someone; *to enlighten and strengthen the faith in the rest of us of course!*

BUT WHICH god?

We have to bear in mind however that unaware people/souls can only work or think within the paradigm they previously accepted, and only through the very narrow, usually religious choices, they are provided through the earth matrix narrative system. Therefore, we can surely understand that mankind is easily redirected back onto the Archon narrative vector of travel via simple *after-life* experience narratives.

To further exacerbate the issue we have a quickly growing segment of scientists and researchers all supremely interested in this field, especially so after the findings and verifications our quantum physics has provided us within the last thirty years. Their great interest, scientific prowess, and professionalism is both a blessing and a curse. The blessing is that they are quickly taking that which has historically been deemed a pariah, and at best esoteric babble, into the mainstream, giving the field, its understandings, and all that their subjects are returning with, great validity. The cursing will be that they continue to take what they are shown at face value, understanding and misunderstanding it all because of their own learned paradigms that are also derived from the Rebellion leaders controlled narratives.

A multitude of souls are shown the same specific controlled theme, with subsequently more and more being returned to reiterate that theme. In conjunction with our somewhat recent ability to hypnotically regress people back into the detailed memories of former personas, again, all appearing to coalesce in their detail with those NDE accounts. All then probed, detailed and meticulously documented by those who make said information internationally available to the masses. Who then consume and assimilate without any additional stream of ancient knowledge or in-depth scholarship applied prior to dissemination of these alleged *after-life* experiences. And for these reasons the Archon rebel usurpation of our original earth creation continues unabated, and they have already won again.

All of the scientific data, and all the systems used to distribute that data, then become the greatest vehicle aiding and bolstering their Archon narrative systems.

For all the points made in this chapter based on the available past-life and near death experience data, the points made in the last paragraph alone are the reason we should stretch out far past our comfortable learned paradigms to seriously consider this Archon "Adam-Eden Matrix" possibility to be our current literal reality.

If in fact, this is our current and mostly unknown reality, then those perpetrating such an adverse possession of men's souls and our creation, will continue to be the only ones that gain from our continued short-sighted lack of understanding. Worse is our unwillingness to consider it! For these reasons, and quite possibly for the sake of life itself as we have yet to know it, I ask that the reader, and all researchers within this field, as well as other sciences, open themselves to the far larger possibilities, and allow themselves to become aware!

"Today, the solitary inventor, tinkering in his shop, has been overshadowed by task forces of scientists in laboratories and testing fields. In the same fashion, the free university, historically the fountainhead of free ideas and scientific discovery, has experienced a revolution in the conduct of research. Partly because of the huge costs involved, a government contract becomes virtually a substitute for intellectual curiosity. For every old blackboard, there are now hundreds of new electronic computers. The prospect of domination of the nation's scholars by Federal employment, project allocations, and the power of money is ever present...and is gravely to be regarded." Dwight D Eisenhower

Chapter 11

The Creator Consciousness,
Our Place and our Ascension

"Not only is the universe stranger than we imagine, it is stranger than we can imagine…" Sir. Arthur Eddington

"The universe shapes itself around our conscious beliefs, which are projected into being by the intention of our living-souls…" S. Asher

The question of what this world is, and how it is created will ultimately bring us far closer to answering *who the Creator is, who we are,* and *why we are here.* A lofty endeavor to be sure.

Thankfully and amazingly, although by design as well, by our own advancements into that virtual electronic world, we are finally coming far closer to the true understanding of our own world reality.

If all of the scientific proofs and correlative assumptions previous to this chapter have left your brain hurting, especially so when combined with ancient spiritual, religious and cultural knowledge, this is to be expected. Most of the ancient texts and precepts provided herein are most likely new to you, and on top of it all the science in and of itself requires us to learn a completely new language, while at the same time trying to comprehend ideas which are far outside of our paradigms, and previously learned and accepted views. For this reason, I ask the reader to please try one more time now to understand and assimilate the following information, which I will attempt to translate in the simplest terms possible.

After you assimilate the following, at the end of this chapter and in the next, I will explain how it all connects to a mercy far greater than previously intuited by man or explained by his two-dimensional religions; but more importantly how mankind as individuals should continue forward with the overall and greater understanding of this book, and the application of a most profound and simple idea, *to treat all souls better than you would have them treat you.* Simple you say? Then why has it not been applied widely and continuously by all people, throughout all generations? Because it has been treated as no more than a byline.

> *"If light is like a classical wave, its speed should depend upon the elasticity and inertia of the medium it travels through. If light travels through the medium of empty space, its speed should depend upon the elasticity and inertia of space. However, how can empty space have properties?"* (Brian Whitworth – The Physical World as a Virtual Reality: Pg. 11 &12)

The **Virtual Reality** or **Holoverse** hypothesis explains this issue quite well, while the *"objective Reality"* hypothesis cannot, and leaves us falling woefully short of true wisdom. Providing the outline of both I present the following: (Based on Brian Whitworths – The Physical World as a VR, pg. 11) (Whitworth)

- **Objective Realist Hypothesis** – Reality is purely physical, it exists in and of itself, and requires nothing outside of itself to explain it...
- **Virtual Reality Hypothesis** – Our world exists by depending upon information processing occurring outside of space-time.
  Observation for both:

1. The Realist Hypothesis relies on the Big-Bang theory which allows for nothing or any creative force prior to its occurrence:
   - **Question** - How can space-time emerge from nothing?
   - **Question** – Who created the Big-Bang?
2. The Virtual world Hypothesis relies on the fact that it must begin from an influx of data – thus, there must exist a data-creator.

As our technology has progressed which is expected due to the fact that we are the co-creators, and thus as any child will eventually do, our tendency is to create to some extent in the same ways in which our Creator or parents do.

"Quantum" - *The smallest quantity of some physical property, such as energy, that a system can possess*

By the observation of science we know that things like light are "quantized" as Photons, this fits the understanding that *we are a virtual reality*, which is also identified by the precept of *quantum minima*, which in digital processing determines that – *(All objects and the events thereof must have a minimal quantity which cannot be reduced any further.)* Of course by our understanding of digital processing the objects being referred to are **pixels**; however we are now able to see that our Plasma based creation/world and its *particle matter* building blocks for the required objects in our reality work in a far greater, but exact same fashion. Thus, by our own virtual space creations (video games, etc.) science has found that our entire creation in its own right, is made up of individual "pixels." Of course to most this automatically sounds outlandish, that is until we are shown what the scientists have found and been able to test and reprove.

Either way, pixels are a great representation for our initial understanding of our own reality, while knowing that pixels are the form in which we create our more inferior virtual reality simulations.

Far more amazing than mere pixels, the Creator projects His creation building blocks in the form of "**all potentiality**", which our science intuits as "<u>waves</u>" of the potential for everything, both imaginable and not yet imaginable. Thus, we can understand all this *wave potentiality* as <u>The Creators "Intention"</u>. Just as we now understand our living souls to also have the much slower and scaled back ability to create our reality by our own "intention".

Meaning, our *intention* literally turns/creates and maintains His storehouse of *wave potential* into the *particle matter* objects that we see and feel. These exist only in waves of <u>*potential creation*</u> until acted upon by even a single consciousness. Our terms for His pixels in their more complex state should be understood as *Electrons, Photons,* etc. The end result of it all proves this place as being what we tend to understand as a virtual reality, or as I termed it in this book, *the Holoverse.*

> *"The universe shapes itself around our conscious beliefs, which are projected into being by the intention of our living-souls…"* S. Asher

Science has found that what we perceive as the universe and space is "quantized", or <u>pixilated</u> into individual atoms – meaning, *space-time, and energy are all quantized.* This is most important to understand, because just like our own inferior productions of virtual realities have a finite number of component building blocks, as well as limited CPU function and storage, so it would appear this creation also has a finite number of building blocks, unless or until its Creator decides to expand on that. *Or could it even be that in our original, unadulterated light-body form, we are able to expand our own playground in this same way?* These finite building blocks are in turn hypothesized by some scientists and believed to be proof by others to mean that this created world also <u>has a finite number of states</u>. *This, in turn, proves a Creator of the space.*

Continuing with the example of our own computer systems and their inherent limitations thus far, scientists believe it can be understood, although in a vastly simplified way here; that the reason the Creator produced our simulation to exists in a state of *wave potentiality* most of the time, and not in a full-time state of *actual particle matter reality,* is because doing so would take massive amounts more energy to keep the entire reality in place, and fully functional all the time.

However, I do not agree with that highly limited assumption. I believe that this system of wave potentiality exists in this form of the *'potential of everything that can be',* rather than *the physicality of what can be,* because of the Creators primary law – Freewill! Simply put, it is one thing to create a small area for children to play out their free will, and express themselves to grow that playground outward and based on the *impetus* within them, as driven by narratives of *Good & light;* vs. creating all that can be created for them to play in, thus leaving them no room of their own to express their souls impetus. Thus leaving no way of testing their free will expressions, ability and heart to always color within the Creators willful lines on their own.

Therefore, given all we know about the Creator and this created place as expressed so far in this book, seeing the proof of His free will system being created first throughout all creations everywhere; then the creation of all souls to inhabit all levels of said creations; then the separation of souls *above and below,* evidently dependent and dictated by the expression of their free will choices; I cannot share the simplistic, science only assumption that its reason for existing in *non-physical wave form only,* to be based on power consumption and hardware limitations alone. Because of course, we are talking about THE Creator of all things here, not a futuristic Apple machine.

Created Limits

Einstein posited that our universe or *creation-space* has a speed limit. However, what he did not prove is why that governing rule appears to be in effect. I see this speed limit to be proof of a creator! *If there is, in fact, a rule, then there must, in fact, be a ruler who created and instituted the rule!*

This proof of *created limitation* has come through the measurement of the Kinetic energy of an electron or more generally known as the *speed of light*, which of course appears to have a top speed which cannot be exceeded within this created space at this time, and in our current less than top spiritual condition – **We have been governed!** *Thus, light speed appears to be the set limit of our creation space-time.* We can continue to add Kinetic energy to the electron, and its speed will move towards its top speed of 186,000 miles per second, but it will not exceed that known limit. As you will see later, I can use our own techno-creation of computer chips to prove the same built-in limiting factor; but for now, we can understand that all of our own virtual reality computer programs, as all programs are, limited or governed by the capacity of the CPU.

Which in turn is *limited* and *governed* by the knowledge base of its creator. Or in the case of the created holoverse, we exist in, limited by the wisdom of our creator, and for specific reasons that should become quite obvious soon.

Another important point to consider in all this, and as it pertains to what we know concerning our own limited creations of virtual reality spaces, is that *all quantum particles/matter are identical.* This is known as **digital equivalence**. Which is to say, *all objects created by the same code are always identical.* Thus by default, being that all of the building block particles of this creation are identical, it is proof enough that they are objects of the same code, and thus, *the same code creator.*

Quantum Entanglement:

"Hence, it is clear that the space of physics is not, in the last analysis, anything given in nature or independent of human thought. It is a function of our conceptual scheme. Space, as conceived by Newton proved to be an illusion" Dr. Max Jammer – The Concepts of Space: pg. 173) Also endorsed by Einstein. (Jammer)

Quantum entanglement or *Spooky action at a distance* as Einstein coined it, is yet another proof of our virtual world as correlated by the lesser technology that we have made. *Meaning,* in a virtual reality world, space and distance will not limit correlations, which is to say that *all points are equidistant with respect to the creative source of the simulation, i.e. – **God is with us!***

This is provided as an example by scientists, as it concerns the processors within a computer; *all points on its screen are equidistant with respect to the location of the CPU. Simplified,* the processor ignores the distance to the projection screen. This is yet another proof found to exist permeating our world reality by what scientists call *quantum entanglement.* In very simple terms here, their tests have shown many times, that when two *objects – particles* like say two electrons, are brought into close proximity to each other, they somehow become "correlated"; *in super simple terms we may think of this as both of them becoming intimately acquainted with one another, like twins.* After which the most amazing thing has been proven to occur; that even when these two or more objects are separated by great distances, when the "observer" affects one of the electron objects somehow, regardless of how it is influenced, the <u>*other* object is observed to mirror that identical change instantly, with zero time</u>

<u>elapsing</u>! These objects can now be separated by a billion miles and the outcome will be identical each time the observer causes a change to one or the other. Therefore, just as Einstein came to understand and express towards the end of his life cycle – *'Space seems to be an illusion created by a virtual construct'*. Now let us remember, his understanding of this was well before he ever saw a computer as you now have them, much less a simulated virtual reality.

This Entanglement, or Einstein's – *Spooky action at a distance* – proves many things to scientists today, and of course has them all reeling with the possibilities it presents, such as Star trek type *transporters,* their *food replication* devices, and much more.

However, what I believe I can add to that from the spiritual side of all this is, *that ultimately all living-souls, whether they inhabit human or animal body-hardware or no hardware, are all inextricably connected.* And that even if we do not all feel the pain or joy of every other individual instantaneously within our current three-dimensional realm *as a disturbance in the Force,* it still does not mean this core point is not true. Moreover, by the way, most of us act towards each other and most animals, this slight disconnect turns out to be an enormous blessing and karmic disaster at the same time.

We are all connected, we have always been connected to each other and to the creator, and we are all equal!

Chapter 12

Deconstructing the wave

by our Conscious Intention!

"…atoms or elementary particles themselves are not real; they form a wave of potentialities or possibilities, rather than one of things or facts". (Warner Heisenberg – Physics & Philosophy: Pg. 160) (Heisenberg)

A s previously stated, it is proven and understood that particle matter, *or that which makes up all that we perceive to be this material world around us,* <u>does not exist in that form</u> prior to a person's <u>*observation of it.*</u> More simply put, and also stated earlier in this book; the Creator's Macro-soul or consciousness from which we all originate and are Micro too, affords us the literal ability to create our own surroundings and emergent futures individually as it were, by mere observation, <u>which is acted on</u> by the *projection* of our soul's *intention.* Which is to say, *the interaction and subsequent influence by our Soul-Consciousness on all particle matter is creating our perceived world.* As science has now shown us, all matter, prior to the conscious interaction by us, <u>exists only as a wave form of potential</u>.

Taking this understanding a bit further; based on the above fact, we should now be able to understand that;

'each consciousness, each individual soul, with its individual knowledge base and personality which has been seeded and cultivated by various narratives, creates their world and ultimately the entire world creation we live in, by those personal influences and the totality of their individual knowledge base — As projected from the soul.'

Never forgetting that all souls have prior life influences stored up and adding to their internal impetus. Impetus for good or for evil in varied percentages.

Our modern video games *create the* *pixel infrastructure* <u>frame to frame</u> as you move and turn throughout that game-space, while at the same time it **deconstructs** the *pixel environment* from which you turned and moved away from while playing. This makes our created game spaces very elemental platforms compared to our *particle-matter* based *super-holoverse,* however, the basic concept is the same.

I find it very interesting how several top physicists have posed the following question or even pose it as a statement of fact that; *'when we turn our attention away from where we are, that like the video game, our reality ceases to exists there; or, as we sleep, how much of our matter based reality continues to exist around us.*

Some Physicists have posed that when we are not aware or physically watching our reality; that it *deconstructs into an out of focus like a soup of matter until we reacquire it with our consciousness.* This, of course, is extreme to think about, however, I believe, for reasons which seem obvious to me, that our virtual holoverse world has a built in mechanism, quite like the *opposite* of our light-speed, *speed limit.* Another mechanism <u>which retards that rate of *deconstruction*,</u> unlike the gaming space we all know, and that which I used in the example here; which literally, totally *deconstructs* as you move through it to save computing space.

Soul-Consciousness-Entanglement:

The glue of our Physicality!

While even more interesting, and as I have posited throughout this book; quantum entanglement seems to suggest that our *correlated souls*, which are pure plasma energy, are so connected, that we all work together, unknowingly, to create that which we all perceive to exist around us, for better or worse.
"This day I present to you Good & Life or Evil & Death"....You choose; you receive, and you live with it!

This quantum entanglement *correlated-Soul state* may just be that mechanism which enables our physical manifestations within this created space to continue to exist in that *constructed* physical state while our individual consciousness is not actively engaging it.

In other words, this deceleration, the mechanism that impedes, is the reason why it all still exists *(not deconstructing)* behind you while you are not influencing it directly with your personal aware consciousness at any given moment.

Meaning, that everything you believe to be behind you right now, or at any given time, is in fact still physically behind you right now, and NOT deconstructing, as they posit. Additionally, what scientists have found and tested proves that we do NOT even have to engage, by *looking* at a wave or particle matter, or in any specific direction within our perceived physical world in order to *collapse the ever present wave of possibilities into a state of constructed physical matter that we identify – i.e. what we see as the physical world.*
The replicated scientific findings have shown clearly that even the **"knowing"** or **"presumptive knowing"** of a particular outcome collapses that wave of potentiality into particles – *(the physical world)*. Thus, proving that everything exists and everything is connected, however only as *potential* until the *"knower-creator"* force, which is our consciousness, our living soul, considers it – perceiving it to be!

Therefore proving, that we do not have to *interact* with our surroundings through our physical eyes, for our surroundings to continue existing in that state while we are away from it - *Surroundings that have been created by many generations of individual and collective consciousness's even previous to our own interactions.*

Meaning, it is, in fact, the continual "knowing or cognizance" of that perceived creation-reality that we left behind, that allows that physical reality to remain cemented by what we call our unconscious state, which keeps it all in place as we remembered it last. *Now, multiply this by all the other people/souls who have that same memory data as you have, within them.*

People, conscious souls from generation to generation, and even up to one minute ago, may have seen the mountains around you, as you do now; their conscious *knowing* and all those after them maintains the mountain creation structurally, albeit even *differently* as all those before them, or as we perceive it, after them. *Please now recall from an earlier chapter, my Eden Effect!*

That although, throughout all time our consciousness's' interact to both, create a new, or maintain an existing creation by our soul's conscious projection of it, or by our souls conscious and subconscious, *knowing* of what already exists; we all tend to perceive the same structures of creation, differently!

In addition to this portion of, and what I call the "Maintenance mechanism"; I believe it to be the quantum entanglement correlation of souls, in conjunction with all of our memories that we have taken in and will take in, all working together 24/7/364 in conjunction with that *Maintenance mechanism* which keeps our realities both near and far, <u>intact</u>! All physical realities being maintained by us and other people who are *correlated* to us, as well as other people *not* correlated to us, but correlated to others, <u>all possessing the same overlapping memories</u> – *(in the knowing of!)*

Although I have never personally heard anyone posing this *Physicality Maintenance mechanism hypothesis,* I believe it to be an extended and multi-layered connectivity mechanism that all scientists should seriously consider in this context of physicality "construction-deconstruction."

In summation of this *construction-deconstruction* theory, it would appear that all roads lead back to it being our powerful, living-souls who work continually to *retard* the *deconstruction* process of our perceived physical world. Which so far has been the prevailing scientific theory of which I do not concur.

By all this and more, the conclusion which is taken most seriously by scientists in these fields is, that this creation acts exactly like a virtual reality. What I am adding to all this as you are seeing, is that the long-ignored facts concerning the Prime Creator entity of this place and of all creations, *and of our living souls,* is that HE has created our *Soul-consciousness in His image, or type.* Which is to say as I have long taught it, *'our living souls are literally the microcosm-soul portions from His Macro-Soul'.* The Prime Creator creates all creations by the *projection* of His awesome *intention,* and thus provided us a place to create *within* His creation by the projection of our individual, and collective soul *intention.*

The main difference being, that most of us have not for some time, nor do most currently, *reflect the Character of His Macro-Soul*!

The evidence of this is simply proven by our historical treatment of each other and all animals within this creation space. Even our treatment of the creation space itself. *Our soul-impetus as individuals, and as a collective still seriously lacks the greater capacity for absolute mercy.*

Inside and out

I find that most people attempting to visualize and understand the concept of their surroundings being a *virtual reality,* compared to how all people tend to believe their surroundings to exist, have a lot of trouble grasping it. I believe most of the issue tends to center on people's understanding of a hologram as they have seen them appear in movies. The far simpler way for me to show you how to understand why your reality *feels, smells* and *tastes* physically tangible to you, and still able to be a virtual creation is to express it in this way; *it is because you are <u>inside</u> the created virtual reality simulation.*

The reason why we can *see* our own created virtual reality holograms, which appear to us so accurately depicted, but still unable to feel them as a physical construct, only to have our hands pass through it, is because we are **<u>outside</u>** of the virtual simulation of that hologram. *We are the creator of that virtual thing!*

Who is the Creator?

> *"The universe begins to look more like a thought, than a great machine"* (Physicist, Sir. James Jeans)

Now that most honest scientists have put the question of *created* vs. *Big-bang happenstance* to bed for the final conclusion of a definite Creator force. The next obvious questions for everyone seemed to be, *how* is this created, and are there levels to it?

From my research and perspective, I tend to believe that the scientists are still missing parts of this, which again may be eluded to by our most ancient knowledge.

A *"mind=consciousness=soul."* It has elements of integrated states, and functions in a state of quantum entanglement to process information non-locally, unlike the previous theory, that we processed everything by a simple hierarchy, as I depicted in earlier chapters by the work of Physicist Dr. Amit Goswami, and other renowned medical scientists. As well, it should be understood that a *consciousness-mind-soul,* does not require matter to exist.

Consciousness is immaterial, unlike the processing hardware that we have created in the form of computers, in which run the faux-consciousness of *software*. That software's ability to run could not exist without first the hardware. Thus *consciousness-mind-soul* does not require the existence of particle-matter in a space-time environment in order to function creatively – *to build*.

It is now of the utmost importance that we must understand and consider, *that this world reality has in fact been created with its known limitations, specifically to govern or limit our soul's ability to create.*

We should also understand from the contrary scientists perspective who cite the *realist hypothesis;* that space-time somehow pre-existed the alleged Big-bang, or worse, was spontaneously created by it - *which of course cannot be, citing; how can space-time emerge from nothing in the first place; i.e. an influx of "nothing" that created everything.* That for the creator to be creating this environment by the classical *Realist hypothesis* of space-time, we are forced to consider, that if that higher world of our creator were a literal, Newtonian *objective world*, rooted in classical physics, that this now becomes an even larger issue for us to solve. That issue being, that the *simulation* is being run by some type of classical hardware, and as such its <u>quantum-bits</u> would have to be <u>unpacked into classical bits</u>. This venture would result in the actual hardware to drive the simulation to be larger than the Creators entire universe! This, of course, is another ridiculous notion. Therefore the truth of our present state must be something else.

"Leibniz's of Indiscernibility of Identicals – States – The principle that if two objects are absolutely identical, then they must be indistinguishable from one another with respect to all of their properties".

Yet another idea of how we exist, which came and went

That our creation is being simulated by future humans as an *ancestor simulation,* however for this model it could be any future, or highly advanced civilization, etc. This idea was set forth by Nick Bostrom - *(Are you living in a computer simulation: Philosophical Quarterly, (2003), Vol: 53, No: 211 pp. 243-255);* (BOSTROM)

Although immediately understood as impossible by him for the following reasons:

- If we are being simulated by other advanced entities, then by default their world would also be quantum bit based, having the same features as our own.
- Which then implies that they themselves are also a simulation by an even higher advanced "simulator-creator" above them, ad infinitum!

This would be understood as *Infinite regression - the intermediate and endless levels of computer simulated life by far advanced humans/entities in the future.* Again leaving us to seek the simulation process and its creator from another direction. Of course on its face this idea of one higher set of entities producing and controlling or manipulating the one below them has been categorically denounced as impossible, but mainly because the physicists are leaning on the hypothesis as previously provided above, that each previous higher, technologically advanced culture's processing hardware would be impossible to build or use to make this happen. *However, I believe we are seeing a self-imposed limitation here.* One that very effectively provides the reason for why our previous world cultures believed that in fact, other higher advanced beings have always existed above us, and influencing us for better or worse.

The scientists employ *Occam's razor* to shave away the notion that there could or should exist any other superior beings above us, and above them. Or more specifically, anyone between our creation and the consciousness that is creating us. However, I posit that Nick Bostrom's intuition may actually be true *in a non-infinite regressive form.* Which is to say, that yes, Nick was correct to intuit other beings far in advance of our own current abilities to exist above us.

I have shown you thus far in earlier chapters how this clear possibility has lived within the knowledge base of many ancient cultures and in great detail. However, they perceived these beings to be gods *because of how these beings presented themselves.* This much has been clearly presented by our ancient writings and cultural beliefs. For this reason, I have depicted and concluded the following throughout this book:

- That yes, otherworldly or ethereal beings, in fact, have and do exist.
- That yes, in most cases some have falsely presented themselves as gods.
- That they have on many occasion ruled the cultures of man in this creation space.
- That they have instituted and left us their own revised legal and social instructions.
- That in our modern times it is still believed by many that they continue to influence our cultures from behind the scenes.
- That there seem to be many people who also believe there exist even higher cultures of beings above them.
- That most religious cultures tend to believe there exist 12 plains of existence, with 2 below ours.
- That modern science as well tends to show the same possibility for parallel universes.

A Created collection of Non-Infinite Regression Realities!

Breathing new life in Nick Bostrom's intuition

Instead of applying Occam's razor to shave away the probable 9 creation levels between us, and our Creator above, let us understand that instead of them all having to create each other by the use of greater and greater impossibly intricate technology, that all of them and us are in fact created by the Eternal Creator Himself - *With no need to exclude any of them, or to limit Him.* Both paths of understanding coexist perfectly, and in fact, they aid to prove the assumptions of this entire books premise. That those entities residing in various *far less restricted* creation levels above ours, who have influenced all of our cultures throughout our known history, some of which who have also misrepresented themselves as our creators at times, do actually exist. As well, other souls residing in even less restrictive creation levels also exist above them. Always bearing in mind the *freewill* aspect which provides all souls at all levels the ability to express their free will choices.

Now the question becomes, *'why so many creations of varied intelligence and ability.'* The short answer is that all souls were created equal and remain equal on all levels except for one – *Impetus!* Our soul's impetus towards choosing good or evil dictates which *creation-space* that a particular soul is allowed to reside in for a time. While speaking to a close friend on this subject, and myself seeking a simple way to answer this question in a vernacular that most will understand but also fit the essence of the overall story, I pose it this way; *that since we see an increasing level of awareness and ability from station to station, that we can look at these creation levels, as stations to ascend to in time based on each soul's individual level of knowledge, but more importantly, wisdom;* for without wisdom one cannot be trusted with higher knowledge, <u>much less greater ability to *spontaneously* create</u>. And ultimately that ability for a soul to create as it wishes is the entire essence of all I am trying to present here.

The goal is to be able to trust any soul to reside within any higher creation space which has far fewer restrictions or governing mechanisms that limit the soul's ability to create. Meaning, how quickly any new creation becomes a reality in that space.

As I already pointed out via both the newer scientific proofs and the obvious logic, that this 3rd-dimensional creation space is highly limited, and obviously governed in order to slow both our soul's *creation construction process*, as well as this creation levels *deconstruction* process.

For your ease of understanding we can look at this in the same way that all governments tackle their system of Security levels; in which each individual person, based on their *knowledge, character* and proven *wisdom* in certain areas, can be trusted to ascend to a higher security clearance level, as well as access to higher security areas; or in the case of creation, higher realms which afford that soul a far less restrictive creative ability and environment.

Conversely, when that person or soul, while within that higher realm or level of security is found to be untrustworthy by *disobedience, infraction* or *subterfuge,* then, of course, they are demoted back down that same line to one of the lower, more restrictive levels. Of course, it would be logical to understand that the position or lower level in which they are sent is directly proportional to the depth and breadth of their infraction.

Thus, there you have it! Not a single creation space, but a series of several creation spaces, all being created and maintained in real time by the Creator Himself, *by the projection of His conscious intention.* All *originally* created and maintained for the **enlightenment, correction** and **elevation** of all created, living-souls. Therefore, we can now understand that any other levels, above this level, not as being filled with other alien type beings, but all the exact same *living-souls* as originally created by The Creator.

All of which enjoy different levels of access and ability depending on the level they are trusted to occupy. *Their trustworthiness directly correlated to the soul's impetus to invariably cling to and uphold The Creators Free will system and His Everlasting Agreement throughout all creation levels.*

The beginning and end of this story or *simulation* has always been conceived and projected out of the creative consciousness of our Prime Eternal Creator. Although the greater understanding of our perceived physical surroundings can be hypothesized in varied ways, most usually disproportionally to a religious bent, I believe the more balanced marriage of both spiritual and scientific core elements provides us with a far greater and more deeply personal understanding, and hopefully, ultimately greater wisdom; that being:

That through it all, all the science and religious dogmas; the layers upon layers of superstitions and apologetics for all those superstitions by later generations, the following constants remain:

The Creator has always been the one projecting and controlling this design.

1. All the control narratives throughout time have been *allowed* as *our* free will choice for our eventual correction, and the correction, or final rejection of those few souls who resist His correction process - Archons.
2. Most of the living-souls remain unaware of the process because of the few, "Archon" souls who, *also unaware,* maintain the narratives and believe themselves to be in control.
3. All souls are here for the same reason, *their consent,* and all must come back to the same wisdom in order to *return* to a higher existence.

I proposed previously, that this creation, its Archon controllers, and all of the rest of the living souls in this creation space as maintaining a hierarchy, the few over the many. I made these accusations based on the solid, high scientific evidence in conjunction with this creations ancient writings, cultural beliefs and long held spiritual mythos. I presented this *action-reaction* event oriented hypothesis showing; *who we are; who they are; and who the Creator is.* I further presented it to depict *where we are; where the alleged Archon power base is; and where the Eternal Creator is within our original estate.*

However, in my initial presentation of all this, dictated more by the known religious and spiritual dogma's of our world's history thus far, I depicted the overall picture in such a way that I made clear separations between all of the above-mentioned entities and localities. Leaving the reader this way, however, may lead you to incorrectly extrapolate the following negative points:

1. The Eternal Creator exiled us!
2. He has forgotten us!
3. He has allowed other evil beings to enslave us!
4. I will never find my way back!
5. Quite possibly He does not want me back!
6. Is this hell?

Now allow me to explain to you how and why none of the above possibilities are true. As well, our science and even our spiritual understandings and misunderstandings tend to prove these to be the Polar opposite of the truth!

As presented in an earlier chapter:

*   Yes, our original estates (heaven) exist, which by default would have to be the highest and final creation we can ascend to, *and,*
*   Yes, our original state of being as eternally living souls exists for us still, *and,*
*   Yes, that is where the Eternal Consciousness of our creator resides. *Remember, our creative living-souls are apportioned from His Macro-Creative Living Soul; and,*
*   Yes, at some point in our most ancient of pasts it must be that many of the created eternal souls, transgressed somehow, trampling the Freewill of others, breaking His Primary Everlasting Agreement. *There was clearly some infraction of the Eternal Creators sacrosanct instructions that got us all entrapped, and keeping us all here.*

So it would appear there are two scenarios to choose from:

- Either both our souls and the souls that all of our religious superstitions incorrectly depict as *higher beings, angels,* etc., transgressed collectively *in heaven,* which got all of our living—souls demoted to this starting point, *or*
- Those *higher-souls* did something to get themselves demoted from the higher levels and trapped here; *Working against us as our combined religious texts and cultures depict, <u>pretending to be gods</u>.*
- In doing so, therein lies the main portion of the second scenario possibility; that this *3ʳᵈ dimension-creation reality* was originally created as a starting point for all new souls, a *Kindergarten* if you will, and not specifically for demoted souls. A creation that these other *higher* souls have been allowed – *via their Freewill* – to believe they actually usurped and reformed aside and away from the Eternal Creator. *For you to understand this second possibility better, you may have to harken back to the early chapter where I explained the two creation stories.*

As a quick recap of that earlier chapters core idea:

- The souls that originally occupied this place (us) existed perfect in our original *light bodies.*
- At that time we were manipulated into mimicking the same sin against the *Everlasting Agreement* by those who needed us to reflect *their character* or *image as those text tend to inaccurately translate it.*
- It is most important here to remember that we all made that choice by our own free will, thus by our own *consent* we gave them jurisdiction over us.
- No one forced our souls to consent! Force is not manipulation, and manipulation by definition is not force. *Already knowing His Everlasting Agreement, we could have chosen to walk away.*
- By our choice to murder the animals, usurping their free will, as it is written in the Hebrew, ***Our light was covered with skin.***

And here you are in that skin learning who you truly are. <u>The time to end all consent and return is now!</u>

Amazingly, regardless if we choose to believe scenario 1 or 2 it makes no difference because the end result remains exactly the same for now. We *chose* to *hear* the voice of another entity, and we *chose* to choose that voice, their plans, their instruction and ideas over that of the Eternal Creator of all creations. We *chose* to follow another entity and put him above that of the Eternal Creator, much as all of the religious cultures tend to reflect their beliefs. Those *Archons* now believe they are the gods of this place, but only because our souls gave them that position over us, via our free will choices while in either scenario 1 or 2.

Additionally, here is the larger rub; having their higher dominion and abilities which far exceed our own in this state, they are being audited and judged daily for the actions they take for, or against all those *souls* which are currently inferior to them, <u>below them as it were.</u>

Exactly, in the same way, all of our souls in this 3rd dimension creation are audited daily and will be judged for our own actions and lack of mercy towards all those *beings/souls* that most of us consider to be inferior or lesser than us. *In most cases, these are those we know as the animals, as well as more defenseless humans.*

From within this *Trinity-6* physical condition, or from within any higher, less governed condition, that is the entire reason for all of these levels of creation, <u>*to test the impetus of all souls*</u> before rising through the various levels of creation. However, I do not believe for a second, which is an opinion backed up by many years of deep academic research and understanding in my field, *that the loving, Eternal Creator intentionally manufactured this obvious soul recycling system which provides on its own, no way out of the rotation.* **No, the** preponderance of the evidence and correlations shown herein, and found in a far greater measure from other sources paints the picture. We have been utterly usurped for a season.

If this was not true, then why do so many prophets of various cultures tell us that there will someday be a renewed universe and a renewed earth; and that all animals and people will again revert to His original, merciful dietary program? Leaving the lion and the lamb to eat grass instead of each other, and led by children?

The original, uncorrupted system was the Eternal Creators multi-level soul sifting process to seal purity!

By the ill-advised free will choices of our ancient past, which are clearly choices we continue to follow through all epochs via the many *false narratives* that have been instituted, our security clearance was revoked for those higher creation levels! All important points to understand before we move on.

As you have just come to understand in this chapter, our virtual reality creation exists as a *super-holographic* VR. And finally after so many years of resistance by the Newtonian scientists, this line of understanding, and because of certain verified findings, most scientists are now inescapably forced to conclude that yes, a Creator does in fact exists!

How these findings should affect all of humanity is simply this; that our creation space has not been lost to, or separated from the Creator at all, <u>but consciously created and projected into being by him in real time</u>. That though it is easy for most reading this to assume we are *captured* here and lost to true freedom, we are not separated from Him at all, nor forgotten or left to be enslaved or tortured by any other defiant entities for their own personal gain. Much less without redress or the ability to relearn some original truth which enables us to *return* from the previous infractions. To exercise that truth is to vote "NO CONSENT!" *And then Return!*

That indeed, by all of the correctly translated ancient texts and coherently applied spiritual perspectives, which are now bolstered by these corrected scientific observations concerning our perceived reality, we can know the following:

- That all of the negative influence narratives are used towards His ultimate gain.

- That all of the souls are free to express their *impetus* for evil, or change from it by our free will to *Good & Life,* **and**
- That all souls are here to endure that which they *consented* to and continue to consent to via so many Anti-creation control-narratives. **And,**
- That the simple changing of one's impetus consciously back to the mercy and love that their soul already knows, should reign supreme, and finally allow their ascension!

In the exact same way that we may teach our own children in quarantine, we have either been admitted into this lower creation level or chose incorrectly while already here without the full knowledge of those entities plans. Ever since experiencing the discomfort of our choices until our souls individually exceed their capacity to absorb the negativity of it all. Like the proverbial wine press, the evil plans of those entities over us, unbeknownst to them, are being used against them and ultimately for the reconciliation of all living-souls. *Again, this is yet another religious narrative portion that most religions retain correctly.*

These evil soul entities believe their processes' are theirs alone, and for their own eventual dominion over all souls.

However, in truth, this appears to be an *allowed* version of *soul-impetus testing* and *purification* mechanism, *albeit a highly unsophisticated version set up by those disobedient ones.* But for a time it is being allowed to test the free will impetus of those evil souls, themselves. In any case, the system is cycling us to a point in which we begin to feel the great depth of our own disconnection from our previous perfected state.

Advancing each soul to a point in which they are eventually, nearly instantly made aware of a greater wisdom towards total mercy. Our *better Angels* as it were, which in most lives we remain meagerly aware of, and too easily dismiss until the dam of our previously firewalled soul's true impetus for *good* and *pure love* comes flooding out. This deep change to our soul's impetus is dramatic enough to make all those close to us become perplexed at our new aversions.

The most ancient of paths for Righteousness and Wisdom, in

which provides a true emancipation from this world's false narratives; our souls now totally aware, are able to consciously project a new life path of pure mercy and love on all levels, with no areas rationalized away as insignificant; THIS is the test!

However, this return and reconciliation process is an anathema to all those around us who still wish to understand the false narratives that we left, as the correct cultural norms.

I would be remiss here to not mention the plight and eventual judgment of those souls who will always resist the small voice and nudging of our Creator to return. Of course as always, virtually all of this world's religious dogmas have their like-minded superstitions on those souls deemed unredeemable.

As I depicted thus far throughout this book, all folklore, myths, and superstitions usually have an original root core of truth to them, as it is also the case with those souls who will never comply. Unfortunately, there is much gray area where those souls are concerned. Where is that cut-off point for them? Logically based on all I can know, that cut-off point will most likely reside in whether or not that soul-person had the full knowledge and understanding of who they follow or served. For there are many, even the majority of souls-people throughout time who have served the side of evil and inequality, but still remained ignorant to the identity of the ones they truly served.

I tend to believe that in most cases, had those people known then and now, the actual identity of the entities they served, that such a realization would be enough to make them stop. Thus, based on this basic logic alone, even without considering the apt words in a multitude of prophetic texts, it would appear that throughout time, regardless of all the manipulations by false control narratives provided by those who believe themselves to be *as god,* the greater multitude of souls will be redeemed.

Therefore the greater and more simplified understanding here is, that the many negative narratives placed here through time, regardless of who we tend to believe designed and implemented them, are ultimately here and *allowed* to be here as stimuli, and not for mere punishment as so many in our religions have incorrectly discerned, _but for awakening_.

Additionally, they are the only stimuli that can eventually direct our return to the Creators state of consciousness, (in His image), which is a state filled with the impetus for _love, mercy_ and _equity_ for all beings and creations, both sentient and non-sentient, and thus void of anything opposite to those simple standards.

All of the narratives of evil or for good, are not only used as proof of a soul's propensity for one or the other but proof of the Eternal Creators vast and ongoing profound ability for mercy. Mercy and love being the lesson, which is the Character of the Eternal Creator in which we must all strive to return to by shining that character back to Him. Only in this can we begin again within this lower creation space to reflect the image of the One who made us, for reconciliation.

It has been said and evidently understood for all time and memorial that the elite families and their Priestly rulers of this world reality have long been aware of the details of all these truths concerning the true nature of our reality.

Keeping the secrets of it close, and the mechanics of how to manipulate it for our gain even closer. They restrict its knowledge for their few, to the detriment of the many. Again, as always we are left asking, why? _Answer: Their god promised them the world!_

Once known to be magic, the few constrained this knowledge for the enhancement of their own power, and the enslavement of the rest. You say that you don't believe that? That such a secret could not be contained all this time.

Well, until our more modern times when science has been allowed to flourish and those practitioners of it do not live in the fear of the king or Papacy murdering them for it _as often,_ these secrets of our reality were far simpler to contain and restrict from the general populations. We can see even in our own times how until more recently, government scientists have been towing the party line of junk science in many disciplines. Take the Physicist _Stephen Hawking_ for instance. He only very recently finally gave into the reality that a

Creator entity did produce all we see and experience here. Until his recent epiphany from the facts which he could no longer ignore, he spent his entire career working to prove that no creator existed!

There are many other scientists such as him who continue to refute and argue against all the blatant evidence that other, more enlightened scientists have found. Now, to be fair, many of them argue against it all because to cave to its truth would be tantamount to admitting they spent their lives and careers to that point being completely incorrect about nearly everything. Every peer reviewed paper and every book ever written by them now proven to be near utterly fruitless. The other scientists who knowingly continue to cast their darkness against the light of such verified truths, and in the faces of such great minds, work for the Kings and Priests in their unending crusade to maintain their grip on the magic, and out of the "knowing" of the masses.

> "Because the understanding of a thing,
> becomes our liberation from it"

Simply put, correlating and providing the knowledge as I have thus far in this book, and the mechanics of it to every man, woman and child within this reality, with their subsequent practice of it, would quite literally change this reality is short order, as we un-consent from it!

Example; If every adult in just one entire country, *say the USA,* became utterly convinced of these truths and the mechanics of *projecting intention* and the *knowing* of a thing, all coupled with the absolute verification within each person that the Creator does exists absolutely, and that he creates ONLY life and wishes us as well to create ONLY life abundantly wherever we can, our reality would explode with positive change!

To have those millions of people's knowledge base expand in this way overnight, and with their collective spiritual convictions re-targeted more pointedly, now able to focus their *intention* on love, mercy and equality for all living things like a laser for longer periods of time as an actual lifestyle, rather than a periodic honorable mention, in all their thoughts and daily actions going forward, our entire Nations reality would change in days and weeks, rather that this slow grind.

No longer would the few elite kings and priests of magic be able to use their negative intentions and false narratives to coax us into waging wars. *Their own ability and main weapon to focus the thoughts and intentions of our masses negatively via their media and staged events would literally collapse overnight!*

Additionally, since all of our living-souls within this reality are truly *correlated* and connected on some level, then quickly thereafter the souls of all other nations would intuit our collective impetus in this direction, and the narrative of righteousness would spread like fire in a high wind.

This, of course, would severely diminish the magical ability of the few kings and priests within those nations as well, and with their ability to influence the mass consciousness of their own people by their media, false narratives and staged events, they would be overcome as well.

Therefore, as the overall truth and reality of our existence which I have been attempting to bring into your consciousness hopefully clings, we must finally take personal responsibility and acknowledge that our world's most negative and declining reality is less the fault of the few evil souls who have hidden these truths, and acquiesce to the more realistic evidence. That it is the fault of the greater collective soul population who allow the few evil Archonian sycophants adverse possession and control over them by continued consensual evil.

It is nothing new - We truly remain ruled by our own consent!

Many people may recognize our greater situation as just explained above within the ancient Hebrew story of King Saul. Even if you are not religious, please read it carefully, because this is all of us. **Sam 8-4** *"All the leaders of Jacob gathered themselves together, approached Sh'mu'el in Ramah, 5 and said to him, "Look, you have grown old, and your sons are not following your ways. Now provide us a king to judge us like all the nations." 6 Sh'mu'el was not pleased to hear them say, "Give us a king to judge us"; so he* *prayed to Adonai. ₇ Adonai said to Sh'mu'el, "Listen to the people, to everything they say to you; for it is not you they are rejecting;* **they are rejecting me**; they don't want me to be king over them. ₈ They are doing to you exactly what they have been doing to me, from the day I brought them out of Egypt until today, by abandoning me and serving other gods. *₉ So, do what they say, but give them a sober* warning, telling them what kinds of rulings their king will make." *₁₀ Sh'mu'el reported everything Adonai had said to the people asking him for a king. ₁₁ He said, "Here is the kind of rulings your king will make: he will draft your sons and assign them to take care of his war chariots, be his horsemen and be bodyguards running ahead of his chariots. ₁₂ He will appoint you to serve him as officers in charge of a thousand or of fifty; plowing his fields; gathering his harvest, and making his weapons and the equipment for his chariots. ₁₃ He will take your daughters and have them be perfume-makers, cooks, and bakers. ₁₄ He will expropriate your fields, vineyards and olive groves — the very best of them! — and hand them over to his servants. ₁₅ He will take the ten-percent tax of your crops and vineyards and give it to his officers and servants. ₁₆ He will take your male and female servants, your best young men and your donkeys, and make them work for him. ₁₇ He will take the ten-percent tax of your flocks, and you will become his slaves. ₁₈ When that happens, you will cry out on account of your king,* **whom you yourselves chose**. *But when that happens, Adonai will not answer you!"*

₁₉ However, the people refused to listen *to what Sh'mu'el told them, and they said,* "No! We want a king over us, *₂₀ so that we can be like all the nations, with our king to judge us, lead us and fight our battles." ₂₁ Sh'mu'el heard everything the people said and repeated them for Adonai to hear. ₂₂ Adonai said to Sh'mu'el, "Do what they ask, and set up a king for them." So Sh'mu'el told the men of Jacob, "Each of you, return to his city."* (Emphasis added)

There you have it in a simple ancient historical account. As we see, nothing has changed under the sun — *"All this has happened before, and it will all happen again!"* The people continue to consent to that which they have little understanding, even after being warned of its considerable negativity. It is easy to say, *that was then and we are* not the same, etc., however again, this would be inaccurate. At that time they had already been steeped in a false religious narrative which had them moving quickly away from that which was originally provided to them, first through *Abrahim,* and then by *Moses.* As clearly depicted by the Creator entity reminding *Samuel* that they had in fact been leaving Him since the time He brought them out of Egypt. *Still slaves with the slave mentality* who yearned to be ruled in the *same manner in which they enslaved and ruled most mercilessly over their own personal slaves and animals.* Imagine! To be slaves of the Egyptians, only to be divinely released and then endorse the slavery of others for your own gain! THIS is the proof of mankind's wayward souls. *The proof is in the impetus of a soul!*

In my ancient Aramaic culture, they would say that your soul's impetus is **marked** on your **forehead** and in your **right hand** – *meaning; that which you believe in your head comes forth out of you by the actions in your right hand!*

No different than any people of any Nation State today. *Give us a King or President, the perception of security, a job, a TV, our steel belted radial tires, and leave us alone!* The only major difference or change in how the elite Kings of this world behave towards their enslaved masses today is, that they eventually learned to allow the masses to *believe* they have freedom and security. By masking their overt controls within systems for the greater good, spreading them out through many diverse systems of control and collection; they became the proverbial armored hand in the velvet glove. *Give them some hope, but never too much hope, lest they break our bonds!*

The parallel and correlation between our new scientific proofs regarding the current limits and greater possibilities within this reality, along with our creative ability to affect it by our soul's intention for good or evil, coupled with the ancient knowledge which points to the same truths of that reality, have proven to be far more than circumstantial.

Rather than continuing down this same controlled path of destruction and continual enslavement, all people-souls must finally now come to the knowledge and understanding of these most simple truths to break free and return to our spiritual, (non-religious) connection to our Creator entity, as King!

The simple precepts in action

- That the Creator exists, and exists forever as our Prime Creator.
- That there can no longer be any man, system or mediator between us and The Creator.
- That we now simply change our impetus from any form of destruction to mercy and equitable life for all.
- To move forward spiritually and culturally within the paradigm of creating and maintaining life for all living beings-souls, as well as all non-sentient life.

This is the simple way to ascension from this lower realm of existence. This is who we all must endeavor to become again!

In our original estate, which is the uncorrupted state of our being, we were able to create all that you see around you now and even so much more, near instantly, and by our own intention we created it and lived harmoniously. We know this because we are, in that way like the Eternal Creator Himself.

With such creative power, there is much responsibility and trust. As you have now come to see by our science, even in this lower creative realm the main properties of our creative abilities which allow us to effect this realms state of being, remain intact; albeit our creative ability has been greatly limited by certain design parameters, I trust you now see that there is very good reason for this. *Our "intentions" cannot be trusted!*

As you have now seen the science and ancient understandings depicted, *our projection of intention,* which is driven by our living-soul/consciousness and the *knowledge, beliefs,* and *superstitions* compiled within it, has the ability to effect change on the quantum level. However, because we are not yet responsible enough, and like most children cannot yet be trusted with such a powerful revolver, all of the changes that we can possibly exert, *thankfully develop in front of us at a far slower rate, and more thankfully in many cases not at all.*

Therefore, this greatly governed state of existence is providing us the *time* required as individual living-soul entities to re-connect the dots, to identify and understand the gravity of its power and awesome responsibility. Of which is a power only afforded to those who learn to *return* to the Eternal Creators original pure path of love and mercy. Some have coined this endeavor as, *"the path to enlightenment."* By whatever label, the core truths remain the same.

The prophet Jesus put it in the Hebrew terms of his day, advising us – *"to treat all souls as you would have them treat you..."* *And that all of the instructions of the Eternal Creator hung on this main understanding.* Our other Hebrew prophets said, *that our Eternal Creator only required mercy and prayer above all else,* as this same sentiment has also been professed by other notable people within other cultures. And in the most notable and apropos words of the Prophet Isaiah:

Isa 24:5 *"The earth is corrupted under the inhabitants thereof because they covered-up the Instructions, pierced the Ordinance, and broke the Everlasting Agreement!"*

The entire earth has been corrupted! And for over 2500 years, not one religious expert from any cult ever thought to inquire as to exactly what this *Everlasting Agreement* being spoken of, even was.

The final takeaway should be; *that we continue, and remain to be somewhat dangerous creative soul entities!* **Who corrupt!**

And this virtual creation in which we find ourselves presently can and will only advance to the level of the wisdom gained and projected by the majority who exist within it. Moreover, unfortunately, the opposite is also true!

We are all correlated and linked as one. One with our surroundings, one with all other souls who seemingly occupy distant places, all linked as one with the Creator Himself. If all of this and all you have come to know within the confines of this book alone, is not incentive enough to make a deep and ongoing self-inventory, and sweeping changes, then try to remember, your ascension up and away from this existence, hinges on whether you can be trusted to move on! Hope to see you there!

Final Chapter

The Real You & Them

IN the beginning there was a Creator, who created many souls from His Macrocosm-soul.

Since then much has been lost and forgotten, once perfect souls enslaved by their own will. Consenting to the works of entities who mislead and misjudge for their own gain and very survival. The scar tissue reaped from these ends and thus far never ending is like so much cosmic debris, spiritual detritus that clings to each soul's interdimensional quantum memory. So densely layered and seemingly inaccessible that our modern sciences scratch and claw, identifying only symptoms which they perceive as their target to heal. With no intuition to consider the root -*A persons Living Soul!*

Of all the mind-bending and soul stretching hypothesis and intimations I have come to envisage in this book thus far, you must concede to Occam's razor to discern and consider the simple intent of it all, and proceed forward at the very least with portions of this new paradigm. A greater mission to save yourself, and in doing so saving others. A paradigm in which we perceive all that was written or understood to be the evident truth from ancient times, as mostly scripted; and to all you perceive as being your undeniably palpable world *reality,* to be something else. Yes, much of the information weaving the hypothesis herein could be internalized as negative, and even frightening. However, its message would serve us better to be processed as a positive course correction to an ancient path that is now again new to us. Fully realizing that our path thus far has been thoroughly manipulated by those who hate us! Returning now to a path rooted in compassion, and focused through a lens of pure love, dispatching all hate or bigotry, and certainly not one of mere tolerance. Because even the slippery slope of *tolerance* is rooted in one breed of orthodox narrative core, or another.

There is no doubt any longer in the mind, hearts and souls of a growing multitude worldwide that a major shift in our consciousness is occurring, and this multitude, which is still a minority at the time of this writing, is quickening the souls of another larger, but still groggy multitude. All of which is proving to supersede borders, languages, cultures, and religions, and doing so to the great distress of Archon controlled governments who have thus far controlled us all. As well, to the distress of those Archon soul entities that control them. Paying closer attention now, you may perceive that this *true* spiritual awakening and its burgeoning growth has an opposite nemesis attempting to run beside us. I believe we are witnessing the controllers and their earthly custodians ramping up their fear and death control-narrative system, spooling up war after war, while dismantling economies.

As stated in the last chapter, I believe this can be understood as them attempting to keep pace in parallel or better with the ascension process of our once again expanding consciousness. I believe the last time in history that this awakening began was in 1960's America. Why America?

Although it may be a topic for another book, I firmly believe it has begun here and spread out worldwide from here, because neither this place nor its core soul-lineages are who even they believe themselves to be. I believe, partly based on specific prophesies by the great prophet Jeremiah, and other related data, that the spiritual majority of souls in America, whose conscious intentions have been salted around the world, were sent here to spearhead the awakening. That they are an ancient population chosen to this end. From its beginnings, America was targeted for destruction through infiltration, and boy are we seeing the fruit of those labors today! The true identity and purpose of most souls in America, which has now grown exponentially worldwide, in my mind is exactly the main reason why the Archon's have introduced their final solution to their earthly sycophants. Their *Singularity-Event-Solution!* The forced merging of all soul energy into one giant AI – *Artificial Intelligence.*

Of course, that may sound so thoroughly over the top to most people. However, if the reader would only do their own research on such topics, they would find that there is a large scientific and political core who have been working towards this very end. And they wholeheartedly believe that it *will* be done. Or might we say; 'the *will* of their masters will be done'.

Although born in the 1960's, I am not a child of the 60's. Even though, having grown up so close to it, and being reared and influenced by so many who were there; my opinion, based on all I have learned is that the 1960's awakening and subsequent movement was still too eclectic, having the basic core principle of *Peace, Love,* and *Pukka beads*, but still lacking the understanding of our need to return to a most ancient core compact for any awakening and subsequent *Soul Revolution* to have true power and teeth; the *Everlasting Agreement,* which is our most powerful weapon. A light bulb requires all of its parts to produce light, not some of its parts!

And although most onlookers incorrectly, even arrogantly might see that principle of the Everlasting Agreement as nothing more than some meek restriction based on some obscure religious tale, I assure you as an expert in that specific field of study, further from the truth they will never be. Moreover, all might do well to remember exactly who will inherit in the end. Meek does not equal weak!

To my knowledge, although they came very close to causing our fulcrum to tip aggressively, no one during the 60's had the truly corrected path for all to follow, which could have assured our victory.

Upon close inspection, it appears clear that the Archon's know when these soul awakening events are beginning long before the *Soul Revolution* begins in earnest. This affords them the ability to get out in front of any burgeoning consciousness tsunami, to shut it down. At that time they initially shocked everyone's naïve consciousness's by murdering JFK so openly, at which time they quickly followed up with a war to regain control of the narrative.

From the year 2000 to this very day in 2016, we see this same scenario playing out again in earnest, and with increasing speed and ferocity worldwide. I believe this is directly due to the quickening of so many souls globally. This was to be expected, but their final authority and control over yet another epoch and the Freewill of our billions of souls is not inevitable, or assured. As many believe it has been foretold, these rebel souls know their reign is going to end badly.

What we, our *living-souls* who inhabit the persona of *mankind* became is due to our poor choices and perpetuated by our individual and collective loss of memory. The introduction of controlling narratives was not inevitable either, but as I have depicted, *chosen* continuously via one form of consent or another.

And regardless of how one wishes to believe that occurred, or by whose hand makes little difference, because the outcome thus far has been the same, as its predictable end will also be the same. The object of this work was to provide a more literal and greatly expanded holistic view from the oracles of our past, mingled with the revelations of our here and now. Provided as such in the hopes that more souls will be enlightened, affected and directed to this original, ancient, elevation of consciousness.

A *Soul Revolution* driven by its cascading effect to overcome the false, narrative driven mind/soul control. A rejuvenation of a most ancient nation, striving to amplify a greater legion!

To this end, I believe this final chapter to be the most important and divinely positive segment of this book. To that end, when it comes, I will end this book's message with the same theme in which I began and carried throughout, which is to reiterate that we all truly begin to – *"Treat all souls as you would have them treat you"*.

In this simple admonition hangs the perfection of all living things, souls or otherwise throughout all creations! So seemingly simple, but rarely lived as a rule by any majority of souls for an uninterrupted period. A bold statement, yet again borne out by the known history of life on this planet. THIS is now the entire basis, and the uplifting feature of our new paradigm shift towards an awakening. No longer merely an ancient saying or religious anomaly to be spoken vainly, but now realized in mass to aid the reawakening of Living-Souls. A seemingly spontaneous awakening to innate knowledge leading us towards Good & Life ONLY! A law that has always been quite literally written on our souls, but quenched and diverted by a generational legend.

Our aim is to become incompatible!

While *projecting* the *intention* of an awakening that disavows and disallows any judgment upon others by anyone for the color of their skin, the slant of their eye, or their nature in general.

Not the law of attraction, or moral relativism, but the common law of LIFE! Do you want your own children, extended family or friends slaughtered for any reason? **NO!** Would it be OK to slaughter them for food? **NO!** Would it be OK for others to slaughter them for believing something differently? **NO!**

If you answered NO to all of the above for your own, then why do we allow those among us to work as our proxy in the indiscriminate death of others? *Government; Corporations; Industry etc.!*

We know who they told us our enemies were. We know who they say they are today, but who will it be tomorrow, YOU and YOURS? Surely as you sit here today reading this, there are dark forced arrayed who plan the silence of so many awakening souls! *Rebel by non-Consent!*

Silence of the Epochs

There are many Great flood stories spanning many cultures, several of them more detailed than the most noted and referred to Hebrew flood story. I touched on this antidotal topic in an earlier chapter, pointing out how some believe the Great flood, *end of an Epoch* story we have today, to be a reversal of its original story.

I wanted to present this mostly unknown concept because it at least circumstantially fits with other apocryphal texts depicting the prophet Jesus teaching the idea of how many such ancient stories and their main facts, were later *turned upside down by the scribes. Reversed, reformatted!*

I will also point out that this idea of *context reversal* also fits tightly with all I have presented concerning the character and misdeeds of the Rebellion-Leaders. Remembering that their main and ultimate goal is the total usurpation and control of all the souls within their domain. Also remembering that by their awareness, and moral intemperance concerning who we are as *eternal* Living-Soul entities, these Archon's do not believe that eliminating entire planet-wide populations to be *literal* murder of anything; since they know better than most people alive at any time, that our souls are eternal, *thus by default no true death exists.*

Specifically, total annihilation is nothing more than a reboot. To them, no more insidious than you reformatting your laptop and wiping out all of the holographic data *entities* within it.

I bring your attention to *Robert Lanza,* a noted expert in regenerative medicine and scientific director of the *Advanced Cell Technology Company;* who turned his attention to physics, quantum mechanics and astrophysics to formulate the new theory of *biocentrism.*

Lanza and co-author Bob Berman, the most widely read astronomer in the world, has a theory codified around the understanding that death simply does not exist. That death as people misunderstand it, *is an illusion that exists only in their conscious state because their identity centers on their physicality.*

That most people, deep down tend to believe, that when the body dies, that their consciousness will disappear with it. *Lanza,* as many top scientists now believe, and as I have posed herein several times now, believes that our *soul-consciousness* exists outside the constraints of time and space.

Going by many of the same NDE and PLR subject data as I have for this book, *R. Lanza* also believes that the soul-consciousness can and will continue to live on in another body, even the exact same body, after traveling through the "tunnel" to another, *similar reality.*
Robert Lanza 2012 (Berman)

As I touched just previously, and as alleged by ancient knowledge, it has been proposed that in fact at the time of Noah the greater populations of the earth were coming to a tipping point of *higher consciousness*, and not at all as our later stories – *controlled narratives* – have presented, and been endorsed by all people.

That, in fact, the people were not at all falling into such great evil as it is written and that the only possible remedy by *some god* was near complete annihilation just prior to their tipping point.

For if we are to believe that at such an early stage in man's history here on earth, that a "god" who allegedly created the plasma and particle-matter building blocks which enables the very existence of all things perceived to exist, could not find a way to instruct His created ones directly, thereby improving their disposition and overall awareness of both Him, His requirements, and their plight to ensure a more perfect union; then who is this alleged "god" that we follow or look for? By our current narrow understanding, *not an all knowing, all capable creator entity at all it would seem!*

So it would appear to a thinking person being truthful with themselves, and having the fortitude to break down old paradigms, even at least for the time it takes to consider another, that mere apologetics for all the alleged religiously inspired texts that we have, especially those stories that came after the flood event, is not good enough. How do we apologize for the unmerciful and sociopathic actions of this alleged god which verifiably extended into many cultures long after that flood event?

There is no doubt that there exists an *accumulation event*, a number of souls at any time who are coming to this enlightened decampment. Souls whom, starting out as a slow spawning and accumulation of both knowledge, coupled with a new ability to explode out of old false paradigms with no remorse or thought for all those around them who scoff. Moreover, spreading wider and faster like infected cells; assembling, concentrating, swelling their ranks without even the conscious understanding of how blatantly and forcefully they are pushing against an unseen enemy, all the while breaking their hold. No one, no soul as yet knows the final number of enlightened souls it will take to tilt their fulcrum forever in our favor.

Some believe that number to be a mere 144000!

However, I assure you, the Archon's know! They watch! And *they* are attempting to reacquire this control as you read this! And if for some reason they are restrained, and positive control of all souls, or at least the vast majority of us cannot be regained, then, in the parlance of Christianity I submit:

"As it was in the days of Noah, so will it be again in the day of the coming of the son of man"...

Thus, the issue may be that no one truly understands HOW it was in the days of Noah!

An enlightening of souls that were instantly washed away and rebooted before the power shifted from the grasp of our controllers?
That appears to be a probable case. With a new reformulated religious narrative provided on the ground, as the reformatted souls housed in their false heaven matrix are slowly filtered back into a new epoch, for another round energy feedings.

A new crop of old souls with recently added scare tissue. Lingering spatial anomalies just outside of their conscious ability to acknowledge their injurious consequence, providing us no ability to discharge their adversarial effects.

Soul scarring

Which now leads me to the greater, and I hope most positive revelation and theme of this book.

If the evidence of how all souls are being recycled can be established and verified as I believe it has been through the sheer number probability of the subject multitudes. If the corresponding fact that the greater majority of people never retain a conscious memory of any past life experience can be proven, *a point I believe to be easily verified by anyone;* then how can so many allow a disingenuous idea from religious narratives which maintain and requires so many to believe that all souls/people are born *one time* and with a *clean slate?*

We are then forced to ask the question which I deem to be somewhat obvious concerning the vast amount and array of people/souls, who are so adversely affected by various and expanding types of mental health disorders of various degrees.

Where do these instabilities *truly* originate from? Debilitating issues that are growing on a grand scale globally it appears. Issues, which in far too many cases are proven to have existed from very early childhood with no clear root cause perpetrated by the standard fair of local environment, parental or cultural stimuli, or biology.

First the Extreme

For instance, what makes a very young *Jeffrey Dahmer?* One agency who has been tracking and profiling these types of serial killers is the FBI, and they appear to have become quite adept at it.

The compiled information on these types of predators does show that they all have some and in most cases quite a bit of unresolved childhood propensities for torturing and killing small animals, as well as abuse towards their siblings and others.

Especially interesting are those cases of very young children who exhibit such shocking proclivities, yet have no known previous life experiences that one would expect to find as the main stimuli and impetus for such super-anti-social behavioral issues, and actions against all living beings.

If the core catalyst did not exist in such a person's early life, then how can this serial killer segment exist? Where did it come from? *What is the root dysfunction?* Of course, there have also been cases where the original negative stimuli did exist, and yes, may, in fact, be part of the reason a person goes off the proverbial rails, but these serial killers and the sheer level of protracted violence appears even to exceed that theory. Yet, no one seems to search for another initiating factor in all this. If science has now proven, *that it is our soul which receives the upload of our life experiences and knowledge, as well as universally intuited data, ostensibly carrying vast piles of data from many lifetimes.* Then we could posit, that all of these previous layers of experience, both good and bad in varying degrees and percentages via the souls' previous incarnation interactions, enforce a high degree of subconscious influence over our emotional condition and brain hardware functions.

It then must be strongly considered, that many peoples' fomenting issues, whether or not their issue is benign or catastrophic, may not at all stem from any negative stimuli in *this life,* but subconsciously bleeding from a past experience which is now flowing through this life. Unrealized consciously, and in most cases unresolved. Much less by pharmacology!

Whether it be law enforcement, religionists or governments, most are driven by societies need to affix some label on these people as they grow to adulthood. Such *two-dimensional* thinking organizations such as medical Psychiatrists', Law enforcement, religious leaders, government agencies and others, tend to apply the most possible negative characterizations on the people who they deem to exhibit these types of anti-social behaviors.

By the revelation of my hypothesis here concerning the probable *point of origin* for most human emotional and mental frailties; and specifically by the correlations of our scientific and ancient data on this subconscious *soul-memory* understanding, which depicts the coupling and interaction between our DNA and living-souls; it now behooves us to contemplate most seriously how many of our modern, socially unacceptable behaviors could very well have been considered normal and accepted in times and cultures past. Behaviors, which could have been quite possibly in some extreme cases, the basis and centermost focal points of some ancient cultures, *i.e. human sacrifices!* It is not hard to envision how any child being programmed by their current life's family culture into being a loving, *insert religious sect here,* learning right from wrong, could also be plagued inwardly on a subconscious level from past life memories, just as we saw earlier with the young *James Leininger* story. Increasingly driven by inward polar opposite thoughts and feelings to those they are learning and being forced to experience in *this* life. In some cases in which many of us are aware, their inward drive increases over time as they infrequently at first give into those emerging fetishes. Only to become more aware of its legitimacy to them, driving them closer to their inherent *former*, even *ancient* urges as time wears on.

As many of us may be aware from living among people, some *phobias & fetishes* can be controlled, and many cannot. It is my contention that most of these should be understood to be driven in each individual by their soul's percentage of previous negative experiences. Wounding by deprivation on many levels.

In many pagan cultures, Archon influenced priests removed live human hearts and ate them. As well the consumption of blood was and is still believed to provide great power and extended life; especially so with the blood of children. The same goes for other cultures who used young, *unblemished* animals for their version of *feeding the gods*. When the facts show, as they have done in many such extreme cases, that no previous prevailing negative stimuli existed in most of the worst *super* anti-social cases, *as with our modern serial killers, etc.,* then a scientist or any thinking person must search for another origination point of contamination and influence for that behavior to have flourished. Merely concluding that every such case is due to a broken and unbalanced brain chemistry does not cut it. That path of diagnosis does for sure however aid big pharma.

As history has shown us, many, if not most of the worst serial killers were known socially by virtually everyone around them to have been highly social people, and always the last person anyone would have suspected to exhibit such gruesome behavior; much less having a refrigerator full of expertly butchered human body parts ready for consumption. So now we have to start asking ourselves when we see such behavior – '*Who was this person before?*' In my opinion it can no longer all be categorized and boxed up as mere *mental illness*, subsequently camouflaged by pharmaceuticals.

Soon an alternate approach and different work must be applied in order to greatly improve the extraordinarily low *actual*, verifiable cure rate of these people. Hypnotherapy is one such light that has been providing phenomenal results in this area because it aims straight at the soul memory level.

Amazing in a severely unfortunate way, the facts show that although pretty much all countries have identified and convicted serial killers, with *Dr. Harold Shipman of the UK topping the charts with the highest known confirmed slaughter of 218 patients, possibly 250; and Louis Garavito of Columbia inching into second place with 138 people murdered, out of a believed but yet unconfirmed possible 400;* the United States has the entire planet beat hands down with the most known serial killers on record; next being our number of known pedophiles.

It suffices to say that we do not require a scientific evaluation to know that of all the countries worldwide, *the USA not being the most populated of them all,* is not a place whose culture and living conditions for children or adults, in general, is such that would lend itself by its nature alone to breed so many violent serial killers organically.

So, as I just previously expressed, we evidently need to be searching somewhere else for the origin of these serial killers super-violent propensities, and or sexual proclivities. I would also like to point out that the entire mental health establishment and all its alleged experts, have yet to truly authenticate the original reason for these predators behavior, nor have they been able to *talk* them off the ledge by any conventional psychiatric means. Nor have their drug programs been able to reverse the *assumed* brain chemistry issue among them. Thus, in large part, it is a last inning, three strikes issued on the part of the psychiatric healthcare community. The drug companies, however, are booming!

Soul proclivities

Surreptitiously motivated, even unto themselves by previously and yet unresolved Soul damage, these types of extreme murderers and sexual predators all present the inability to fend off their innate drive towards horrific nightmare scenarios. The medical community should peer far deeper, considering the internal soul-drive as the dynamo for such behavior.

Remembering from earlier chapters how Russian quantum physicists and other biophysicists have now proven how the majority of our DNA, *erroneously labeled as "Junk DNA" by the epic failure of the Human Genome Project's final results,* do in fact work as memory storage receptors and transmission nodes, which transmit most of our lives experienced memory information to our soul for final capture. At which point most life memories are stored forever. And as I posit herein, may lay the issue to it all.

Probable Hypothetic scenario: *In the well-documented case of serial killer Jeffery Dahmer, who killed people and removed internal body parts for his private consumption.* Could such an extreme case be driven by a past life in tribal South America living as a Mayan high priest? Or for that matter at any point in history as a pagan priest who sacrificed people and animals, eating their freshly removed body parts? Of course many might recoil from this possibility, calling it fantastical, but in the face of a couple hundred years of modern science not being able to prove any repeatable results in this area, the hypothesis at least bears further consideration.

Moreover, there is and has been ongoing, repeatable results of people being healed of many horrifically debilitating phobias by *hypnotic regression therapy,* also once laughable, as it remains in the minds of most Western medical practitioners.

Again, we have to ask, where have these phobias come from? So many of the cases where the subjects are adversely affected in profound ways have no previously known or experienced dysfunctional preadolescent background in their lives to accuse as the source. Of course, this is not precluding that some people have established phobias from *known stimuli* in their lives; but if only ten thousand people in the world had debilitating phobias with no known or traceable source for them, then this question remains valid.

However, as most might imagine, the numbers of people with phobias, fetishes and super extreme behavior abnormalities for which their source cannot be accounted for, is far higher than that.

Touched on already, hypnotherapy has proven extremely effective in many documented cases. Also proving to have a very high cure rate. So, if so many people have no known, previously learned or inflicted source causing their phobia's, fetishes, psychotic or sociopathic behavior; to now find many people with known and unknown causes being verifiably cured by top hypnotherapists and even past-life regression processes; does this alone not lend enough evidence to consider the hypothesis as actionable? A case for these injuries to be originating from a higher, soul source? A soul evidently scarred by extreme emotionally charged circumstances in a past life cycle, but having no conscious memories of them!

To the contrary, if the Western medical community is correct in their two-dimensional prognosis, and all of these psychiatric issues emanate from the human brain's inability to cope or occurring strictly from a chemical imbalance; then how can they account for so many of these issues in people who have no correlating, original trigger mechanism for the psychiatric issues in their current lifetime? The logic stands on its own and needs no defense, much like all truth. *A clean slate that has no history of being written on, nor signs of influence by extreme adversity, and therefore remains a normal slate.* Such a clean slate *soul* should have no historic adversity attached giving cause to that person's extreme phobia or super extreme anti-social behavior. Much less a clean slate being the root cause for such extreme cases as serial killers or any highly violent or sexually driven propensity.

The proof then is not in the pudding, it's in the soul!

Serial child molesters, proven by medical science to be uncorrectable or redeemable, with the only option being to isolate them until death. *Or recycling as it were.*

Other sexual proclivities in seemingly normal men and women, although in most cases not dangerous, still exhibiting much of the same animalistic drive in the character of those people as well. Much as we saw in the story of *Aristophanes* as presented by Plato in an earlier chapter; that quite possibly some of these lesser urges between people can be attributed to the original dividing of our living-souls by the demigod of this creation, into thirds.

Urges that cannot be fended off or subdued for long. Urges that eventually, just like in our serial killers, pedophiles and other classes of phobias, if left to their own ability to *self-edit*, will always give in to their inner *souls'* unquenchable drive.

I believe all this to be yet another sub-routine of the Archon leaders' control-narrative system. Part and parcel with, and why all of the memories of all lives, in all souls, is continually firewalled. A sub-system of fear and negativity played out in generally negative ways upon the person that houses a phobia or psychotic propensity, as well as upon all others around them.

Inflicting pain and suffering atop of the main negative narrative routines playing out in our daily lives. *Accumulatively!*

Marking & Labeling to create deeper soul scars

As I have previously pointed out many times in earlier chapters, how religious organizations and their death cult based narratives have turned *inequality* and *intolerance* into sport with erroneous labels. By their own ancient narratives which have been provided to them by some demi-god who is characterized as equally narcissistic, and known by his own sociopathic tendencies throughout many ancient religious texts; they fabricate and command allegiance to other sub-narrative, social intolerance routines. Narratives to instill yet more fear salted with the more than occasional social stoning for one alleged sin or another. Even today the main control narrative and sub-fear narratives march on under a thin veil of *false love, tolerance* and *equity* within the halls of certain large religions.

There are many Christian leaders who appear quite ready to begin stoning homosexuals in a New York minute if the right authoritative figure gave the nod. At least Islam makes no pretense about their unrighteous misadventures. When they find a gay person among them, or even suspecting one, it's over rather quickly. And if a homosexual is not present, any female will do in a pinch. The moral of the false narrative story is; *the Archon manipulators are in all the details and sub-details!*

What better way to create sub-narratives within the main control narratives to cause more fear, dissension, loathing, and of course many eventual deaths for "god", over many generations of recycled souls, than to create anti-establishment narratives!

LAWS, like, *stone all gays* and *uncompliant women*, burn all alleged witches, cut off the head of a resistant Ox here and there, etc. First, they incorporate these sub-narratives into our main religions, and *then* they purposely return souls to new bodies in such a way as to all but guarantee these socially *unacceptable* behaviors to emerge in greater and greater numbers from within the people in which those souls were implanted.

Have you ever consider that a predominantly male or female soul may be reincarnated into an opposite type *Trinity-6* body hardware, *purposely?* Having all the dominant experience and emotions of a man or woman from his or her past life experiences, to now be completely out of sorts with no understanding of even themselves, or why they feel like they do?

I, as also you may have experienced; many of these consciously confused people/souls tend to turn against their Creator after being told by the vast unwise priestly class that, *god created you this way...* Well yes, *some demi-god* entity may have, but NOT the original Eternal Prime creator.

All mostly meek and un-confrontational people/souls, whose purpose built condition becomes greatly exacerbated and exploited by the even greater UN-wise leaders and pundits of the aforementioned religious cults who label and target these people/souls as *abominations, sinners, infidels,* and the tired like.

Levitical intolerance narratives

Under these intentionally, Archon directed perfect storm conditions for those *mis*planted souls, who, during their current life cycle ultimately receive more fear, regret, death and generally negative *soul memory-scarring,* which later moves forward into their next recycle. Thus, causing and perpetuating this proverbial *overlapping* wave in the pond effect. An effect which causes more soul-scarring, and all but guarantees additional layers of negative emotional effects, in both this life, the next, and thereafter!

Additionally, and on a much greater scale globally and generationally, this overlapping effect adversely scars the souls by varying percentages of everyone else involved with those socially and religiously unacceptable people who have now been destroyed by the intolerant love of chosen priests, and their superstitious automatons. Your own child, family member or friend may even be considered one of these religiously and socially unclean, control narrative derived bit players today.

Souls whose past life *soul-memories* have been recorded and stored up as predominantly male or female from previous life cycles. Now purposely placed into the opposite sex *body-hardware* for the *Soul* purpose of creating narrative scapegoats to be the whipping posts for all those who assimilated opposite narrative streams. Streams, superstitiously driven by the majority of people who consent to and believe all narratives to be of righteous origin.

These are the majority of sleeping, controlled souls who remain awash in and manipulated by their own assimilations.

Where is there room for – *"Treat all souls as you would have them treat you",* in any of this, then, or today in our more allegedly *enlightened,* modern times?

The problem with false paradigms is such that, as long as you remain in yours, you will never see or identify anything you hear or read differently than you did previously.

If we are to LIVE by that most basic and everlasting golden rule which has its root in the immutable law of *free will.* To live it daily in every single waken moment. Making it alone our individual and collective ruling touchstone. Moreover, identifying it as a law that already exists and resides within each of us regardless how enshrouded and veiled in overriding narrative propaganda it may be. It must be then our individual and collective *duty* to *insight, uphold* and even strenuously *drive outward* the understanding and details of this knowledge to ensure the victory of this current awakening, and ascension of souls!

We have in recent years been experiencing another emerging giant rising from its long slumber; lifting many to search new things, awakening souls seeking its simplistic ascension causality. If this is where we are headed again, then I ask, *'what other or additional laws outside of the immutable law of Freewill, applied to all equally, would we then require to guide us all?'* **None!**

If every living-soul person truly and fully believed they should live by this single rule, then there would be no need for any other rule! In every culture without exception, people/souls are *driven* without question or delay towards the overwhelming compassionate aid of others in trouble, even in far off lands!

There is almost no greater proof, albeit periodic, of our innate, soul driven propensity to act in total and complete opposition to every single, Archon influenced, anti-life narrative!

This alone is the law within us seeking to escape!

If we are to seek only *LOVE, compassion, empathy, equity* for all others before seeking it even for ourselves, then we would not have to seek it privately at all, as it would already have been given freely.

Then, if the true prime Eternal Creator is as most believe Him to be - only LOVE; and if we can agree as most seem to be willing, that He is a literal part within us all, then by default it must be our true and primary nature to also be only LOVE. Just as we tend to see people act on a large scale, periodically.

However, if we are to judge our physical species *humanity* by our known history within this world paradigm, it clearly appears to paint us a very different picture than that of pure love.

Therefore, as I continue to advocate within the academy of these pages, there exists a very real and active opposing force which restrains and inhibits us from exhibiting our true soul nature on many levels.

What we should see, elevates our true nature

Knowing all this and so much more, I can attest as a teacher of many souls from diverse cultures, that I have experienced many people who were frozen and incapable of lasting change by past life scarring events. However, we must as spiritual leaders, healers, scientists and the people in general, seek the cause of their psychopathy, phobia, dementia, or general irresponsibility from within their soul, and not initially from their physical body, or what we perceive as their conscious mind.

In example; regardless if it is some cosmic Archon joke, planned negativity campaign, or just the odd luck of some other cosmic lottery, if I am to live in love only, then for example - what I will "see" when confronted by two homosexual people who truly seek each other in *love,* must be this way;

That I do not judge them on the basis of some ancient archaic ruling, but I only seek to understand what *their* souls *see* through *their eyes,* first!

*Again, remember my hypothesis of the **Eden Effect!***
That each person/soul, literally, see's everything within our creation space differently! The importance of this truth cannot be overstressed!

In this way my understanding and perception of these two gay people will always be correct, inflicting no judgment or pain. And in that, *I neutralize the soul-damaging, negative effect of the false narrative fabricated for that context.* Damage that not only affects their souls, but also my own! By understanding and *projecting* outward this *corrected* spiritual paradigm, I have now quite literally, and by my new *intention*, eliminated the negative result of that false control-narrative stream. And more importantly, I removed my negative energy output from their Archon life support system! Becoming incompatible!

And in that, by choosing a corrected knowledge base and narrative stream, and by *choosing love,* we can starve those who seek to enslave us in cycles. Think of this **Times 7 Billion!**

Although there remain many *learned* socially unacceptable lifestyles and activities even today, as most of us already know the majority of these perceptions to be remnants of long outdated, ancient religious control narrative paths.

The homosexual discussion and topic today is, as usual, fervently opposed by the unwise concubines of religion and their illustrious leaders, who themselves have been caught near countless times in their own depraved sexual positions. I would name, names, but decided to keep this book under five hundred pages. Amazingly, but not so unexpected, unfortunately, is the ongoing discussion and tensions among lawmakers and fractious religious leaders here in the land where all men are alleged to be created equal; is whether or not we, by decree of spurious law, should allow two people to LOVE EACH OTHER!

STOP the presses and quite literally "by god" STOP the LOVE!

Gay people! STOP trying to convince us that all you wish to do is get married, LIVE and LOVE one another, in PEACE and EQUITY, and without becoming a religiously driven bigot, lurking about fomenting hate and discontent in others. We will not have such benign behavior among us! Haven't you heard? It turns out that love is NOT the answer!

What is the soul but an eternally living, energy based, super-sentient entity with the highest awareness and creative power when left to its original form and nature. It is as I have discussed herein, an entity that acquires _some of its knowledge_ here in this Adam-Eden matrix we call earth through the transference of learned and emotionally assimilated input. But now we have the knowledge of what the ancients believed us to be, coupled with our modern discoveries of both our physical and spiritual tapestry. By these we should better identify and determine the nature of certain people/souls who sometimes defy their outward appearance; _i.e. men who we know to be heterosexual, but outwardly exude tendencies that we have been socially engineered to identify as being exclusively female._ Equally, we have all encountered the Tom-boy effect to varying degrees.

The question is, why is it we find souls/people exhibiting portions of both, male and female traits?

By the modern science, I explore herein, it would appear obvious why this might be, especially within a system of continual revolutions, cycling souls in and out through various eras. Add to this the fact that so many souls have been traded back and forth between genders, and I believe this is where that dog lays. If our modern quantum and biological physicists are correct in their findings, and our DNA does, in fact, transfer our life experiences to the soul directly making an eternal record, _then it would also make logical sense that a large part of any emotional life experience revolves around one's gender!_ Of course, after many lifetimes having accrued the eternal records and emotional ties to a female gender, to then be placed rather abruptly into a male body, would obviously create quite the stir within that soul's conscious experience each time around. Trapped inside what that soul deems to be the wrong _Trinity-6_ hardware, is how several gay people have expressed it to me. Trapped indeed!

Not only trapped within an opposite body-hardware but also trapped more thoroughly by their lack of very important knowledge such as all this. Trapped both physically, mentally and emotionally all at the same time, with seemingly no way out, or to even adjust.

So then as I stated earlier, what we have here is a matter of degrees. A soul who has spent their predominant life cycles as a male, possibly a few as female, maybe at one point exhibiting both mannerisms, but not being so influenced by any deeper urges to play outside of his socially accepted sandbox.

Whereas other souls who have lived only a male or female existence through many cycles, now shocked from the subconscious level to find themselves cycled indiscriminately for the first time into the opposite body-hardware. No matter how long and hard I ponder this situation, or what depth of scholarship I apply to it, I cannot at all identify any logical answer for how such a situation could possibly serve the soul involved. Conversely, I find many answers coming to me when I seek to understand how this and other like situations would serve the Archon usurpers. For them so far it is all mostly coming from the subconscious level. A primarily female *experienced* soul acting out as she only knows how to do by the predominance of her female nature. However, doing so while inside the wrong hardware package. So far, in most cases, this has been highly problematic for those people socially, and especially religiously for the reasons stated herein. Additionally problematic for everyone close to them because of all the traditionally entrenched false religious narratives which have worked so diligently to influence and drive our world by - *Accepted norms and non-accepted behavior.*

So this would lend an answer to why some women portray more masculine traits, and why some men exude more feminine traits, while neither are actually attracted to their same sex. While others are more deeply committed to their desires and need to couple with like sex. Much like those people we touched on earlier, those with minor phobias or other issues who are influenced by their urges, but not led by them. While others like our serial killers and the like who, no matter what they do or how socially unacceptable the action, cannot hold back their need to fulfill their deep, subconscious urges.

Yes, the soul has its *original* nature, clean-skinned and without destructive or unbalanced tendencies. However, as we are seeing within the entirety of this reformatted creation understanding, that all the preexisting and newly emerging false control-narratives, along with their sub-narrative routines, have gone a long way to scarring our souls and attaching considerable baggage. All of which, and unbeknownst to most people, these formerly unresolved spiritual issues are being subconsciously driven out and *projected* into subsequent life cycles.

By the combination of their existence, and the affected person's lack of conscious understanding through literal memories of their personal soul-scarring, this condition, while growing in frequency among us is causing greater social conflict, crossing all borders and languages. It has been poison upon poison, and all generations wonder openly why they see the next generation becoming worse, and not better. But of course, isn't that the Archon objective?

My disclaimer

I am absolutely in no way correlating or painting gay people or any variation thereof with the same brush or vein as the aforementioned examples of criminal murderers or pedophiles, etc. The deeper understanding in all this, and as the entirety of this book should be understood to exhibit is, that virtually ALL souls, ALL people have been and are being continually scathed by this soul recycling system. And as I already expressed, it all boils down to the percentage of soul damage done. This, of course, can only be assessed on a case by case basis and in no way can be used to single anyone out for any reason.

Consider the Soul!

They exist, they have always been among us, some have been terribly violent, or horribly destructive to women and children in other ways. Some are disturbed, and some have odd proclivities in which others find it difficult to adjust. Thankfully, the most prevalent of all the uncomfortable souls among us are those who have gender issues and NOT the ones with horribly destructive natures.

So maybe instead of drugging the person, or religiously demonizing certain segments of people, everyone, medical communities included, need to start considering the soul – **who's in there?** And, how can we help you? Would be a good start.

Look closer, and SEE differently!

The religious control narratives are quickly becoming as dry dinosaur bones, just as all destructive, dogmatic, ritualistic control vectors should become among a growing enlightened people. The narratives have all been found guilty of pernicious evil from our ancient times to this very day, but many show no signs of abating that divisive nature. Their collective existence can be swept into the ash pile of ill repute so easily and simply, and only using our mere thoughts and directed *intention* to disregard them all totally and completely, they will disappear.

No longer can we allow ourselves to be controlled and manipulated into damaging others by the hate that established itself within us through those false narrative systems. Run from all those who would feign LOVE, but spew hate against their brother or sister because she is gay, or because they dress differently, or speak differently than them. Like a great spiritual leader once told another, *'if you want to be stoned yourself, then feel free to cast the first stone!'*

Since the gay issue has been growing for many years now in America where all the Levitical, superstitious, witch hunters live, then allow me to paint this overall picture concerning how we should be seeing **everyone** from here on.

I use the example again of those who society has labeled

homosexual, because in many, especially within America, this is a growing and divisive topic that has turned once loving people and families against each other. To SEE with LOVE, and not hate or bigotry filtered through some false ancient religious narrative, we all have to recalibrate our paradigm before we will ever SEE anything differently. For instance, when we see two females embracing each other in a typical loving manner as we might do with our own spouses:

> **"What we should correctly identify and SEE, are two predominantly <u>male influenced souls</u> who themselves are both SEEING exactly what they are naturally attracted to – a FEMALE! And of course vice versa with men. IT'S SOCIETY WHO HAS THE PROBLEM SEEING!"**

When a man is driven to wear woman's clothing and make-up and yearns to be accepted as such by his family and peers, it is NOT because that man has a broken brain! It is clearly the consequence of a deep internal drive to be female. Why? Because the SOUL believes, and or feels more naturally female for the reasons I previously described. The Man, on the other hand, not being conscious of this soul condition, or knowledge concerning his/her soul attributes, is psychologically imprisoned. That person is chained by the debilitating constraints of our – *social norms,* all of which are driven by ancient religious control narratives. These people spend their lives hiding their emotions and needs. This overriding, fear induced dilemma then becomes the new emotional scarring transmitted to her soul over time again. Another layer of soul-scarring to be resurrected in yet another life cycle in the form of a compounded phobia.

Moreover, this predicament may even turn into some actual physical dementia in this person's life after being forced to live in this adverse and most hated condition. Yet again, as a whole, we ostracize and fear these people into dark, dank corners. Again, adding more and more soul-scarring!

This sounds like moral relativism!

Is that what love your neighbor as yourself means? No, of course not, more clearly it implies not doing to someone what you wouldn't want them to do to you, which by default then means, *"do not ostracize or create fearful conditions!"* From that angle, loving gay people means being *respectful, considerate, not insulting or bullying,* and certainly not *physical violence, mental anguish* or anything else through government action or religious intolerance!

In love, we would refrain from poor conduct and not judge someone because of their sexual preference, as we wouldn't judge people of a different race, color or other religion. Yet, having discernment when they or anyone is not choosing life, good or moral ways of acting towards others; no matter what their race, color, religion or sexual preference.

Hopefully, now having this specific depth of correlated information and understanding will enable many on both sides to come to terms in this life. Especially so for the indiscriminately labeled souls in this area of faith and spirituality to which they are most generally cut off!

If you take away nothing else

The overall and final context of this book may be summed up, and clearly understood as being a *call to arms to ignore the Archons on all levels!* A call to all souls, shaking their long slumber to awaken a truly massive, sleeping giant. We must take total responsibility for ourselves, *our souls,* for past deeds and reawaken to the fact that it has always been us, and not only some other convenient evil entity. We must individually first, and collectively take a more conscious and deliberate stance and action against all those entrenched control narratives – And IGNORE them!

Drive out the negative *intentions* you may be harboring inwardly and *projecting* outwardly as others do towards one's self and those people who society demonizes based on their lifestyle, sexual orientation, or beliefs. *All coalescing around a narrative cult which only seeks for you to assimilate and express death and destruction to all, and on many subtle levels.* All of which has always and will continue to originate from societies systemic, dogmatic and mostly misrepresented religious narratives. If we are truthful with ourselves, and now able to identify the *narratives* as a real trap, then you understand how truly powerful and invasive they have and continue to be. *If we continue to consent!*

Everyone regardless of language or culture on this rock needs to change, and above all IGNORE EVERYTHING, they constantly throw our way via TV and media, etc., and the sooner the better. No longer can we be driven like chattel by so many negative *control-narratives,* all of which breed only fear and hate on many levels, some even almost imperceptibly. LOVE and MERCY in all things, *projected* in all ways to all people, even the bad ones, as evil does exist, must be our primary, driving motivator. Quite literally working in this way of *projecting positive intention* on to all things and all people, we can succeed.

Our overall dynamic *intentions* must change towards the endlessly consistent positive of love and mercy. I eluded to such changes by using this phrase as a mantra in my first book many times

"If you want to change the world, first, change yourself!"

In this single ancient understanding lies more wisdom than anything previously stated in this, or any other book.

With these understandings as I have attempted to lay out and connect herein, just as any truthful ancient religion scholar should not remain ignorant of current scientific data corroborating ancient beliefs, then it would also be the due diligence for any truthful scientist not to ignore useful ancient writings and beliefs that align with his findings.

Consequently, this requires both coming back together and considering a holistic point of view as they attempt to determine the truth of our current reality. This reunification would then aid the greater multitudes still enslaved within the many diverse systems of *control-narratives* to recognize the need to make the choice of returning "above" or remaining captive "below".

Can changing the world be this simple - _To IGNORE the Archon's completely_ and the fear narratives as perpetuated by their earthly sycophants? Well, their polar opposite of _making the world increasingly negative_ has appeared this simple for those forcing their agenda on this world. Thus, maybe this is the last reality view they want anyone to truly assimilate and live daily - _"Treat all souls as you would have them treat your own child"_...

In summation

The overall takeaway should be; that there are some very evil soul entities lurking about out there who vehemently hate our souls because we were not judged and un-tethered from the Eternal Creator as they were, for what they believed to be the same crime against free will. That we naively consented to join their will and did so without knowing the fine print of their contract. We have been used for so long we have forgotten who we were, and more importantly what we are! However, though it all the Prime Eternal One continued to drop His bread crumbs for our return. _We need only once again see them, consent to return, and begin once again to project His intention for all life abundant._

And on that day, when the fulcrums weight finally tips, unable to reverse, then the evil will just quietly pass away...;

The moral of the story?

UN-Plug and IGNORE everything negative or fearful at all times! Shun it all and project none of it again! Ignore them utterly and completely! _Break their tether and they will die!_ This means living the Everlasting Agreement above all!

Bibliography

Alain, Nickolas Gisin &. *Quantum Chance*. Copernicus, 2014. Paper back.

Alexander, Dr. Eben. *Proof of Heaven: A Neurosurgeon's Journey into the Afterlife*. Simon & Schuster, 2012. Paperback.

Allan, Sterling D. *(pesn.com/2010/10/27/9501716_Hutchison-Lazaryan_frequency_generator_clears_polluted_Gulf_waters/)*. 2010. Website article. 2015.

Asher, Dr. S. *The Asher Codex*. Avinu Publishing - CreateSpace, 2013. Hard and Soft cover.

Asher, Dr. Shmuel. *The Land of Meat & Honey*. Avinu Publishing, 2012. Hard and soft cover book.

Berman, Robert Lanza & Bob. *Biocentrism: How Life and Consciousness are the Keys to Understanding the True Nature of the Universe*. BenBella Books, 2010. Paperback.

Bludorf, G Fosar & F. *Vernetzte Intelligenz*. 2001. Hardcover.

Bohm, David. *The Essential David Bohm*. Routledge, Fransis & Taylor Group Inc. , 2003. Soft cover.

BOSTROM,NICK.
https://www.fat.bme.hu/student/pub/Programozas3/SimulationArgument.pdf. 2001. PDF.

Century of Self. Dir. Adam Curtis. 2002.

Charles, R.H. *The Book of Enoch*. CreateSpace, 2013. Paperback.

D.D., The Rt. Rev. Lino Sanchez. *http://www.christianism.com/articles/19.html*. 2007. Website.

Emoto, Dr. Masaru. *The Hidden Messages in Water*. Atria Books, 2005. Paperback, kindle, Audio.

Federal Bureau of Investigation. "A Memorandum of Importance." Memorandum. 1947.

Giorbran, Gevin. *Everything Forever*. Enchanted Puzzle Publishing, 2006.

Goswami, Amit. *Physics of the Soul*. Hampton Roads Publishing, 2001. Paperback.

Greyson, Bruce. *The Handbook of Near-Death Experiences: Thirty Years of Investigation*. Praeger Publishing, 2009. Hardcover.

∞ Soul Revolution ∞

Heisenberg, Werner. *Physics and Philosophy: The Revolution in Modern Science*. Harper Perennial Modern Classics, 2007.

Henry, Richard Conn. "The Mental Universe." (2005).

James, Cliff. "Of Bodies Changed." James, Cliff. *Of Bodies Changed*. FeedsRead.com, 2014. 324.

Jammer, Max. *Concepts of Space*. Dover Publications; Third Edition, Enlarged edition (March 16, 2012), 2012 Third Edition,

Jowett, Benjamin. *http://www.anselm.edu/homepage/dbanach/sym.htm*. October 1, 2014. 4th Edition, Oxford U. Press, 1953 (189c-189d) p 520 to (193d-193e) p 525.

Layne, Meade. "Fly, Loka, Fly." July-August 1947. *boarderlandsciences.org*. <<https://borderlandsciences.org/journal/vol/03/n06/Fly_Lokas_Fly.html>>.

Leininger, Bruce. *Soul Survivor: The Reincarnation of a World War II Fighter Pilot*. 2010. Paperback.

Lonnerstrand, Sture. *I Have Lived Before: The True Story of the Reincarnation of Shanti Devi* . 1998. Paperback.

Martini, Richard. *It's A Wonderful Afterlife Vol 2: Further Adventures Into The Flipside*. Homina Publishing, 2014. Paperback.

McCloud, S. A. *Id, Ego, and Superego*. 2008. <http://www.simplypsychology.org/psyche.html>.

Mooney, Sharon Fish. *http://www.equip.org/article/descending-masters-a-history-of-the-raelian-movement/*. 2002. Christian Research Journal.

Pribram, Karl H. *Brain, and Perception - Holonomy & Structure in Figural Processing*. Lawrence, Erlbaum Associates Inc., 1991. Hardcover .

Prophets. *Ezekiel - Chapter 1:4-5*. Stone, 6 BCE. Hebrew Prophets.

Rabi, Morai V'. *https://youtu.be/-H0MDGIXZ0o*. 2015. Video.

Robinson, James M., ed. "The Hypostasis of the Archons -The Reality of the Rulers." *The Nag Hammadi Library*. Vol. 1. Trans. Bentley Layton. HarperCollins. San Francisco: HarperCollins, 1990. PDF. <http://khazarzar.skeptik.net/books/nhl.pdf>.

Sagan, Carl. *The Cosmic Connection: An Extraterrestrial Perspective*. Dell Publishing, 1975.

Page | 340

Schaff, Philip. *http://oll.libertyfund.org/titles/1903*. 2014. website books.

Schopenhauer, Arthur. *The World as Will and Representation, Vol. 1* . Dover Publications, 1966. Paperback.

Studies, International Association of Near Death. *http://iands.org/home.html*. 2015. Website. 2014.

Walker, Ethan. *Finding Gods love*. Devi Press Inc, 2003. Paperback.

Whitworth, Brian. *The physical world as a virtual reality1*. Massey University, New Zealand, 2014.

I implore the reader to go to this YouTube video interview and listen first hand to one of Judaisms most renown Rabbi's in NYC prove every single, long hidden precept that I have ever taught existed within that ancient Babylonian religious cult.

(IN THIS INTERVIEW RABBI ABRAHAM FINKELSTEIN REVELS THE JEWISH CONTROL OVER THE US GOVERNMENT, THE JEWISH INVOLVED IN 9/11 AND THE MIDDLE EASTERN WARS, THE JEWISH FOUNDING OF COMMUNISM AND THE JEWISH RITUAL SACRIFICE OF NON-JEWISH CHILDREN, etc)

https://youtu.be/vyuDNsTSXl8

About the Author

Dr. Asher is a Hebrew Scholar whose main area of study has been in Ancient Middle Eastern Comparative Religion and Semitic languages, with an emphasis on the Hebrew biblical, and later period Judaic cult sects influence and effect on Islam and Christianity.

Although breaking from the modern version of his original Karaite-Hebrew roots, Dr. Asher hails from an uninterrupted family lineage of Karaite Torah scholars whose family ties originate in the Galilee area of Northern Canaan. Dr. Asher's earlier teachings advance the *original* ancient Karaite tradition of uncompromising data extrapolation and dissemination, and specific to the original Hebrew culture, traditions, and language from a more spiritually based root.

Dr. Asher's ongoing teaching emphasis has been to free people from manmade religions by distilling more ancient truths via the eldest texts available, and in lieu of the later period *corrected* texts and cultural traditions.

Dr. Asher spent most of his childhood in NY & NJ, continuing his learning in his early twenties in Israel, where he also received his citizenship. During his formative years, Dr. Asher was exposed to the Christian religion extensively by those around him. Learning the Torah from the age of seven, he quickly identified that most Judeo-Christians and Jews of other sects were deeply misinformed on all levels of ancient Hebrew history, and in need of clarifications. Thus, he ignores no opportunity or circumstance to teach anyone who would listen. In doing so Dr. Asher has dedicated himself to the teaching of the Eternal Creator's *original* spiritual laws and path among all who wish to know, and be separated from their narrative-driven religious slavery.

To this end, and before publishing any of his books, Dr. Asher formed the *Ancient Hebrew Learning Center*, which has been the focal point for his free online and personal instruction worldwide. Those who glean insight from Dr. Asher include people spanning all religious faiths; all of which are people searching beyond their fundamental religions for a more original truth which eludes them. His factual, hard-hitting teachings demand a paradigm shift. To most strident religionists he is at best controversial, and at times even hated. So, it would seem his exercise in truth must be hitting some very raw nerves; and with this latest spiritual adventure, ***Soul Revolution***, he does not disappoint.

Other Works by Shmuel Asher

The Land of MEAT & Honey

The Greater Exodus

The Asher Codex

Christendom's False Prophesies

Greater Exodus Radio Show

Coming Work by Shmuel Asher

The Ben'Asher Torah
A literal and highly corrected translation

Midian to New Egypt
A fact-based fictional story depicting how the Hebrews and mixed multitudes of people leaving Egypt split between Mt. Horeb and Mt. Sinai; their religious and cultural separation into two peoples; and their advancements and influences into our modern times.

No Power in the Verse can Stop Me!

S. Asher

Made in the USA
San Bernardino, CA
24 September 2018